Changing Library Environment Concepts and Contexts

Changing Library Environment Concepts and Contexts

M. Ram

Changing Library Environment Concepts and Contexts

ISBN 978-93-5111-477-2

Published in 2015 in India by

RANDOM PUBLICATIONS

4376-A/4B, Gali Murari Lal, Ansari Road
New Delhi-110 002
Phone : +9111-43580356, 011-23289044, 011-43142548
e-mail: sales@randompublications.com,
info@randompublications.com, randomexports@gmail.com

Type Setting by : Friends Media, Delhi-110089
Digitally Printed at : Replika Press Pvt. Ltd.

Preface

Information and Communication Technology (ICT) is rapidly changing the whole world creating new challenges and opportunities. Revolutionary advances in ICT have now transformed the way information is gathered, processed, oraganised, accessed and disseminated to the user community.

Today, the libraries are increasingly viewed as outdated and under rated with the use of modern web- based services. The pressure on libraries to modernise the way of delivering their services is now intense and more demanding. The user expectations on libraries to deliver high quality, comprehensive, user-friendly new generation services have grown tremendously in recent years. The survival demands change, updation and modernisation. Libraries need to change quite dramatically to modernise almost every aspect of their operations, information resources and services in order to meet the rising users expectations of the modern world.

Library and Information Service (LIS) professionals are confronting challenging dynamic technological environment demanding the extensive and effective utilization of ICT in order to survive and meet the changing complex information needs of user community. The change is the law of nature. ICT is a driving force for change in library. Change is inevitable for the survival and success of any library in the changing technological world. LIS professionals must develop expert technological competencies required to make best use of the opportunities, the ICT offers in order to provide a gateway access to wide range and variety of information resources and services.

The present book explores the various upheavals and changes in the library environment as they are evolving from concrete structures to digital. It is an attempt to help students, teachers, professionals and researchers of LIS in getting information of recent trends of library environment.

Author

Contents

1

Digital Libraries and Distance Learning

Access to education has become increasingly important for individuals who need to gain a competitive edge in the labour market through acquisition of specialised or new knowledge. This demand for new information, coupled with the ever-increasing quantity of information available in digital form, has led to a change in traditional teaching methods. Face-to-face teaching is gradually being replaced by distance education. In order to make this form of education both effective and efficient, advanced information and communication technologies must be exploited. To this aim, digital libraries of distributed complex multimedia data can serve as suitable repositories of continuously changing up-to-date information, which are indispensable for distance education.

In the new information society era, knowledge and innovation are certainly the basis of the added value and competitiveness of most successful corporations. Successful corporations strategically promote a knowledge exchange culture. The organisations of the future will certainly rely on a set of virtual technical communities, exchanging corporate database information and communicating through mail, bulletin board and conferencing systems. In a knowledge era economy, the learning enterprise is strategically crucial. Digital libraries may play an important role in the organisation and management of information flow and cooperative work. Libraries may act as the interface between the research community and the commercial and industrial worlds, by means of the dissemination of scientific and research work and of the learning and collaboration facilities supplied.

Digital libraries are learning centres, the nodes of knowledge in the worldwide information society networks. The technological evolution of storage and representation of different media made possible the development of digital multimedia libraries, integrating in a single support text, image, audio, video, and also interactive content, like simulations and presentations. Meanwhile, the standardisation of catalogue and classification procedures led to flexible and open networked search and retrieval systems. Nowadays, other promising new technologies are also being applied to digital libraries, introducing radical changes in the intellectual practices and in the social and economic organisation. Transparent worldwide interaction is aimed at distributed systems and component software technologies, while automatic content description, object-oriented and agent technologies enhance the collaborative and productive work.

The functionalities of a digital library service should satisfy the needs of such different users as students, teachers, researchers or teleworkers, and make them collaborative and interdependent in the search of the relevant knowledge for their activities. Administrative support and security procedures are key system facilities for the correct management and maintenance of the databases, the access control and the protection of intellectual property rights. Powerful and relevant document search and flexible browsing methodologies are needed for an efficient use of the digital database resources available, in particular when distributed services and large multimedia contents are available. Content creation and cooperative work facilities should be available to users, so that everyone can contribute as a content provider and digital library access can be considered as a learning experience. Commercial exploration of the digital library resources must be considered, requiring accounting and billing mechanisms, for electronic publishing purposes.

The library wants to constitute a reference, in the access to information resources in the scientifical and technical areas of engineering and related fields. Besides providing the traditional library services at a high level, the plan has a great component related to information technologies, both by the service enhancement they provide and by the new habits of access, production and dissemination of knowledge they will produce in the future.

A possible model for the development of distributed databases of learning content considers multimedia information entities, the learning objects, cross-connected in tematic subject paths, allowing for the representation of several associations of ideas, or annotations, on the primary contents. In an operational view, the model is divided in four different levels of structured information: the assets pool, which are monomedia elements referenced in the cataloguing system, the learning objects database, where documents that group objective elements are stored, the subject path connection service and the annotation facilities at each node.

The combination of these four levels creates a dynamic and evaluative system: the hypermedium. The mediabase is supported in a conventional relational database, where the contents are multimedia entities, self-described and objective, and that can even be interactive. An entity acquires significant relevance in the context of an argumentation, described as a tematic subject path connecting several entities. The long term success of this model depends on the massive involvement of active users in the system, multiplying the entities and the subject paths defined on them. Intellectual property rights related with the annotations inscribed on the subject paths are protected by the nature of the hypermedium, as any copied entity.

Annotation Layer from the system loses the most important quality, which is the relational information inscribed in the subject paths. Mediabase objects can include any kind of multimedia standards and formats. The initial content will be based in the large number of monographies, thesis and papers available in digital support. Video cassettes can also be converted to any suitable digital video format for distribution all over the campus. More elaborated multimedia objects, such as, presentations, application demos or interactive simulations can also be developed. A team including experts in multimedia production, interface design and pedagogic aspects will assist teachers and researchers in their development, providing also training courses and online support.

Annotation functionalities will provide for the user creation of subject paths connecting those entities, which can then be exported, if desired, to a restrict group of users or to all the research and learning communities inside the campus or in the internet. Agent technologies will allow the development of pro-active and user configurable information services, providing a better exploitation of the available resources. Accounting and billing mechanisms will provide the needed security procedures for searching, editing or distributing the contents, and for statistical analysis of the users behaviour and taxation of commercial services.

Digital libraries are emerging technologies for document management. These documents includes multimedia objects. It requires new methods of all aspects of multimedia data management. Starting from the source through storage to delivery, digital libraries have to use all modern network and servers technologies in order to supply services of a high quality. Its universal nature makes the digital library an excellent foundation for other multimedia-based services such as distance learning.

The digital library (DL) is based on a few components. The main components are:

i) metadata management application (DL Logic)

ii) content servers for storing and serving multimedia objects

iii) web server for the presentation of library content

iv) GUI (Graphic Use Interface) management application for content load and management.

Based on metadata stored in the database forms are generated for searching library content as well as web pages presenting library content. For presentation purposes a graphical three dimensional interface using VRML scenes was developed which allows simple and fast browsing through the library structure and content. A very important component of this installation is the GUI application supporting users with a functional interface to library content.

The application uses system access control rules implemented in the database, which allows restricted access by particular users to specific library branches or documents. The application allows the loading of new documents. The document can be assembled by putting together objects of different types (text, images, video, audio) and defining the structure of the document manually dividing it into chapters and pages containing selected objects. Objects are then described by simple metadata such as: author, title, description or keywords.

This problem is solved by using HTML as way of presenting library documents. With this concept a user creates an entire publication using any HTML editor and stores it on a local disc. After pointing its localisation document is analysed by the application. All objects included in the document are described by metadata and sent to content servers and data describing the whole document and individual objects are sent to the database. Links contained within HTML pages are fixed in such a way that they point to new physical locations of used objects. The document is then presented using its own HTML, not automatically generated pages.

New services, new requirements caused new design principles. The most important of these are presented below:

i) *Distributed library and interoperability*: Especially in the broadband network spread over the whole world an important aspect is the possibility of creating multiple local digital libraries serving local users, but allowing their global integration as well. This requires a new mechanism for exchanging information on library content between libraries, so a user can see all of the content through one entry point. In the future, intereoperability with other libraries should also be provided.

ii) *Quality of service*: New methods for the presentation of multimedia objects according to a user's requirements and technical possibilites need to be developed. This is especially true for access network bandwidth and streaming media.

iii) *Performance and resource management*

iv) *Access control*: Creating new mechanisms assisting digital libraries is a mistake. It forces users to remember another password and creates new problems in existing security policies.

A digital library system was designed as the framework for several multimedia service scenarios, which will be realised within it. The main topics addressed in this area are:

i) The management of different types of data including stream-based data,

ii) The creation of multimedia publications,

iii) The storing of documents and objects contained in these documents,

iv) The possibility of describing objects and documents by simple metadata for searching, and

v) Access control for content.

The digital library framework is foreseen to be the operational environment for these multimedia services. The first of the mentioned services is the distance learning system. It is planned to realise the distributed teaching environment composed of three different levels: offline lectures, interactive on-line lectures and remote exercises in virtual laboratories. In the scope of off-line lectures, there is projected to provide a set of lectures stored in the database.

The digital multimedia library system is the natural environment for preparing, storing and distributing the content. Having assured scalability and flexibility of the system the content can be easy prepared and managed. The video broadcast extended with some content-depended information is stored in the digital library environment and served by it to the listener synchronously. The internet access to lectures makes this service easily accessible but the quality of media will be decreased.

Especially when the content will be served in multicast groups, students can access these lectures when they study a subject at home for the purpose of knowledge consolidation. It does not put high requirements as far as quality is concerned but only aims at helping students with home exercises. Another approach is to prepare an environment for distributed online lectures.

Another example of service, which will be implemented in the digital library framework, is the digital edition of a book. The original printed text form will be extended with parallel multimedia events. An animation and sound served by specific content servers will be synchronised with text presented by management applications on web pages. The content will be created with the usage of specific applications for data input. The publication decomposed into basic multimedia objects will be formed when data will be accessed.

The digital library will be used to digitise the work, store it and finally provide it to the user. The most important thing is to concentrate on the implementation around the digital library concept as a framework for other services based on media transfer to an end user. The role of digital libraries in the delivery of recommended readings could be in the near future important, because of the access to ITC connection all over the world. Distance education is the pedagogical technology, how to support the student in the self-study process. The major difference between face-to-face study and distance education is in the separation of the teaching and learning process. To ensure this process successful, there is a lot of supportive tools, which are organised by the DE delivery institution.

The advantage of distance education is in the independence on the study place and time of study. In the public libraries, there is the problems with students, who have not access to the such a library in the region and they had to cross to long distance, spent time and pay additional expenses connected with their study. From this reasons (democratic and comparable study conditions for all students), the obligatory visits of libraries are not the part of DE generally. The recent time is significant by the growing application of internet (or other electronic networks) for transfer of information and delivery of study materials. Of course, that without strict keeping of the principles of DE the final effects are usually very modest. The online study is well possible and the amount of information can be sufficient. The problem is only with the "overloading" of student by the non-relevant information. This tendency is typical for academic, who are not able to separate the relevant and non-relevant information for practical use.

The DE student looks for study to improve his position on the labour market and no to accumulate huge amount of its say useful, but not relevant information. The technical problem with the storing of whole library in the net is in the hands of ICT experts. From the point of view of DE technology, there is a good perspective to use the digital libraries for all students, because the access to internet is practically in each place. The application of ICT in the distance education is necessary to consider the approach of con-temporal students of secondary grammar schools and universities, and the potential students of Life-Long-Learning programmes including distance education. Also the approach to the LLL changed in the recent time according to development of learning society. The learning society will give more and more emphasis on the individualisation of study opportunities with the growing share of interactive contact with the teaching institution.

Electronic links are only a new way of information transfer, but definitely it is not a new teaching/learning technology. Flexibility in the educational processes must be supported by the corresponding learning environment and this is the good chance and challenge for digital libraries.

Impact of New Technologies

Knowledge has become a power, a determinative element of competitiveness. The growing clamour and move to revolutionise the educational sector with the aid of computer technology is clearly a part of an overall desire to be globally competitive. To qualify for global competition, it has been suggested that human power must be sustainably developed. Human development has been defined as the process of widening people's choice and the level of well-being they achieve.

Many aspects of our social, cultural, natural, etc., environment are changing from day to day. The motors of this dynamics are the globalisation of communication and information processing technologies, and the globalisation of industry, business and trade. People are faced with the need to retrain themselves, as existing workforces, to ensure that their skills are relevant and meet the needs of the current technological, cultural and social changes. In contradiction to the needs of the past a cyclical retraining becomes nowadays non-sufficient and there has arisen a need for permanent further education possibilities, so-called continuing education. Various emerging information and computer technologies dramatically expand options for opening up a space that support the development of full human potential by challenging the rigidity and conservativeness of traditional schooling as well as by empowering learners to be engaged in diverse processes of learning.

These technologies force us to rethink our education systems, giving more attention to adult learning, reshaping preparation of young people for adult life, stressing the autonomy of a learner, shifting the focus of the systems and processes from teaching to learning, and redefining the ways in which people get access to information and knowledge. The new information and computer technologies raise quite new questions about how knowledge is created and who owns it. Educational institutions, schools and universities, which used to have control over knowledge and over its dissemination now find themselves in mediatised environments where schooling is simply one of many different cultural experiences.

Education was traditionally conceived as a fairly one-way street where knowledge travelled from a teacher and textbooks to students who tried to memorise all they could remember. Students were expected to store information in their mind, but not necessarily to use their mind to process the information. The technological advances that characterise our current age have changed everything and we have to reconstruct the cognitive map of education. To remember information and systematically repeat skills has been not enough in current epoch. The world no longer needs human databases or robots, such people are dysfunctional in it. It needs learners who can adapt their activities to what is happening each new day. Learning to know and learning to do must be replaced by learning to become learning-oriented. Actually this is an orientation with which we are born—because learning is a never-ending experience taking place with different intensity from the cradle to the grave—but later we tend to lose it.

Traditionally individuals have tended to begin and end their formal education within defined segments of education systems in their early years. Today, the ongoing movement calls for lifelong learning and in its frame for continuing education. Continuing education is a broad concept which includes all of the learning opportunities all people want or need outside of basic education and primary education. It extends well beyond the completion of formal studies and into the less formal area of adult education. People involved in adult education undertake courses for many reasons. It may be for mental stimulation, personal growth, acquirement of new knowledge and skills, for social interaction and self-confidence. Regardless of a person's reasons for studying, one thing is certain, continuing education makes a major contribution to the well-being of society. The various information and communication technologies present dynamic new opportunities to support the diversity of learners and learning processes.

The information and communication technologies are conceived as alternative delivery mechanisms which facilitate mass broadcasting of information to learners in a low-cost way. Usually there is little concern about whether the learners actually understand these broadcasts. Often times a mistaken assumption is that information is in a sense neutral and that all receivers will extract the same meaning and ideas that the creator intended. Adult learners often need to attain new or improved skills in order to better meet and solve work and real-life problems. To acquire these concrete skills they intentionally actively look for the adequate opportunities of further education. Adult learners prefer to deal with problems, which are meaningful and known for them, it means with such problems which they encounter or might encounter in their particular life situations.

Adult learners are usually willing to participate in the learning process. Many motivational theories suggest that individuals prefer activities involving an optimal level of challenge. This is a very important fact in adult education which instructional designers must deal with. They must very carefully consider an appropriate, not non-estimated, level of such a challenge. Motivation can also be used for gaining adult learners' attention. The adult learners are usually willing to take an active part in the learning process. To support them to be active it is very important to present them adequate stimulus material. Since adults tend to be problem-centred, skill-seeking, independent and active participants in the learning process, clarity and relevance are the key principles in presenting information to them. It is also very important to engage the adult learners in the tasks with a very strong necessity to attain a relevant goal.

There are many individual differences among learners that interact strongly with kinds of teaching. These are called learning styles or strategies. Learners who are highly motivated and actively involved can often respond almost constantly while learning. For adult learners it is important to feel that they are effectively learning new skills. In the last decade, the widespread introduction of personal computers led to their use in training. As computers became more powerful, sophisticated multimedia computer-based training allowed learners the freedom to work on their own, much as they might with a traditional correspondence course.

The training and education requirement today has changed radically from the past, in particular because of:

i) Increasing training costs

ii) The need for continuous reskilling

iii) Shorter product lifecycles

E-commerce and network digital economy as trends that will affect almost every area of our work and life, consider education in this line too. In the world, where the king is information value, continuous learning and reskilling will be necessary. The classical way of attending classrooms will have to be replaced or combined with distance education.

Internet or generally public information network brings to the side of supply an effective tool for educating the customers and to the side of demand a chance to decide more by real information rather than by advertisment slogans. Moreover the intranet (or other forms of corporate information system) is a suitable tool for an organisation to provide employees with cheap and efficient education and to maintain corporate know-how. Schools have to prepare for a fundamental change of their society role. Regarding IT development they cannot compete as encyclopedic information sources anymore. Their unsubstitutability is especially in performing as training and live communication centres, in providing space for such activities that cannot be virtual. The Virtual Learning Environment (VLE) could be created under the umbrella of the internet services. This VLE is going to be used as an support tool for the managers education. Many people are fond of receiving new information but only a few of them are willing to get the information from books, learning them by heart.

Web-based Digital Library System

The use of the web is the delivery mechanism for digital libraries. It was important therefore to modularise the digital library so as to allow each teacher to organise the materials according to their own desires. However, it was realised as the library developed that in moving from a lecture presentation mode of learning to a self-paced, web-based learning environment, the peculiar influence of the librarian/webmaster diminishes and the needs of the learner could be fulfilled better with a less structured strategy. This approach also has the advantage that, by eliminating a fixed structure, the contents can be readily updated as new problems arise, new laws are promulgated, precedents are established in court cases, or international diversity is recognised.

The digital library has been expanded by collaboration with faculty at several other institutions. The development of a digital library to support teaching and learning in computer ethics, web-based learning is a growing phenomenon that has yet to reach its full capability. Much has been made of the web simply as a passive searchable resource, and our experience already records that many learning opportunities have been satisfied through this mechanism, but "data-mining" is truly only a precursor of data analysis and refinement. Substantive learning can only be achieved through the management of data acquisition, and the collaborative development and reinforcement of concepts. The general tenets of Computer Aided Instruction (CAI) can now be implemented in a web-based learning environment built and maintained on the basis of a digital library. The study of the social impact of the computer and computer ethics should not be limited to post-secondary computer education, but should be available to all users of computers. As a result, a new infrastructure has emerged, our pedagogy has been transformed, utilisation of the courseware we developed has grown rapidly both locally and remotely, and many tools have been constructed. Students learn new topics, often in new ways, and we have continued to progress in developing digital library content, systems, and interfaces.

The International Centre for Distance Learning which is located in the Open University's Institute of Educational Technology, an essential resource of the Centre built up over 15 years, is its digital library which includes information on 1,200 distance education institutions, 31,000 courses and 10,000 abstracts from the literature of distance learning.

ICDL promotes international research and collaboration by providing information based on its library and databases; it reaches other audiences through publications, including *ICDL Update*, compilations and reviews; teaches both face-to-face and online in the UK and abroad, undertakes international consultancy; and conducts its own research. An essential knowledge resource of the Centre built up over 15 years is its distance education library and databases:

The main paper-based library has the largest collection of literature on distance learning in the world. There are over 15,000 items—books, journals, journal offprints, conference proceedings and papers, research reports, surveys, dissertations, and newsletters—so-called grey literature. ICDL aims to obtain copies of all new books and monographs published in English on distance education, open learning and related fields. It subscribes to all the specialist distance learning journals and receives newsletters published by institutions and organisations involved in open and distance learning.

Most of the collection is in English, but there are significant numbers of documents in French, German, Spanish and Chinese. Institutions also have the largest repository of information about institutions across the world including prospectuses, calendars and course handbooks. Included are institutions dedicated to distance teaching, open universities, institutions which have distance teaching departments and conventional, e.g., dual mode; or have programmes or courses taught at a distance. Coverage includes all education and training levels. ICDL also contributed to a database and is a partner in the World Bank Global Distance Education network, which has been established to provide core and regional information online for development policy makers. The largest group of users are those online. Currently ICDL receives up to 10,000 hits a day from 25,000 users in over 130 countries which adds up to 300,000 hits per month. The main countries from which users log on from are shown in table 1.

While the content of ICDL's digital libraries are distance learning and its methods involve collaboration and networks, it is not a distance learning system in the same sense as an open university or other programmes of distance education. This is mainly because it does not provide teachers or a tutorial system, nor does it accredit the learning it promotes. However, it does operate key functions which promote and support distance learning.

It collects and creates knowledge resources, which are organised in a structured and systematic form; makes these resources accessible at a distance and delivers to individuals wherever they are; provides tools to assist users in identifying their needs and engaging with the resources; furthermore it is open to all and not restricted to fixed times or dates.

Table 1. Top 20 countries where log-ons originated (figures for one month)

Country	*Total hits*	*% of total*
US	85591	27.56
UK	33414	10.76
Canada	16506	5.31
Australia	6246	2.01
Singapore	4995	1.61
Malaysia	4958	1.60
Japan	3573	1.15
Germany	3405	1.10
Netherlands	2927	0.94
Greece	2758	0.89
New Zealand	2504	0.81
Brazil	2204	0.71
India	2144	0.69
South Africa	2056	0.66
Hong Kong	1922	0.62
Italy	1825	0.59
Sweden	1776	0.57
Belgium	1669	0.54
Spain	1629	0.52
Ireland	1406	0.45
		(59.08%)

ICDL is used mainly by:

i) distance learning researchers, scholars and students engaged in the field.

ii) distance learning specialists who are developing opportunities for others to learn.

iii) potential students or their advisors seeking appropriate distance learning opportunities.

It promotes collaboration between creators and users of knowledge and is part of a global knowledge network. The classification system used by ICDL is one example from a library tradition and there are other classification systems applied to the field. With digital libraries the potential for computer analysis of their contents can be exploited.

The main elements for the analysis of the contents and use of a digital library are represented in table 2 below. The main actors are authors and users. Authors apply the words and concepts of their discipline to construct documents which are entered into databases. The entries include author names and over time represent the productivity of each author in the field. Users access documents using search words and author names, and some documents and authors are more popular than others.

To model the contents of a digital library it is necessary to use a measure of association between the items under each of the main elements. Generally used measures are based on either author or user behaviour give values of co-occurrence and proximity between pairs of items. However, the role of a particular library in enabling the connections is not clear-cut and authors may have found out about and obtained documents from many sources. User surveys can gain some information regarding the contribution of a particular digital library. Research on the utilisation of information has shown that this is a complex process.

Table 2: Main elements and main actors

Element	*Authors*	*Users*
Key words/concepts	Word frequencies	Frequently used in entries search words
Names	Productivity	Popularity of authors
Documents	Number per author	Frequency of visits

All forms of information are not the same and there is a need to specify typologies of information and uses and the conditions and circumstances under which various types of information can be employed for different types of problems. In other words, to take a contextual and contingency approach in order to assess the use of information and the impact of what has been learnt. Knowledge does not exist in isolation, its use depends on contextualisation both upstream and downstream.

The role of digital library support for distance learning can be assessed through content analysis of transcripts of online collaborative learning and students assignments. The university created, assembled and delivered all the teaching materials students needed for their studies, except for a limited number of published set books which they were expected to purchase.

Digital libraries and new technology generally are not distance learning systems. They can provide a means of facilitating learning but do not provide the value added by a learning system. Value added functions include:

i) Entry, admission, registration, a learning contract of some kind

ii) Definition of the curriculum, knowledge and skills, what is included

iii) Series of tasks, instructions, learning activities

iv) Motivation, progression and commitment

v) Feedback, support and guidance

vi) Accreditation, certification

To organise these services a learning system with infrastructure, management, operational logistics, resources and scale is required. The idea that all that is needed for resources can be loaded onto the web and learners can simply access this material is attractive to policy makers. In essence a learning system must provide an appropriate degree of structure. With too little structure sustained progress and success are more difficult, too much and rigidities and inflexibilities create barriers for participation, increase possibilities of failing to meet deadlines and induce frustration in learners.

The work on the analysis of the content and structure of a field of knowledge is important for monitoring the development of the discipline and its coverage in a digital library. The resulting measures of association and structures can be used to help users navigate the field, either to find related documents, or to explore related concepts. Incorporated into a distance learning system a digital library can have a central or supporting role. The crucial issue is to provide appropriate structure for the curriculum and pedagogy for successful distance learning.

In fact, to look at the world wide educational material, as a virtual distributed archive of courses interacting with digital libraries is today only an attractive hypothesis: the educational information domain has not yet benefited of the digital libraries research efforts and requires a qualified and adequate indexation. The problem is burdened also by the fact that even the basic terminology and concepts for representation, organisation, and management of knowledge are still unsatisfactory.

Libraries and Flexible Learning Environment

Today, new ICTs have created a flexible learning environment and discipline boundaries are breaking down on the net. Groups of connected scholars globally have more in common with each other than their increasingly managerial university environments, where there is an emphasis on performance and delivery rather than the historical collegiality. The net web of intellectual anarchy replaces campus anarchy—the wheel barrow of academic frogs analogy.

The research undertaken by OCLC into distance and web-based learning could lead to partnerships with organisations like the open university. Lifelong learning, or lifelong retraining, will become the norm so the underpinning of such needs for structural information will be required. In the UK 70 per cent of jobs now require cerebral skills and less than 30 per cent manual skills.

The virtual universities will need virtual delivery of content. Mass physical lectures are clearly outmoded in the future. Students should be able, particularly as many have part-time jobs, to access to their lectures, plus associated material, whenever they want and increasingly it may be from whomever they want. In a higher education market research collections will have to be linked at a global cooperative level. There will be an associated growth of specialists in organising knowledge and the development of niche markets.

A multimedia environment, the nature of copyright, e.g., in interactive visual images becomes more complicated but the concept of 'fair use' in a university environment is one which is in need of universal protection. Electronic access rights could actually inhibit free flow of information in a number of cases as witness the quagmire that the Australian Copyright Agency (CAL) has got itself into an electronic reserve. Academics will have to retain their intellectual property particularly the electronic rights. It was noted that many publishers initially did not allow electronic retention of an archive. In the current Australian round of negotiations with Academic Press, the firm was unwilling to allow retention of their electronic archive. A design for living in the digital age, the information age may see a return to the pre-industrial revolution values. As individual themselves become producers and distributors of information, the dichotomy between gigagiant conglomerates and cottage industries will be evident and be mixed.

The rise of ICOLC (The International Coalition of Library Consortia), currently comprising about sixty library consortia, shows how the building bricks of library organisation might be erected *vis a vis* the well known multinational information providers. Thus the Australian and New Zealand university library community carries relatively little weight on their own but allied to the European and American groups it can provide increased leverage. Partnerships and strategic alliances may well be the way of the future.

In October 1997 more than 10,000 libraries in 53 countries were using OCLC First Search. OCLC more directly liaising with the Asian market may predict better the duration of the current Asian downturn on those countries and thus the educational/academic market. The global economy obviously impacts on global information access where costs of international information are often priced in US dollars.

OCLC's automation initiatives with the National Library of China in the early 1980s met with some hurdles and probably reflected the gap then between Chinese optimism for technology and the lack of necessary infrastructure to underpin it. In many Asian countries infrastructure support has to be evaluated for the long haul. For several years the Australain National Univertsity Library was able to support the Sino-Australian Electronic Centre in the National Library of China and also 'kick start' internet Chinese and Indonesian article indexing on the net, but this has now virtually ceased because of significant budget cuts to the ANU Library. The OCLC Tsinghua University office in Beijing is one example of another long-term support mechanism. The work OCLC has done in Hong Kong with JULAC (the Joint Universities Library Advisory Committee) may well provide a showpiece for China which has the second largest market for PCs in Asia.

The Middle East is again an area whose countries could be regarded as one. So on the one hand get, as mentioned earlier, a significant joining of interests in a mass globalisation and then in other sectors the need for recognition of local diversity is necessary as global sharing of resources is greatly accelerated by a more global use of the OCLC databases. The University of Queensland Library, which has uploaded its records into the OCLC database, has seen a decided increase in ILL requests which transforms into credits on the OCLC operations.

The linking of libraries from their catalogues and/or websites to the major providers of new books like Amazon.com or Barnes and Noble.com, or to the antiquarian book providers like ABE, Antiquarian Arcade and Interloc, opens up new dimensions to material which transcends the traditional library networks. It may be cheaper in the future to buy a volume from the Antiquarian Net than borrow and return on a one off basis the item from an overseas library. The US net is far more advanced in this context than the UK where second-hand booksellers seem less organised and more idiosyncratic despite the richness of the collections there. Global traffic will follow the best value, irrespective of country loyalties, and this pattern will be reflected in content access and dissemination.

The 'bulkinisation' of information allows costs to be spread across the globe via organisations such as OCLC. As foreshadowed earlier the size and variety of OCLC global stakeholders may provide both a challenge and a hindrance. The diversity of visions will need to be carefully balanced especially re-economic and cultural sensitivities.

Intellectual Access to Digital Information

Today most libraries, invests heavily in cataloging its collections. It probably has the largest cataloging operation in the world1 and is a source of both cataloging data and standards for much of the library community. In the world of paper-based publication, its role is second to none. One enduring role of libraries during the transition from physical to digital information will be the intellectual task of cataloging—imposing order on diverse resources with the goal of making those resources easier to discover and manage.

Cataloging is arguably among the most expensive tasks in the library. Current estimates range from $50 to $110 for the creation of a single full cataloging record. What is responsible for this high cost? While some of the tasks of cataloging—for example, recording a title—are indeed mundane (in the majority of but not all cases), others are intellectually challenging and time consuming:

— *Subject analysis*—The usability of library catalogs for finding resources "about" a particular subject depends greatly on the nontrivial task of understanding the content of a resource and tagging it with a controlled subject heading.

— *Authority control*—While the subject of assigning authorship may seem superficially simple, it is confounded by the fact that people frequently use different forms of their name, and different people frequently have very similar or identical names.

There is the problem of the multiple spellings of historical figures (is it "Shakespeare" or "Shakespere" or "Shakespear" or ?), the problem of aliases ("Mark Twain" and "Samuel Clemens"), and the seemingly random use of initials, shortened names, and the like ("Samuel Langhorne Clemens," "Samuel L. Clemens," "Sam Clemens," etc.). Authority control, in the context of author names, is the task of, first, associating these name variations with a canonical name in the cataloging record to show that the variations are indeed the same person and, second, differentiating between ambiguous and overlapping names.

The development of standard cataloging practices from the end of the nineteenth century through the twentieth century made it possible to share cataloging records, leading to a significant cost savings for libraries. "Copy cataloging" exploits the fact that the overwhelming majority of resources in an average library are not unique. Rather than produce original cataloging records for the duplicated resources, libraries can use cataloging records from other libraries. In US, the development of the machine-readable cataloging (MARC) record by the Library of Congress, in concert with the library community, in the 1960s was a landmark event in the automation of library operations. As recalled above, preautomation catalog sharing involved the physical shipment of catalog cards to fellow libraries. The introduction of computers into the library environment allowed sharing computer catalog records among libraries by exchanging magnetic tapes.

MARC consists of both an encoding scheme for labeling cataloging elements (e.g., "author" or "title") and an exchange format for packaging the encoded bibliographic data into a record for transfer purposes. The MARC record remains a critical technical foundation of existing integrated library systems and permits the transfer of records among these systems. The Library's Network Development and MARC Standards Office leads and coordinates international efforts to further develop MARC as a standard for the efficient and long-term interchange of bibliographic information.

In recent years, the office has been analyzing the relationship of MARC to standard generalized markup language (SGML) and the use of MARC for digital media. Such a catalog could have been a natural product for a national library and, perhaps, could have provided a revenue stream to underwrite the Library's cataloging operation. In fact, the Library, for reasons not entirely obvious to the committee or the individuals, failed to take advantage of this key opportunity and ceded it to the Online Computer Library Center (OCLC) and the Research Libraries Group (RLG).

While MARC provides the markup and transfer syntax for bibliographic records, the Anglo-American Cataloging Rules (AACR2) provide the rules for the actual description of a bibliographic item. The Library of Congress plays a major role in coordinating activities in AACR2, and its Library of Congress Rule Interpretations defines common practice for the use of AACR2 in cooperative cataloging. The result, in combination with the MARC standard, is that both the meaning and encoding of cataloging records can be shared among a large number of libraries.

These activities are centered in the Library's Cataloging Policy and Support Office (CPSO), which provides "leadership in the creation and implementation of cataloging policy within the Library of Congress and in the national and international library community." In general, archival and manuscript items are handled differently from monographs and serials. Whereas the latter are cataloged at the item level, the former are described at a coarser level of granularity (for example, a manuscript box or folder). Tools for locating such items are referred to as "finding aids." The encoded archival description (EAD) was the product of a project at the University of California at Berkeley in the early 1990s to develop a standard for machine-readable finding aids. The EAD standard utilizes SGML to mark up structured descriptions of units of archival information. The Library's Network Development and MARC Standards Office serves as the maintenance agency for the EAD standard, an excellent example of the Library stepping in to play an important role in the new metadata environment.

Challenges to Traditional Cataloguing Practices

A user of the Web who has sampled any of the numerous search engines (e.g., Google, AltaVista, Excite) might argue that digital content, networks, and full-text indexing have made human-mediated organization through cataloging obsolete. Web search engines demonstrate the great utility of such searching and the benefits of over 30 years of research in information retrieval and, to a lesser degree, natural language processing. However, there are numerous inherent limitations to the technology underlying them:

— *Scalability*—Most Web search engines accumulate indexes by scanning the Web and downloading full content from sites. As the volume of Web content grows, it has become increasingly difficult to keep these indexes current or complete. One study indicates that even the best search engines index only about 12 to 15 percent of Web content. Even more problematic are the limitations of the information retrieval (IR) technology used in most popular Web search engines. The nature of the Web as a corpus presents some difficult scalability challenges for IR and often leads to poor results. The sheer size of the corpus is a notable problem; a typical Web query will retrieve a very large set of potentially relevant documents. In addition, the Web corpus is usually presented as a single, unorganized collection of documents, which makes synonym clashes inevitable. Synonym clashes are well understood and can be addressed with a variety of techniques (e.g., thesauri, user feedback, local context analysis, phrase structure), but these techniques are generally not exploited by Web search engines.

— *Access limitations and databases*—While a great deal of useful content is freely available on the Internet, there is a growing and equally valuable portion of Internet content that is proprietary and held in protected systems. Much "valuable" content is held in databases on special servers that require a password or other means of authorization for access. These databases also provide enhanced functions beyond what can be done with simple, static Web pages. However, they do not in general support access via crawling, the method used to build most Internet search services. Thus, while Web indexers are able to access and index a large percentage of the total content on the Web, an ever-growing percentage of the most-sought-after material is not available from Internet search facilities.

— *Format*—Existing Web search engines are limited to textual content. They index words in documents and process textual queries—for example, "digital imaging"—returning lists of documents ranked according to the appearance of the query words in their content. Extending this approach to images will require tools to analyze image content and respond to queries such as "find images with cars in them" or, at an even more advanced level, to queries that ask for images with features similar to those of another digitized image. The tools to retrieve images, video segments, voice, and music are being actively researched but are currently beyond the capabilities of Internet search engines.

— *Context*—At a more abstract level, the usefulness of indexing based solely on the text content of a resource is compromised by lack of context. The best tools to help a person locate a resource are those that are tailored to the context in which the resource occurs and to the knowledge context of the searcher. For example, content-based searches of MEDLINE (the medical index at the National Library of Medicine) might be appropriate for a professional familiar with medical terminology and with the body of medical literature indexed by MEDLINE. However, a high-school student might not be able to select documents that are appropriate to his or her background and might not be familiar with medical terms, so he or she might find content-based searching to be difficult. The lack of context is a problem for both human and automatically generated representations, but different representations can often be combined to good effect.

— *Markup*—HTML, the main markup language of the Web, provides only a very simplified set of tags for labeling the parts of a document. These are primarily oriented to supporting the appropriate display of the document and in general tell little about the meaning of the various sections of the document. Many search engines utilize smart markup to provide more powerful retrieval facilities, allowing users to limit which parts of a document are used to satisfy the search argument. The simplicity of HTML markup severely constrains Internet search engines' use of such facilities, which are very useful for limiting and refining search results.

The creation of structured descriptive records for resources (e.g., traditional cataloging records or, more generally, surrogates) can help to address some of these limitations. Scalability can improve if surrogates are used instead of the full content for indexing. Content providers may be more willing to distribute freely descriptive surrogates for indexing, in lieu of the full content. Surrogates can be created, and standards are being developed for describing all manner of digital objects.

Finally, surrogate records may include descriptive information that is not part of the document itself (usually the result of human analysis). For example, surrogates to facilitate searching MEDLINE by high-school students might associate more common medical subject terms with the resources, thus making searching easier for this community. On the other hand, there is broad agreement among the committee members and in the general information community that the nature of resource description needs a thorough examination in the context of digital resources.

Traditional cataloging is one kind of resource description, which, in turn, is one kind of "metadata (information that describes the structure or content of a document but is not part of the document). The nature and use of meta-data are evolving to accommodate the great variety of digital objects.

Traditional library cataloging has scaled up to serve institutions of great size—prominent among them the Library of Congress. However, over the past year the number of resources on the Web has grown to the point that they exceed the number of books in even the largest of libraries and even the number of book pages in the average library. The growth rate of these networked resources substantially exceeds the growth rate of traditional physical resources. Sheer size presents considerable challenges to the economics of traditional library cataloging, in which metadata records are characterized by great precision, detail, and professional intervention.

The high price of traditional library cataloging makes it impractical in the context of such growth, and less expensive alternatives are needed for many, if not all, of these resources. There has always been a trade-off between the cost of creating metadata and its value in facilitating access to document collections. Large print collections generally cannot be accessed without some sort of metadata, so the value of the metadata is high. The appearance of digital objects in commercially interesting collections during the 1970s changed the economic model. Then, access could be provided with relatively little investment in metadata, although higher-quality metadata could still be justified for high-value materials. Now, the steady increase in the volume of electronic materials has increased pressure to reduce the cost of metadata, although manually produced metadata are still common.

The lifespan of networked resources differs dramatically from that of physical resources. The well-known problem of "dangling URLs" bedevils any librarian who is trying to incorporate Web pages into a collection. The impermanence of networked resources is rooted in the economics of networked dissemination. The cost of distributing networked content is low compared with the cost of printing and distributing hard-copy content, so there is little benefit to the publisher of maintaining older versions of a document. With no incentive to retain older versions, the management of objects is haphazard and object permanence is problematic.

Such an environment has a strong impact on the economics and incentives for producing metadata and also points out the critical need for preservation-oriented metadata and mechanisms to manage the preservation of digital objects. The breakdown of traditional publishing roles has disrupted some of the traditional mechanisms for establishing the credibility of an information source. Since metadata is itself an information resource, the credibility issue applies to the quality of metadata created by external sources (outside the traditional library cataloging community).

The creation of bad metadata can be nonmalicious: for example, an author who lacks training or who doesn't care may assign a bad subject classification to a descriptive metadata record. It can also be malicious: so-called "index spamming," whereby content creators seed metadata fields with misleading or incorrect information to affect the ranking of their pages by search engines, is a real problem on the Web. An important challenge for networked information is developing the mechanisms and policies to verify the origin of any information, including metadata.

Libraries, deals with a considerable variety of resources, including books, serials, maps, software, movies, images, and, now, digital resources. The Library's efforts to create metadata for this spectrum of resources can be divided into two categories. First, much attention has been paid to enhancing the traditional cataloging mechanisms—AACR2 and MARC, for example—to accommodate these new genres. These efforts are motivated by the central role that the traditional cataloging formats play in the Integrated Library System and in the cooperative cataloging efforts.

Second, the Library has employed a number of other vehicles for resource description—metadata schemata tailored for individual resource characteristics. Some schemata have been coordinated with external communities; others have been developed internally. The use of other metadata vocabularies raises the issue of how these vocabularies interact to provide integrated information spaces for users of digital libraries. After all, one of the major strengths of the standardization on AACR2 and its expression in MARC records has been the uniform search interface provided by library catalogs to large and heterogeneous collections.

The field of metadata has exploded into a major area of investigation and development over the past several years. As information becomes more of a commodity item--and, as many would argue, is the largest product of the "new economic paradigm--its management is of interest to a broad spectrum of organizations. This stands in rather strong contrast to the situation in the pre-Internet era, when the standardized management of information was more or less restricted to libraries, with the Library of Congress playing a key leadership role.

This broadening of the metadata environment will include many new players and applications and require the Library to think in new ways if it is to reassert its leadership in this area. Descriptive cataloging, exemplified by the traditional library cataloging record, is but one of many classes of metadata. Real-world applications need to make use of a much broader range of metadata than descriptive cataloging. Some other metadata types are listed below to provide a sense of this range.

— *Terms and conditions*: metadata that describe the rules for use of an object. Terms and conditions might include an access list of who may view the object, a conditions-of-use statement that might be displayed before access to the object is allowed, a schedule (tariff) of prices and fees for use of the object, or a definition of the permitted uses of an object (viewing, printing, copying, etc.).

— *Administrative data*: metadata that relate to the management of an object in a particular server or repository. Some examples of information stored in administrative data are the date of last modification, the date of creation, and the administrator's identity.

— *Content rating*: a description of attributes of an object within a multidimensional, scaled rating scheme assigned by some rating authority; an example might be the suitability of the content for various audiences, similar to the well-known movie rating system used by the Motion Picture Association of America. Note that content ratings have applications far beyond simple filtering on sex and violence levels. Content ratings are likely to play important roles in future collaborative filtering systems, for example.

— *Provenance*: data defining the source or origin of some content object, for example, of some physical artifact from which the content was scanned. The data might also include a summary of all algorithmic transformations that have been applied to the object (filtering, reductions in image density, etc.) since its creation. Arguably, provenance information might also include evidence of authenticity and integrity through the use of digital signature schemes; or, authenticity and integrity information might be considered a separate class of metadata.

— *Linkage or relationship data*: data indicating the often complex relationships between content objects and other objects. Some examples are the relationship of a set of journal articles to the containing journal, the relationship of a translation to the work in its original language, the relationship of a subsequent edition to the original work, or the relationships among the components of a multimedia work (information on synchronization between images and a soundtrack, for example).

— *Structural data*: data defining the logical components of complex or compound objects and how to access those components. A simple example is a table of contents for a textual document. More complex examples include the definition of the different source files, subroutines, data definitions in a software suite, SGML or XML tagged books, or other complex works.

The need for additional metadata types and for traditional metadata for a larger volume of materials challenges traditional means of metadata creation—manual techniques cannot be scaled up to meet demand. But automated techniques are available that can help in the production of metadata. These techniques have yet to be integrated with more traditional manual techniques; such integration will be a huge task for the library community.

References

Achatz B and H. Chen, "Digital Libraries: Technical Advances and Social Impact", *Computer*, vol. 32, February, 1999.

Hartley, S., et al. "Enhancing teaching using the Internet", *Report of the Working Group on the World Wide Web as an interactive teaching resource. SIGCSE/SIGCUE ITiCSE '96*, 218-228.

Marchionini, G., and H. Maurer, "The Roles of Digital Libraries in Teaching and Learning", *Communication of the ACM,* Vol. 38, No 1, 67-75, 1995.

Nikolaou, C, and M. Marazakis, "System Infrastucture for Digital Libraries: A Survey and Outlook", *SOFSEM'98, Lecture Notes in Computer Science 1521*, Springer, 186-203, 1998.

Rajashekar, T.B., *Digital Libraries, Information Studies,* October, 1995.

2

Net and Information Access

Digital libraries have a major influence on the design of future information systems. They are the cradle from which future advanced information technologies will emerge to provide 'transparent' services to a variety of users. They have already attracted many real-world agents, which participate for various economic reasons. For example, publishers of books are in the process of presenting their collections in digital formats in order to reduce production costs and increase profit margins.

Digital libraries are housing information objects in various media, such as text, audio, video and image, and provide information access services to a variety of users. One can envision a plethora of applications, such as collaborative computing and virtual classrooms, using such services. Users of these applications, being heterogeneous in their preferences, could request for different qualities of service for information access. The preferences of users could be based on the charge to access information. For example, users browsing through a digital library of video clips or image clips would prefer different qualities of service based on the charge and the availability of local resources (local software and hardware). The fact that current networks have limited bandwidth, and efficient usage of bandwidth is necessary to support many concurrent accesses to the digital libraries. Therefore, one can envision several levels of services being offered by digital libraries to access information objects.

In designing service mechanisms for accessing information objects in digital libraries, several issues arise. One of them is the issue of pricing services (and multiple service levels) to access information objects, and accounting and billing users for QoS. These are economic issues, however, they play an important role in allocating resources such as processing time, network bandwidth, buffer, memory and cache for storing, searching, accessing, transporting, and presenting various information objects in a coherent way to the users. For example, users might want to know the prices for different qualities of service to access an information object, such as a video clip of a lecture based on a specific day and time.

Globalisation and Information Services

Global politics are both multipolar and multi-civilisational, and that modernisation is distinct from Westernisation. The movement to increasingly large and dominant global providers will continue to emerge. E-commerce already surmounts national boundaries as major internet providers have found. The globalisation of business has already undermined the prerogatives of the nation state. Transnational corporations are increasingly paying tax in the jurisdiction of their choice and directing investments to countries offering special assistance. The internet accelerates the trend by bypassing established distribution channels which governments tax as goods and service move from producer to consumer. Local VAT taxes on electronic publishing could be overcome by global distribution. If the UK introduces a 17 1/2 per cent VAT on electronic publishing in 1999 this could have a devastating impact on library budgets, as could a first ever GST in Australia after the forthcoming election in 1998.

Globalisation is accelerated by the development of virtual organisations which might also become virtual feudalisms. The rise of the network society urges us to address the cultural and institutional effects of such rapid changes in the access to and exchange of information. The segmentation of knowledge encapsulated in the net may be reflected, in an extreme flexibility of work patterns and the individualisation of labour. The struggle between diverse capitalists and the miscellaneous working classes is subsumed into the more fundamental opposition between the bare logic of capital flows and the cultural values of human experience. Local providers will have to provide niche markets in either service or content, which, of course, in turn can be global.

The corner store will be replaced by the hypermall, the local bank by on-line commerce, the local bookshop by the internet super bookstores, while the local library could be challenged by the future super information providers. As keepers of the information prison the age-old social responsibilities of libraries may re-emerge in the internet society. Not for profit organisations like Online Library Centre (OCLC), have perhaps an increased societal role to play.

'Research Library Briefing' to the March 1998 OCLC Research Directors meeting outlined the stunning pace of technological change and revealed how earlier predictions are now hopelessly outdated. Retrovision is a useful perspective but the ability to predict the future is notoriously difficult. In an article in 1985 'Managing catalogues without cataloguers' 'the cataloguer and the librarian are no longer the somewhat remote and static recorders of information but the guides and pathfinders to the proliferation of electronic information data', but based this on CD-ROMs and not the net. Information would be delivered via punched cards and inter library loans in the far future would be via fax output. Sooner rather than later CD-ROMs will be seen as an interim technology like microfilm. In 1982 Bill Gates predicted that 640K of main memory would be sufficient power for user workspaces in operating systems and Microsoft failed to recognise the importance of the internet in the early 1990's. Internet Technology, believes in the relatively near future telephones, pagers, churches and vending machines will be all web connected.

OCLC need to recognise regional diversity and cultural attitudes but also be aware of the global economies of scale. Some concern has been expressed in Europe as to the nature of the American content in OCLC references services. Major American ILMS providers often shape their deals and practices in the US and then trying to impose them on to other global environments. US historical rigidity or practices may not be the best practice and comprise more flexible approaches internationally. OCLC may also wish to expand its 'think tanks' like Dublin Core in various sections of the globe. Bodies like OCLC need to both recognise and ignore national boundaries.

OCLC's management believes that what is good for OCLC must be good for the library world". This has clearly not been a dominant stream in recent years, as OCLC's interface has deepened with its users and the nature of libraries and their information resources has changed. One of the flavours of that early period and throughout the 1980's was the 'competition' between OCLC and RLG which was largely based on a general utilities provision.

If one looks at where the two groups are positioned in 1998 it is evident how different the two organisations look.

OCLC has positioned itself to become the springboard for global information provision across a wide system of activities, while RLG has focused itself, as a specific resource in the context of research collections. As chair of the OCLC Users Council in 1985, most OCLC users would be amenable to new ventures as long as OCLC continued still to provide the basics, which she called cataloguing and ILL. Eighteen years later these are important service but no longer, the core for the end user, who increasingly will not be a library, even though libraries may be a conduit for some users.

OCLC's Linking Strategy foreshadowed the impact of the internet and the aim of OCLC to become the easiest and most cost-effective way to integrate libraries into the emerging digital, global community. Furthermore, in the new systems approach are going to have to be concerned with the users' costs as well as the cataloguers' costs.

Reproduction of the card catalogue entry on OPAC terminals continued for some time, as has the replication of a printed page on the screen in the e-journal environment. In an era of increased coordination the constituent elements will include electronic library facilities, multimedia interactive classrooms, virtual reality laboratories, design and innovation centres which sit within or by the side of traditional print libraries.

Resource discovery will increasingly be a global activity with the focus of information access being in ever expanding circles rather than focusing back to a local print library, as has been the situation in the past. The net will empower centralised services such as OCLC and the search engine facilitators and that small groups will be effective globally in niche markets. It will be the middle ground, which will be weakened and libraries fall into that space.

A Recent study *Searching the World Wide Web* by Steve Lawrence and Lee Giles published in *Science* indicates that there are 320 million pages on the web that are accessible to search engines. They estimate that of the search engines studied, the best engine HotBot only covers one third of the Web. They suggest that tools such as the Metacrawler and software robots that can use multiple search engines and then combine the results into a single list will provide the best result. In future indexing services will be less and less popular unless they are linked to full text sources, either of the original creator direct, or by document access. Traditional catalogues are equally endangered unless seen as multi-source entry points to full texts and/or include metadata resources.

In areas of electronic access services, where funds are tight, there has been established definition between "core" and "value added services". Intelligent agents or "data miners" in many areas will replace some services by librarians. As users can delineate their requirements in terms of access to 'x' or 'y' topics in their specialities then commercial and non-commercial providers will increasingly provide customised access profiles. Material inside that profile delivered by the agents will either be free, available under an institutional site licence, or at a price as the user pays to open a particular envelope of information.

The identification and listing of the outside of books to the manipulation of the "deconstructed" text into chunks of electronic information is increasingly surrounded by subject value added services. Thus electronic journals cannot simply be the replication, both in cost and structure, of the print originals. ECO (Electronic Collections Online) provides an excellent one stop shop, e.g., for Australian libraries which have consortia deals. Pricing models however will be crucial for future subscriptions as budget cuts dig deeper and some major publishers continue to maximise profits over delivery of services to their academic providers.

Material Acquisition in Electronic Libraries

Following are the four principles for material acquisition in electronic libraries:

i) Link to the Original Source.

ii) Identify or Implement Reliable Mirrors.

ii) Identify or Implement Value-Added Features.

iv) Maintain the Links.

These principles attempt to address the issue of how to include items in an internet electronic library once a decision to add the item has been made. Principles for identification of appropriate items for inclusion and overall organisation of libraries are an area for further work. In addition, the principles suggested here are a first attempt at standardising electronic materials acquisition practices; additional experience and changes in technology may require the development of new or modified principles.

Implement Reliable Mirrors

Mirrors are useful to provide an efficient means of access to clients that are 'electronically closer' to the mirror site than to the original archive. Mirrors also provide greater reliability: an alternative source for the material when the original archive is unavailable (either temporarily or permanently). Mirroring is widely used in ftp-space based on the mirror software package. This software automatically tracks changes at originating ftp sites and duplicates those changes at the mirror site, with a variety of options. True mirror technology for other protocols is less well developed. For gopher, proper mirroring does not appear to be available, but copying of remote gopher directories and hierarchies is possible using the gopherdist and gopherclone utility programmes available with the Unix gopher software.

Implement Value-Added Features

In the case of the PACS Review, there is a searchable full-text index (freeWAIS) available in the North Carolina State menu, a facility not available from the Houston archive. This represents a *value-added* resource for PACS Review and is worth including together with the link to the Houston archive. As a more elaborate example, consider the Communications of the ACM entry in the computing science journals collection of the SFU Electronic Library. This menu links to the publisher (both the ACM Web Page and the ACM gopher server), contains a description of the journal from the publisher, includes three sources for bibliographies in different forms, links to a full-text archive at Arizona and also to a WAIS-searchable full-text archive.

Maintain the Links

Internet links are often dependent on several attributes, typically including a protocol (e.g., gopher or http) for accessing the item, an internet address for the computer (server) which provides the item in question, a port number at which the server listens to requests using the given protocol and a local filename, pathname, or other string that the server uses to retrieve the specific item in question. For example, the *universal resource locators* (URLs) used to make links in the worldwide web are essentially notations for specifying such attribute combinations in a form which allows unambiguous retrieval of an item.

Unfortunately, this means that installed links in an internet electronic library will need to be updated whenever any one of its attributes changes.

Reasons for such changes seem frequent and varied: reorganisation of material to a new structure, moving information to a better maintained or more powerful server, switchover from one protocol to another for providing information, and so forth. Even though most serious information providers attempt to provide relatively stable access to their resources, in the present context of the internet, 'stability' may mean no more than one or two years without change. At present, then, internet librarians must expect a significant percent of installed links to be changing each month. Link maintenance is a two-part activity involving link monitoring to check for broken links and link correction to repair, replace or delete broken links.

Many electronic libraries include e-mail contact addresses to report problems in a top-level menu. It may be more valuable to include a 'feedback' selection with every menu or information page, so that it is immediately visible to the user whenever an error occurs. Indeed, the top-level directory of a library may not be directly accessible to a user who has accessed a submenu through an external link or as the result of a search. It is now fairly common to find WWW servers with contact addresses on every information page, but the corresponding practice in gopherspace is rare.

The limited monitoring technique is to have the gopher or Web server software log all attempted accesses so that the logs can later be checked for errors. This can catch internal errors in data directories as well as certain types of error in gatewayed external links. However, errors in most kinds of external link will not show up in server logs.

Once a server has returned such an external link to a client, it will not be involved in any attempt by the client to access the external resource and hence there will be unable to record any log entry for such an access. On the other hand, errors in external links from other sites to your server will show up in the log file. By analysing these errors, it may be possible to track down outdated external links at remote sites and request that they be updated.

Resource Management in Digital Libraries

Current networks and systems have limited resources such as link bandwidth. Therefore, allocation of resources, such as processing time and network bandwidth, can be crucial in providing efficient services. In the future, bandwidth and processing time will be more than sufficient, and information objects will be priced based on the demand for them rather than on the digital library system (DLSystem) that houses them. A DLSystem is a complex computer system that provides storage, indexing, and access services to various information objects. Assume that a set of resource allocations make up a service. An information object could also be a resource, but do not price information objects in the current models; however, plan to incorporate this in the near future.

The main approach in pricing and accounting for QoS is an economic model of the players in large digital libraries. This involves modelling and understanding the various tasks that are required to support digital libraries. There are several reasons why this form of modelling helps in understanding the interfaces between the various elements of digital libraries. The main reasons are as follows:

i) *Limiting complexity:* Economic models provide several interesting contributions to resource sharing algorithms. The first is a set of tools for limiting the complexity by decentralising the control of resources. The second is a set of mathematical models that can yield several new insights into resource sharing problems.

ii) *Decentralisation:* In an economy, decentralisation is provided by the fact that economic agents attempt to achieve their goals in competitive fashion. There are two types of such agents, suppliers and consumers. A consumer attempts to maximise its benefit by obtaining the services or resource allocations that maximise its preferences under a wealth constraint. Suppliers compete in order to maximise revenue and minimise costs, which means attract more users and provide the best services.

iii) *Pricing and coordination:* Most economic models introduce money and pricing as techniques for coordinating the behaviour of agents. Each consumer is endowed with money, which they use to purchase services or resources. The price a supplier charges for a resource or a service is determined by its supply and the market demand.

iv) *Usage accounting, billing and dimensioning:* In using economic models for service provisioning in distributed systems, usage accounting becomes a part of the economy. Suppliers have to keep track of resource usage in order to price resources effectively, and thereby charge/bill the users for access.

v) *Administrative domains:* Large distributed systems and computer networks are spread over several domains. Each domain is typically managed and controlled by an administrator. An economic model of such an environment would imply that administrators advertise their services and prices. Therefore, provide a simple interface to negotiate between domains.

vi) *Scalability:* A key issue in designing architectures for services in large computer networks and distributed systems is scalability. Models of competition provide—in a natural fashion—mechanisms for scaling services appropriately based on the service-demand and resource-availability.

The novelty introduced by the economic approach is not only in modelling large decentralised, autonomous systems, but also in designing efficient systems that account naturally for user QoS requirements, and optimally allocate resources for the various services in digital libraries.

There are three kinds of players in the economic model of digital libraries: Suppliers (storage and indexing), Agents (who search, transform and present information) and Users. The three players are described below:

i) *Suppliers:* Commercial DLSystems buy works from various publishers and authors, and provide services to a variety of users for a fee. The DLSystems not only price information but also price QoS to access the information. Pricing is based on the user demand, and users represent their demands through agents. The prices remain fixed every time-interval, assuming that time is divided into intervals. For example, a time-interval could be six hours in a day. The time-intervals are decided by each DLSystem independently based on the market demand. The suppliers provide storage, access and local indexing services.

ii) I*nformation agents:* These are suppliers that provide *Value-Added Services*, such as transparent searching and presentation of objects to the users. From now on, we refer to information agents as agents. The agents charge users for QoS provided. Agents contract services and resources from DLSystems over a period of time, and provide stable set of services to the users. The stability is provided by a flat service fee over a period of time to the users. Agents renegotiate for services from each DLSystem provided it is profitable, else they release resources. The agents compete to provide *One-Stop Shopping* services to the users.

iii) *Users:* They present complex queries to the information agents, and request for a service in viewing or obtaining the objects. Users could be grouped into query classes based on similar access patterns or just based on service required. Users within a group or class share the costs of the services. Users are free to choose among the various agents based on the QoS and charge.

The economic model with three players. There are many classes of users who obtain services from one or many agents. The agents buy services from one or more of the DLSystems (library systems), and provide searching and presentation services to the users for a fee. Users are shown to get services only through the agents; however, one can also model users obtaining services directly from the DLSystems, which means that users have to search, on their own, for information about digital library services.

In the economic framework, agents compete for resources and services from DLSystems. They buy information access services ahead of time, and provide a set of integrated services to consumers (users). Similarly, DLSystems which have common information objects naturally compete to attract users and maximise profit. In designing pricing schemes for such services in an economic framework, several considerations need to be taken into account. The main considerations are the following:

i) Resources (such as buffer, bandwidth and CPU time) and services, based on performance parameters such as response time should be priced. Services for quality of search can also be priced. Information objects, in general, will be priced, plan to study this in the future.

ii) Prices must be set such that demand equals the supply. This is done to make sure that resources are not over-booked, and service quality is always maintained.

iii) Prices should reflect user query-request behaviour (load). This is essentially to control congestion of requests to a single digital library system.

iv) Prices should not fluctuate rapidly as users can get confused. In practice, prices should be stable for a reasonably long period of time.

v) Prices need to be negotiated ahead of time. This means that arriving users choose the services from agents based on the price information and the service levels.

Agents, post their prices and services offered for all the time-intervals on a certain day. For example, agents might offer low prices for a service between 6.00 a.m. and 4.00 p.m. and offer a higher price for the same service between 4.00 p.m. and 10.00 p.m. Agents, based on factors such as user demand profile and market behaviour, might compete to buy more services from the DLSystems. Agents have bugdets for buying services from DLSystems. They compete among themselves for services from suppliers. They charge the users based on QoS requested in searching and presentation. Suppliers price resources/services based on demand from the users. The time-intervals, where prices are fixed, are set independently by each supplier.

For example, supplier *A* might have 6.00 a.m till noon as one time period, and from noon till 6.00 p.m. another time period and price structure, and from 6.00 p.m. till 10. p.m. a different set of prices. Supplier *B* might have fixed prices between 6.00 a.m. and 5.00 p.m and another price structure for 5.00 p.m to 11.00 p.m. The behaviour of the suppliers is an economic one, the change in prices is due to the market demand. The suppliers operate indepedently in selecting the time periods for stable prices, however, they are driven based on the collective market demand. Similarly, each agent independently selects the time periods for stable prices to the users.

The suppliers, based on the demand profiles of the agents, decide on times when negotiation of the services and prices is done. For example, the price negotiation times everyday could be 6.00 a.m and 4.00 p.m. for supplier *A*, and 6.00 a.m and 5.00 p.m. for supplier *B*. Negotiation of prices and services by the suppliers is done at the beginning of every time period. Prices could be announced just after the negotiation. In economic terms, the negotiation protocol between the agents and the DLSystems could be done using the tatonnement process: agents are endowed with some wealth. Each agent computes the demand from a benefit function and wealth.

The aggregate demand from all the agents is collected by each supplier who then computes the new resource price. If the demand for a resource is greater than its supply, the supplier raises the price of the resource. If there is surplus supply, price is decreased. With the new prices, agents again compute and present their demands to the suppliers. This process continues till the equilibrium price is achieved where demand equals the supply. Bidding and auctioning for resources/services are other forms of price fixing. The basic philosophy behind auctions and bidding is that the highest bidder always gets the resources, and the current price for a resource is determined by the bid prices. The digital library system has a simple computer system with CPU and storage (discs, memory and cache).

The storage is very large and therefore the charge is negligible, however, assume that processing power and network I/O bandwidth is limited, and users are charged for them. Users who wish to get a good response time pay for network I/O bandwidth and processing time allocations.

One can argue that prices should be set on a monthly or weekly basis. However, this can cause potential problems as multiple levels of services cannot be supported flexibly for the various users. For example, users may not want services on all days, instead they would prefer to get services on demand.

If the agents in the information economy do not exist, then users will have direct access to the DLSystems. In such situations, users will send requests for information at arbitrary points in time. Therefore, guarantees for services and prices can be complex, as several thousands of requests could potentially arrive. If prices are not stable for long periods of time, then users can get confused about choosing the right agent.

Users will see a charge for access ahead of time, and will have a choice in choosing the right agent for searching and access services to the information objects. Assuming that prices fluctuate slowly, several practical issues of billing and payment can be resolved very easily.

Digital libraries contain information about companies and newspapers. The user first queries the digital library for stock information such as stock price, earnings and performance plots of a specific company or a collection of companies. The user then decides on stocks to invest and contacts a stockbroker to submit the request. The stockbroker buys stock for the consumer using the consumer account in the bank. The interesting issues are in storing and presenting information about companies in digital libraries and payment mechanisms.

Changing Library Environment

Information users that have served creators of electronic content in more established formats such as CD-ROM and local access databases have been rendered obsolete by recently emerging technologies—particularly the world wide web— complicating this endeavour further. Not only is this a new environment we are now designing in, it is changing at a daunting pace making relative experts out of anyone with an understanding of and skilled in the latest innovations. In this environment, experts seem to be generated on-the-fly much like a lot of web-based content.

There are numerous guides to authoring HTML and designing effective and useable Websites, there are few resources available to help more experienced content providers of web-based information systems to organise and manage their sites for the future. Perhaps one of the biggest challenges to such professionals is to develop and maintain a holistic approach to managing information in the fast lane of the information superhighway.

The University of Illinois at Chicago (UIC) has embarked, over the past several years under the auspices of the Great Cities Initiative, to explore numerous models for addressing how to bring traditional library values and librarian expertise to the organisation and management of information in this new and slippery environment. Some of these projects include the Chicago Public Library Website, the Chicago Council on Foreign Relations, the Illinois Department of Employment Security, Online, Incorporated's publications, the Apple Library Users Group, and most notably the US Department of State Internet services.

Acquisitions roles are also relevant to the digital environment as library staff have adopted the roles of receiving data files via the internet, validating the data for transmission errors, tracking and securing missing documents, reviewing files for completeness and accuracy and converting files from a number of proprietary formats for electronic access. This later responsibility has also led to expanded roles for librarians who find themselves in the position of developing access mechanisms via file conversion and interface design. In addition to the technical side of library roles of designing and managing content for the internet, library staff assume public services roles in the electronic environment.

Librarians provide assistance to users with accessing and navigating an often bewildering information environment, provide technical assistance in understanding the broader context of the information landscape (mediacy) and provide reference desk services and specialised services to remote users from around the world who access the information from a multitude of platforms. These public service roles also translate to collection development issues. Detailed log analysis and the high volume of e-mail user feedback and reference inquiries provide much data for librarians to decide about new content areas to develop.

Through the public service roles, librarians are in a unique position to understand user research and information needs, to determine what information is available and to look further by finding unpublished information sources, to identify and select content for local electronic publication, and to advocate to information providers to make new documents.

Librarians are in a unique position to assume consulting and advocate roles. Librarians serve as catalysts for the information explosion and advocates of free and equal access to information for all. This later advocacy role also translates to their historical role as advocates for preservation of information for future generations of users.

The traditional internal library roles are merging and evolving, the relationship between librarians and the rest of the world are shifting—the entire communication and information paradigm is being transformed. As a result, new partnerships are developing between professionals in a wide variety of fields, including publishers, the entertainment industry, technology enterprises, utilities, service industries and government. Time will show that the most successful projects will be those that take advantage of this redefinition of information by bridging expertise to give users better access to more reliable information resources. As more sophisticated means of tracking and measuring internet site usage are emerging every day, electronic information content providers are in a position of better knowing who users are and what their information needs and habits are.

A related concern with many web site administrators is how users find their sites. There is frequently discussion about the usage of HTML meta tags and the practice of 'spamdexing' or index spamming. This issue is complicated by the rapidly evolving information indexing and retrieval tools being made available to internet users. The speed and depth of such search tools and indexes is truly impressive, yet, it is important to remember that most of these sites are not in the information retrieval business. Such sites are marketing tools and indexing standards are not as issue.

Consequently, the use of tagging to improve retrieval can be a dubious endeavour. However, a look at from where users are connecting to a site can give designers an idea of what search tools and subject guides to pay close attention to if they are using HTML tagging to improve the accessibility of their sites.

Intellectual Freedom in Digital Libraries

Intellectual freedom is the right of every individual to any information they seek regardless of the subject, format or philosophy expressed. Intellectual freedom is at the heart of librarianship and the library is the most available and important point of access to information for all. It cannot exist as long as the right to information is challenged by censorship and any library may be a target of censorship.

The American Library Association (ALA) affirms that all libraries are forums for information and ideas, and that the following basic policies should guide their services:

i) Books and other library resources should be provided for the interest, information and enlightenment of all people of the community the library serves. Materials should not be excluded because of the origin, background or views of those contributing to their creation.

ii) Libraries should provide materials and information presenting all points of view on current and historical issues. Materials should not be proscribed or removed because of partisan or doctrinal disapproval.

iii) Libraries should challenge censorship in the fulfilment of their responsibility to provide information and enlightenment.

iv) Libraries should cooperate with all persons and groups concerned with resisting abridgement of free expression and free access to ideas.

v) A person's right to use a library should not be denied or abridged because of origin, age, background or views.

vi) Libraries that make exhibit spaces and meeting rooms available to the public they serve should make such facilities available on an equitable basis, regardless of the beliefs or affiliations of individuals or groups requesting their use.

Globalisation and Intelligent Library Services

Information is one of the most basic requirements for survival for all who living in this information age. How can we use computers, the most powerful devices yet devised, to enhance human intelligence, in particular to help us organise, find, get, and utilise relevant information? How we can specify such a computer solution to the universal problem of information need? How can we make intelligent digital libraries. Scenario-based design is one of the best ways to develop a solution. Seek an optimal design, posit a set of oracles that can undertake the desired services, with the support of the best possible description of the available collection of information. Thus, oracles can serve as ideal librarians and intelligent agents, and can work with a perfect information catalogue. By considering upper-bound or best-of-all-possible-worlds scenarios, we should be able to develop requirements for an ideal computerised system to help with today's networked information systems.

Discourse analysis techniques have been used to study what happens when an expert intermediary assists an end-user. The basic scenario is that a user approaches a librarian, who helps that user find relevant information. In the optimal case, the user works with an oracle (i.e., expert librarian) who: helps elaborate the problem (or anomalous state of knowledge), describes the user and user background, understands the topic or subject, constructs queries or other requests for desired information, knows how to access and present the relevant information, and provides explanations as appropriate. While scenarios and systems have been devised for this situation, even though the computer solution calls for a distributed expert-based information system, the overall architecture of (user)-(intermediary)-(information-base) is still fundamentally centralised.

To build a global information infrastructure one must deal instead with a distributed architecture. In the conventional situation this involves the following chains of communication: (i) (user)-(intermediary)-(catalogues)and (ii) (user)-(collection-of-intermediaries)-(collection-of-information-bases).

In the electronic version of this situation, electronic librarians will replace the human search intermediaries who assist end-users, intelligent network agents will replace the collection of intermediaries and other librarians who work with catalogues and indexes, and information catalogs will help with resource discovery and information retrieval. Then can serve: patrons of libraries scattered around the globe, internet clients dealing with the set of thousands or millions of disparate information servers, or, in the most general case, users of the emerging worldwide (virtual) digital library.

Specify the new functions to be carried out. They deal with: constructing catalogues, searching in catalogues, discovering desirable resources through the use of catalogs, effectively utilising the information network, searching in parallel or in a serial sequence through the distributed collection of information resources. Since agents are involved there are additional functions, such as building of knowledge representations by agents for record keeping and continuation of sessions, interchanging knowledge between agents to facilitate their cooperative pursuit of user goals, and communicating directly or indirectly between users and agents.

In the context of digital libraries, there are additional demands from information providers regarding: market analysis, economic modelling, quality control, intellectual property rights management, copyright protection, subscription handling, personalisation for users, version control, usage analysis, and tuning of services offered. In the context of collaboration among users there are further requirements regarding group access control, tailored information sharing, communication between user agents, and support for distributed problem solving.

Designing the ideal digital library system (IDLS) to support the humanities can be accomplished in part by providing detailed scenarios involving: expert electronic librarians, intelligent network agents, and information catalogues. The scenarios below deal with a sampling of representative situations, focusing on the handling of textual information.

First, consider the work of constructing a new dictionary. Picture a talented lexicographer working with a collection of oracles to construct a new general purpose dictionary of English. One oracle takes the job of collecting works to make up a representative corpus. Using the IDLS's catalogue of entries, it samples them to provide a suitable mixture of genres and to balance according to economic, educational, geographic, political, religious, and social distributions of the target population. The catalogues agent helps with the sampling and balancing tasks, calling on agents that work with the various aspects of user models. Each significant work selected for inclusion in the corpus has its own 'work agent.' Each work agent has collected data on the most commonly accessed parts of its work. The work agent can use that data along with a word-sense level inverted file to find the best quotations and usage examples available to accompany the definition for any given word.

A clustering agent works with the word-sense disambiguated concordance-type data extracted from the full set of works, to assemble the raw material for constructing dictionary entries. A browsing agent coordinates with the clustering agent and an entry agent to allow the lexicographer to experiment with groupings, orderings, annotation and hypertext-style linking back to the contexts of appearance in the corpus. An assembly agent identifies all the parts for the dictionary entry, generates suitable SGML according to a Document Type Definition (DTD) based on the TEI guidelines, and produces links to other dictionary entries as well as to the original works in the corpus. Finally, an editor agent communicates with the lexicographers and the dictionary editor, ensuring consistency and high quality in both the electronic and print versions of the dictionary.

Second, consider the task of assembling and analysing the works of a great writer. A humanities scholar is the world's expert on Miss X, and wishes to assemble and use an electronic archive of the works of X along with all the relevant interpretive commentary, background (cultural, historic, and social) information, correspondence, and biographical documentation. That archive must be defined by an electronic catalogue of suitable works, which can be derived from the IDLS catalogue by an agent that constructs subsidiary catalogues for specific areas of interest. The subsidiary agent works not only with the IDLS catalogue but also with search agents whose expertise is to handle the short, semantically rich, highly structured catalogue entries. The scholar cooperates with an electronic librarian through a number of sessions of searching and browsing to provide various result sets, which, after suitable culling, provide the basis for the subsidiary catalogue for Miss *X.* Through a type of scatter-gather operation, the subsidiary catalogue is repeatedly expanded and refined to give optimal coherence and coverage. A citation network agent uses the transitive closure operation to chase down citation chains, and the literary clustering agent uses co-citation and bibliographic coupling measures to organise the many levels of interpretation.

A timeline agent prepares an historical organisation for the corpus, and a variety of special purpose indexing agents prepare views for each genre found in the collection. Our humanities scholar can employ agents to help look for patterns, e.g., those found by Ide in studying Blake, or those related to repeating sequences, work with raw frequency data or higher level statistical analyses, browse at high speed and with great flexibility, construct a wide variety of hypertext trails, visualise new organisations, or prepare courseware.

A frequently-asked-questions (FAQ) agent monitors accesses to the archive, noting users' interests and what they find, as well as the additional material recommended by the humanities scholar, and prepares an optimally structured collection of questions/needs and replies/pointers. A collaboration agent helps groups of students, historians, writers and others to work together to discover new perspectives, that can in turn be added to the emerging, dynamic digital library for X.

Finally, consider developing a digital library from the research of graduate students. ETD International is a hypothetical non-profit corporation seeking to facilitate graduate education as well as technology and knowledge transfer for the benefit of society. Its focus is on electronic theses and dissertations (ETDs). It maintains a comprehensive electronic catalogue of all graduate student publications and an electronic archive containing them all. It constructs agents to help with ETD preparation, review, abstracting, cataloguing, archiving, searching, browsing, and reuse.

Digital Library Collaborations

Now many of the collaborative relationships between librarians and computing professionals are developing in many institutions. Teaching faculty and researchers have evolved in the context of networked information resources and services. The relationship is based on the work of writers in the fields of communications and organisational behaviour. The range of existing collaborations in the networked information environment will be categorised and factors which motivate collaboration, and those that hinder it, will be examined. The implications for library administrators, computer controllers and higher education institutes, both now and in the future, will be considered.

The roles and job functions of librarians and information professionals have been subject to significant change over the last five to 10 years—firstly as a result of automation and, secondly, as a consequence of the advent of networks. In some higher educational establishments this has led to the administrative merging of libraries and computing centres; in others it has resulted in increased collaboration between two administratively separate units and there are yet others where the consequence has been duplication of some functions.

As the information environment has become increasingly networked, librarians and information technologists have begun to move from contractual arrangements to new patterns of relationships characterised by a move towards shared responsibility in:

i) conceptualisation of projects;

ii) authority;

iii) allocation of resources.

The process of shared creation is two or more individuals with complementary skills interacting to create a shared understanding that none had previously possessed or could have come to on their own. Collaboration creates a shared meaning about a process, a product, or an event. The concept of collaboration focuses on the characteristics of the process of interaction among the partners, with emphasis on an intangible—shared meaning—and a quality of interaction between the participants that can best be described as mutual respect.

Rosabeth Moss Kantor in 1990 described productive partnerships as those which evolve and continue nevertheless to yield benefits, create new value and work through interpersonal connections and internal infrastructures which enhance learning. She identifies eight characteristics of best partnerships:

i) each partner contributes something of value;

ii) the strategic objectives of all partners are addressed;

iii) partners have complementary skills and assets;

iv) each partner makes an investment in the other (as distinct from a contractual relationship, in which there is no such mutual investment);

v) communication is reasonably open;

vi) mechanisms for smooth working together are in place;

vii) each partner becomes both teacher and learner;

viii) there is integrity and mutual trust.

Now most campuses expect that a Campus-Wide Information System (CWIS) is either available or is being developed by one or more units—and both the library and the computing centre would have a valid claim to its being within their strategic province. By combining resources, pooling professional talents and learning from each other, the two units can implement a collaborative project which will enhance the information environment of the campus and yield shared meaning.

In a true collaboration, each unit considers the endeavour to be mission critical, while in a contractual relationship only one party would have that view, the other having provision of support services as the primary goal. Also, in a collaboration, risks and benefits are shared, whereas in a contractual arrangement, the contracting party reaps most of the benefits if the project is successful and is the major loser if the project fails. Success, as far as the party providing services is concerned, may still provide a limited share of some of the benefits, but failure will not prejudice the agreed remuneration.

Only a few years ago, the provision of information services to the campus community had a very different meaning for both libraries and computing centres. Advances in the networked information environment in, for example, library catalogues on the internet and universal access to information via gopher and the world wide web, have brought library and computing centre services closer together. The traditional division of complementary skills into 'content' for librarians and 'conduit' for computing professionals, which has served as a good starting point for collaborations, has become increasingly blurred.

Collaborations on service projects with a concrete outcome, such as the provision of reference facilities, or the establishment of a help desk, or the development of an internet training programme, offer opportunities for staff from library and the computing centre to begin to discuss common mission, can provide mechanisms for sharing skills and will encourage the concept of shared meaning. The development of a campus information environment, including information policies, creation and distribution of electronic journals and the development of websites and pages, provides a fertile ground for the exchange of ideas on the mission of the library and of the computing centre, promotes convergence of the principles and practical experience of professionals in both disciplines, and encourages the adoption of the concept of shared meaning.

Administrators of libraries and computing centres have a critical role to play in the successful implementation of collaborative projects between their respective units. Firstly, they must share their vision of a project and the way in which it addresses the mission of their unit, with all staff involved;

secondly, they must demonstrate a demeanour which discourages power struggles between the units; finally, they must make evident a mutual respect and help to create a climate in which others in their units can develop shared understandings.

There are many creative and forward-looking ways to foster partnerships between librarians and information technologists. Most important, however, is to begin with an open mind and an attitude that each group has much to gain from the other. Successful partnerships between libraries and other professionals, such as the teaching faculty, publishers, media designers and instructional specialists, are also becoming increasingly common in the environment of the world wide web.

There is a strategic advantage for libraries and librarians in securing collaborative relationships both within the academic arena and out of it. No one individual or profession has all of the skills now needed to create an information infrastructure for a community of users. The establishment of a collaborative relationship should provide a stake in it which relates to the mission of all partners. A shared understanding of the way in which a project contributes to each partner's mission will have a beneficial effect on all team members, and the individuals concerned must also pay as much attention to the relationship among the partners as to the outcome of the project. A fundamental appreciation of the complementary skills of each team member and of the viewpoints associated with them is crucial and must be accompanied by open and easy communication, opportunities for mutual teaching and learning and the building of mutual trust and respect.

Architecture for a Global Digital Library

The architecture for a global digital library is simplified by considering the following infrastructure levels:

i) *Application/configuration layer*: This level provides tools to help select digital objects for assembling a new digital library, as well as tools for defining context as concept spaces. Concept spaces support description of users and collections, facilitate matching of levels of expertise and content.

ii) *User services:* Multiple services are provided by a global digital library, including presentation, translation, mining, and query support. Presentation services can dynamically define the user context and modify the presentation context to be compatible, controlling user specified presentation versus collection specified presentation (such as choice of character set). Translation services can help develop correspondences between thesaurus-like concept spaces. Mining provides tools to seek out the existence of explicit relationships, thus aiding query support and content-based information retrieval.

iii) *Domain knowledge management*: Ontologies organise collection concepts, and require explicit tools to facilitate their maintenance. Tools can integrate existing ontology representations or can extend a specific ontology to include new concepts that describe common sets of information about the collection. Tools also are needed to support the creation of metadata for concepts contained within the ontology, but not expressed within the collection metadata.

iv) *Collection management:* The ability to build an infrastructure independent description of a metadata catalogue is needed to support migration of collections between different types of database systems. Effectively, this consists of tools to support creation of schema, modification of schema, and publishing of schema for use by other applications. The collection then can be distributed across multiple information repositories, with local control over the digital objects, and access control lists used to protect intellectual property. A distributed collection can be implemented across multiple administrative domains, including internationally distributed sites.

v) *Data handling system:* When digital objects are distributed across multiple storage systems, data handling environments are needed to manage access. This is essential for integrating collections that are distributed across file systems, archives, and databases provided by multiple vendors. Distributed digital object management provides persistent identifiers, replicas of data sets, containers for aggregating digital objects before storage in archives, and archival storage interfaces.

vi) *Storage system:* The fundamental level of a global digital archive is the set of storage systems used to hold the data objects. The storage systems will be distributed internationally, with each site maintaining local control. A global digital library only becomes possible when the storage systems are integrated.

Fundamental to modern scholarship is the notion of distributed collections. Each nation, state/province, town, university, department, center/group, or individual may run a server, with collections of data, documents, and other resources. Building upon this base, digital libraries add unique types of support.

i) Digital libraries allow sharing not only of various digital objects but also of information describing those objects. Such descriptive information often is called metadata. In many cases metadata is adequate for discovery of useful resources, and generally is more freely shared than are digital objects themselves. Through the Open Archives Initiative (OAI) Protocol for Metadata Harvesting, metadata can be shared, from personal collections (e.g., built using tools that run on laptops, such as Kepler), to group or department or focused collections, on up to global repositories. The OAI concept is powerful. Scholars can easily share metadata, without also having to provide services. Others who desire can use specialised tools to provide tailored services, after harvesting just the information really needed.

ii) Distributed collections allow virtual documents to be constructed. A collage can be assembled from a group of images of art works. A homework assignment can be assembled by an instructor from a small set of problems, each made available as an educational resource. A report can be prepared by a student, drawing upon diverse materials, to argue a particular viewpoint, supported by data, images, and video. Further, virtual collections can be prepared. A portal might provide access to a virtual collection that is built up in turn from smaller subsidiary collections. Smaller virtual collections can be assembled in a particular specialty area, or larger virtual collections may be built as national resources.

One way to assemble a global digital library is to integrate multiple existing libraries. As with PRDLA, this can be achieved through varied mechanisms. It is possible to integrate collections at the following levels:

i) Data level, through replication of resources. Each site continues to provide their original services, but on a much broader set of primary source materials.

ii) Access level, through implementation of a data grid. As before, each site continues to provide their original services, but they are now able to access material that is managed and archived at another site.

iii Service level, through implementation of common web services. This makes it possible to apply a service developed at another site to digital holdings on your site.

For these integration mechanisms to work across cultural and language domains, interoperability mechanisms are needed for both semantic and procedural knowledge. One can think of semantic interoperability as providing mechanisms to describe relationships between terms to define equivalent meaning. Procedural knowledge is the expression of the manipulation context that one expects to associate with a collection. This can be as simple as the organisation of material for presentation for societies that read right-to-left, or bottom-to-top, or back-to-front. Procedural knowledge defines the manipulation context for the presentation of the material within a digital library.

One of the interesting challenges is that procedural knowledge is typically assumed by the style of display used within a portal for accessing the digital library, to conform to a cultural standard. It is interesting to note that the emerging support for handicapped persons is challenging the ideas of cultural standards for presentation of data and information. A fruitful area of research will be to understand how support for handicapped access addresses the same procedural knowledge issues that are encountered by multi-cultural access.

User access to digital libraries brings an additional layer of complexity to the definition of procedural knowledge. The challenge is to preserve not just cultural context, but also the individual user perspective when exploring information. Users can define their preferred access context as a combination of their historical access patterns, their current interests, and their personal level of knowledge. In a multi-cultural setting, each access to a digital library should result in the presentation of a context that meets not only cultural expectations, but also personal preference expectations.

The area of digital library infrastructure where legal, policy, and technical issues most strongly interact is in the management of user access. The specification of what an individual is allowed to access, the rights they have to reuse material, and the rights they have to remain anonymous represent possibly conflicting requirements. The resolution of these conflicts requires policy decisions for use of the digital library infrastructure. For multi-cultural situations this can become a 'catch-22' situation. To correctly identify the rights of a person to anonymous access to material, the digital library may first have to identify the culture or organisation through which the person is obtaining access. By representing individuals as members of a combination of cultural/organisational groups, it may be possible to decide which policies to invoke without having to explicitly identify an individual. This implies the ability to authenticate membership within an organisation or cultural group. This type of identification is being pursued as part of the Shibboleth authentication environment, and is being promoted for use within digital libraries.

Digital libraries that span cultural systems have substantial operational management concerns. Many of these issues can be cast in terms of policy management decisions, for the criteria under which actions will be taken. Operational management also includes management of user load, by redistribution of accesses to sites where resources are available to meet demand. This in turn implies the replication of data resources between sites to enable access load to be shifted. The mechanisms to manage replicas across sites are provided by data grid technology. Thus operational management for global digital libraries will be linked to the emerging global grid infrastructure.

An international effort has been underway for two years to develop consensus on the services and protocols that will be provided by global grids. The grid community meets at Global Grid Forums that are held three times per year, traditionally in the US or Europe. An effort has been made to plan for grid forum meetings in Asia, to promote a truly global grid environment. The creation of global digital library infrastructure should carefully track the emerging grid technologies.

The typical services include grid authentication mechanisms, support for remote job execution, support for characterising grid resources, and data grids for building distributed data collections. These services will form a core operational framework for global digital libraries. The second community that is providing relevant technology includes the standards efforts led by the world wide web consortium, ISO, and industrial consortia such as the Object Management Group. These communities are developing technologies to support semantic webs, network protocols, and model driven architectures for infrastructure independent representations of services. The hope is that the technologies developed by the digital library community, the grid community, and the standards groups will be able to interoperate, and create an infrastructure that minimises the operational management requirements. The idea of the 'digital library' includes solving many of the technical and logistical issues in current libraries and information seeking. The digital library, if improperly considered, could lead to a problematic future. Many of the scientists have spoken with wistfulness about the past, remembering themselves in a single physical room. They do not want to go back; they do not want to lose the independence of separate workstations. But, they do miss the camaraderie and social cohesion furthered by the interaction in that room. Such interaction is too easily lost and regained only with great difficulty. Considering only the mechanical aspects of access can lead to ignoring the positive and useful social interactions in information seeking. Social interactions can be quite helpful to information seekers in four ways.

i) One may need to know what to know. In general, it could be argued that as access to material becomes easier, emphasis will shift from the mechanical aspects to knowing what material to access. If we can have every book in the world, we will need to know what handful of books to read. Help in selecting materials can be alleviated through technical means. None the less, one may need to have the help of other people as well.

ii) Social interaction is helpful in providing mechanism for seeking informal information. Informal information includes unofficial information such as technical fixes, organisational work-arounds, and personal corres-pondence. Since this information is often quite volatile and transitory, it is seldom written down, let alone indexed. Other people are often the only source of informal information. Current libraries do not handle this type of information seeking, but digital libraries could.

iii) Information seeking is often *ad hoc* and highly contextual. Information seekers often have highly specific interests and needs. It is often more simple and efficient to go to others for information than to written materials.

iv) Current libraries do have some important—and useful— social functions. For students, the university library can have an important

> socialising function. Students meet one another and talk in the hallways and canteens, and faculty members bump into colleagues in elevators and stacks. Libraries serve as a place to co-learn. Moreover, community libraries offer a number of social outreach and care programmes. Many of these useful social functions exist secondarily, as by-products of the library's information access goals. None the less, they are not only useful functions, they also make life more pleasurable and rich.

The design of a digital library does not have to eliminate the social world. Quite simply, there are important elements of the social world, including a sense of community, that we do not want to lose from our notions of "library". Many social mechanisms are important and useful in information access, and social interaction provides an enjoyable and community-building function.

The British Library is one of the world's great research libraries. It has served scholarship, research and innovation for over 450 years. Now, tremendous changes are taking place at a rapid, and increasing, rate. Some of these transformations arise from the demands of users who are themselves influenced by new phenomena, such as the internet; some are due to the sweeping changes affecting equipment, particularly computers and communications.

The British Library is preparing for this new environment, not only by initiating programmes to exploit information technology, but by forging new partnerships to meet the challenges ahead. Its main purpose is to serve scholarship, research and innovation. In this respect the Library is not primarily providing resources for undergraduate teaching, but acts rather as a research material provider.

Computer literacy is becoming more and more commonplace, from the schoolroom to the workplace. This process has been encouraged by the exponentially increasing use of the internet. In its own services and collections, the British Library is sure that digital materials will not replace all traditional library materials and that people will continue to want to use them as traditional materials. In parallel, there is an inexorable rise in the demand for digital materials.

Information Technology (IT) is polarising in respect to its equipment and activities. Convergence on a global scale is manifest in computers and communications, media and publishing and education and entertainment.

The same technology trends are catalysing great individuality, creativity and variety. Access to electronically held information is distance-independent and in the near future the cost of using powerful communications over long distances will be negligible.

At present, one hour of such use would cost about five cents. Although this might be perceived as relatively low and although it will undoubtedly fall, the level of charge is currently two orders of magnitude above costs and significant changes are perhaps unlikely over the next five years. Nevertheless communications is now viewed as a global commodity, though the infrastructure is not in place as yet in many parts of the world.

Software tools are becoming increasingly inexpensive, easy-to-use, powerful and sophisticated. This, combined with the development, price reductions and availability of hardware advances, such as massively parallel processing, will allow desktop computers to interact very quickly and a great deal more naturalistically. The British Library is preparing for the new environment, where access will be a primary factor. It has initiated the Initiatives for Access programme of pilots and demonstrators to exploit IT, test new services, examine organisational implications and provide a vehicle for collaboration and public relations—including PR on exactly what a great research and development library is capable of.

The vision of the British Library is of integrated access to its digital collections and those of other organisations. It will, therefore, be organised, and indexed for such access and will work towards increasing the access, both in terms of people and materials, while maintaining availability of digital archives. Other aspects of that vision will include staff having 'digital competencies', establishing a balance between the requirements of Intellectual Property Rights and fair dealing with information and the commitment of substantial investment, from both the Library and its partners, be they government or private sector. The priorities will be:

i) the extension of United Kingdom legal deposit legislation to electronic materials (microform and digital);

ii) the expansion of British Library document supply services, built on article alerting and improved delivery;

iii) the expansion of patent services, based on Patent Express (all patent offices issue patents on CD-ROM and it is unlikely that any patents will be on paper beyond the next five years);

iv) improved access to the British Library's historical collections via services to researchers, schools and the general public.

The global digital library clearly requires cooperation, not least on standards, protocols and on services based on access to digital collections. Different kinds of partnerships will encompass agreements on standards, collaboration with other digital collection owners and joint ventures with the private sector. Different partners could be derived from the academic community, from industry and commerce and from public libraries. Partnership will provide opportunities for developing improved, more comprehensive services and a means of sharing development costs. In addition to nationally-based partnerships, the British Library will be seeking to extend collaboration with relevant organisations in both the European Union and the United States.

Overall, the great changes now taking place worldwide and at an accelerating rate will transform the nature of all libraries and the British Library will not be exempt from that process— far from it.

In the digital world, libraries face number of challenges. But it is also about every non-commercial institution — from public TV to the freenets — that provides information to the public. It uses libraries as an exemplar of what can happen to even our most cherished public institutions when they face the onset of the digital revolution, a seismic societal shift. Libraries have their work cut out for them if they do not want to reside on the margins of the revolutionary new digital information marketplace.

The younger generation— wedded to desktop computers — may provide a particular challenge. But this battle is not the libraries' battle alone. At issue is the very notion of a public culture—that nexus of schools, hospitals, libraries, parks, museums, public television and radio stations, community computer networks, local public access, education, and government channels of cable television, and the growing universe of non-profit information providers on the internet.

Library leaders want the library of the future to be a hybrid institution that contains both digital and book collections. And they assume that it will be the librarian 'navigator' who will guide library users to the most useful sources, unlocking the knowledge and information contained in the vast annals of the information superhighway.

Some library leaders envision a digital 'library without walls' in which users gain access to almost unlimited amounts of information through home computers or at remote terminals located around the community. They also envision a time when one library's collection will, because of growing electronic capabilities, become everyone's collection. Library leaders see a continuing role for the library building. As a central and valued community meeting space, the library will become more of a civic integrator and a locus of community information on health, education, government, and other local services.

Library leaders also express considerable concern about the information have-nots, individuals who do not have access to computers or online information. And they argue for a social activist role for libraries in which citizens could receive literacy information or acquire health and job information. They nevertheless express reservations about the library becoming marginalised by taking on exclusively the role of information safety net.

The public loves libraries but is unclear about whether it wants libraries to reside at the centre of the evolving digital revolution or at the margins. Trusting their libraries and seeing them as a source of comfort in an age of anxiety, Americans support their public libraries and hold them in high esteem.

They support a combined role for libraries that links digital and traditional book and paper information resources. And they accord equal value to libraries as places where people can read and borrow books or use computers to find information and use online services. Americans also strongly support the key roles of libraries, ranking the following roles as very important:

i) Providing reading hours and other programmes for children.

ii) Purchasing new books and other printed materials.

iii) Maintaining and building library buildings.

iv) Providing computers and online services to children and adults who lack them.

v) Providing a place where librarians help people find information through computers and online services.

Moreover, men were less enthusiastic than women on almost all aspects of the library. And a strong plurality of Americans said they preferred to acquire new computer skills from 'somebody they know,' not from their local librarian. While only a fifth of respondents said they thought libraries would become less important in the digital age, those with access to computers were most likely to feel this way. A focus group of frequent library users affirmed much of the polling data, endorsing America's trust in libraries and sounding warnings about the need to remain relevant. In many respects, focus group participants saw libraries as playing an important role in their communities.

For example, they seconded the library leaders' vision of a hybrid institution, containing both books and digital materials. They also warmly endorsed the concept of the library as a place that provided equal and free access to information, especially to the information have-nots. Libraries should take a reactive role, adapting to new technologies.

Some library leaders fear that computers and bookstores will increasingly draw library users away from libraries, at least for now this concern appears groundless — one market seems to draw sustenance from the other markets. Americans favour spending more tax dollars and charging extra fees to supplement library operating funds and to purchase computer access and information. Given $20, they would rather spend it on taxes to aid libraries that want to purchase digital information and make it available through home computers than spend that $20 on their own computer software.

Library users favour increasing taxes more than non-library users, who prefer a pay-as-you-go fee system in which individual charges would be levied for certain services. Like library leaders, Americans place high value on library buildings. But unlike the library leaders, Americans are less sure that the library is a significant community meeting place.

The public ranks high the notion that librarians should take on responsibilities for aiding users who want to navigate the information superhighway. But when asked where they would go to learn more about using computers, a strong plurality said they would ask somebody they know, not their local librarian. Families with children were particularly strong library supporters as well as heavy computer users.

Minorities favour providing computer services to information have-nots and are strong supporters of building more libraries. They are also willing to pay extra taxes and fees for more library-based digital services. Lower-income Americans are least likely to ask a friend for help in mastering computer skills, so they might be particularly receptive to librarians acting as digital information trainers.

The public policy issues which will affect the realisation of library leaders' visions for their professions and the ways that people use libraries, include:

i) Universal service and access, through which libraries would provide affordable access to and use of computer networking tools.

ii) Freedom of speech and the host of policies that support or limit libraries' ability to collect, create, and make available materials— including those that invoke controversy — in the digital age.

iii) Intellectual property issues, including copyright and the moral rights of artists and authors to their work, which will affect both libraries and library users.

iv) Funding or support mechanisms, especially with the decoupling of library services and the local tax base as more collections are part of digital networks with no geographic boundaries.

Today, libraries are at a crossroads, for they must adjust their traditional values and services to the digital age. But there is good reason for optimism as libraries and their communities take up this challenge. Libraries have enormous opportunities nationwide to influence and direct public opinion because strong public sentiment already supports key visions for the future of libraries. Moreover, the growing use of home computers seems, at least at this juncture, to complement library use. So libraries and their leaders now must chart a role for themselves, giving meaning and message to their future institutions and their central role in community life.

References

Chen, C., "Global Digital Library Development," *Knowledge-based Data Management for Digital Libraries,* Tsinghua University Press, pp. 197-204, 2001.

Gopal Krishan, *Digital Libraries in Electronic Information Era*, Authorspress, New Delhi, 2000.

Hulser, Richard P., "Digital Library: Content Preservation in a Digital World", *DESIDOC Bulletin of Information Technology*, 17, 1997.

Lynn, M.S., 'Digital Preservation and Access', *Collection Management* 22, nos. 1998.

Schatz B., and H. Chen, "Digital Libraries: Technical Advances and Social Impact", *Computer,* vol. 32, February, 1999.

Sproull, L. and S. Kiesler, *Connections: New Ways of Working in the Networked Organisation*, MIT Press, Cambridge, MA, 1991.

3

Digital Archiving

Archives have been involved in great changes with the use of modern information technology to automate archives management, especially through the application of computers for the arrangement and description of records. The result is faster and more accurate arrangement and description, as well as more efficient information retrieval. The use of computers in Asian archives is not widely developed, but the employment of word-processing or database systems to produce finding aids or to undertake other aspects of the management of archival material is now to be found in Australia, China, Indonesia, Japan, Macao, Malaysia, the Republic of Korea, Singapore and Viet Nam.

An Asian computer network for exchanging archival information does not yet exist. Archives in Asia play an important role as an indispensable instrument for the history of both the whole continent and the individual nations. Consequently they must offer well-organized and structured services in order to give easier access to citizens and researchers. Until recently most archives in Asia were very isolated and unprivileged institutions. They have been gradually developed and provided with increased resources, as a result of the growing awareness of the important role they play in society. Yet the present situation is far from ideal.

The scarcity of economic resources and the lack of proper archival policies are the main problems. The situation of archives in Asia, assume that all countries have archives at the national level, together with archival legislation which defines and establishes general policies and standards for the preservation of the national archival heritage. Many archives use microfilming technology to preserve records and a few have now started to implement and develop computerised systems to help with the arrangement and description of archival materials. Almost all the archives issue archival publications and are members of international associations.

However, there are less positive aspects: lack of specialised human resources and almost non-existent professional archival education and training. In the absence of qualified personnel the archives are experiencing difficulties in tackling the problems of records and archives management. Another major problem is the uncertain financial background -often archives institutions have very limited budgets which do not guarantee them adequate resources for the implementation of a proper archives policy. The statutes of most countries in the Arab region have appeared in various publications.

The number of countries without any real legislation on archives none the less remains high. However, apart from Morocco, they are small countries where the state apparatus is relatively new, and whose institutions until recently amounted to local governments. Furthermore, many of these countries are still monarchies. Morocco is a special case: archives are kept for the King's private administrative offices but little is done in the sphere of public administration. The shortage or absence of legislation on archives is a function of the lack of importance some decision-makers attribute to it. The public conception of archives and their purpose is another factor here.

Almost everywhere archives are esteemed only for their heritage value; the role documents play in managing the country's affairs and assisting the decision-making process is forgotten. As record-keeping practices are not changing, there is no incentive to draft new legislation. Standardisation is everywhere less developed in the archive sector than in other information sciences. In the Arab States, standardisation is at best confined to applying known standards, particularly as regards conditions of conservation and building construction. Archival institutions are relatively recent in Arab countries.

Many countries took over the archive system established by the colonial power; others set up archive services much later. Some countries, such as Oman and Jordan, still have no real administration for archives. The attachment of an archival institution to a supervisory body can have an enormous influence on the development of the archive sector. Archival institutions under the supervision of a body well placed in the political hierarchy have more facilities at their disposal for the accomplishment of their task, provided that decision-makers are willing. Many Arab archival institutions are not only attached to ministries of culture with little political authority, but are often dependent on other cultural sectors such as archaeology.

The subordination of archive services to other structures often results in the marginalisation of the field. As far as the administrative organisation of archives is concerned, a distinction can be drawn between institutions regarded as departments coming under a ministry and those established as autonomous bodies with a legal status and financial autonomy.

Organization of Arab archives at regional and local levels is embryonic. Except for Algeria and the Sudan, which have set up regional archive services, such organization is non-existent in Arab countries. The same is true of municipal archives, which exist in only a few large Arab towns. Purpose-built premises for archives are important tools for any national policy in this field. This type of building is still rare in Arab countries. The comprehensive view of archives which sees documents as records from the moment they come into being is not widespread in Arab countries.

Records Management Programme

The aim of the records management programme is obviously to improve the efficiency of government agencies. For some public establishments and businesses the tools have already been prepared and applied. As regards government departments, the plan has just begun and should be completed by the year 2000. Records management in the private sector in Arab states is no better than in the public. The strategic sectors of the economy are still controlled by the state, so the private sector consists essentially of small and medium-sized companies, many of which have become aware of the importance of records management as an aid to the decision-making process and a factor in more rational management.

Records management is not a common practice in the administration of Arab countries; it is not inherent to Arab civilization. Although the Arab world had a highly developed administrative and documentary tradition in the Middle Ages, the region went through a long period of decadence marked by political instability that lasted until the colonial period.

The collection and organization of records determines the development of historical studies. It should be noted in this respect that records concerning the twentieth century are relatively little developed in Arab countries, and the same is true of historical studies of the modern period. Historical study often remains the prerogative of specialised researchers. Some research on genealogy or local matters is carried out by individuals, especially the elderly, but not much in comparison with that in developed countries.

Few catalogues of inventories or archive documents, or books based on archive documents for a general audience or for educational purposes, are published. In contrast, the publication of annotated manuscripts, particularly religious and even scientific manuscripts, is flourishing. Multimedia techniques are making slow progress in the Arab States. Their use calls for financial resources and a propitious administrative and human environment. Information retrieval applications are being developed in some countries and a few CD-ROMs relating to heritage have been produced including the CD-ROM on the fragments of the Sanaa Koran produced within the framework of UNESCO's Memory of the World Programme, and the CD-ROM on archaeological sites produced by the Regional Information Technology and Software Engineering Centre (RITSEC) in Egypt.

The spread of multimedia in the archives sector, however, encounters the question of the medium's durability; conservation of original documents, because of their probative value, is indispensable. Multimedia at the moment, therefore, is more useful for distribution than for conservation. The archival situation in Africa is as varied as the multiplicity of nations that make up the huge continent. In as much as the more than fifty countries that comprise Africa vary in size from a geographical coverage of less than 1,000 square kilometres to 2.5 million square kilometres, populations of less than 100,000 to over 96 million, Gross Domestic Products (GDP) ranging from US$279 million to over US$110 billion and per capita incomes of US$60 to US$6,000, so too does the archival situation vary enormously.

At one end of the spectrum are nations that have only the most rudimentary of archival infrastructures and where even the most basic of archival services are absent; at the other end are countries which have established advanced archival services and whose facilities and infrastructures compare favourably with other nations in the developed world. While some countries in North Africa have archival institutions that date back several centuries, most sub-Saharan countries established national archives only after the Second World War. Benin, Burkina Faso, Namibia, Senegal, South Africa and Zimbabwe are among the few exceptions in sub-Saharan Africa that established national archives before 1950.

Most countries have promulgated national archives or public archives acts which provide the legal framework under which national archives institutions operate and which control and preserve the archival heritage. The very few that as yet have no archives legislation, such as Uganda and Ethiopia, have draft legislation which is in the process of being formalized.

The legislative instruments in general give the national archives the authority to deal with the records and archives of public entities such as central government, local government and parastatals. The degree of authority and control differs from country to country, ranging from giving advice to the right to inspect records and issue instructions for their proper management and handling. In most of the legislation, the destruction of public records is forbidden without the consent of the national archives.

In a number of countries the national archives also administer the legal deposit or printed publications acts which require the deposit of copies of all publications produced in the country. This in effect creates within the national archives the national reference library. The ministerial placement of national archives is varied, but the vast majority of the national archives are in the ministries of home affairs, education/ sports/art and culture, and the president's office. In a few countries advisory boards or committees have been created to assist the national archives. The standards applied in the acquisition, processing, preservation, conservation and usage of records and archives in general are those that have been developed by the International Council on Archives (ICA). In West Africa, standards from the Association Française de Normalisation (AFNOR) and the International Standard Organisation (ISO) have been adopted.

There are also standards which have been developed by other organisations such as the International Records Management Council (IRMC), the Association of Records Managers and Administrators (ARMA) based in the United States, the Records Management Society of Great Britain, and other specialist organizations. Standards also tend to be influenced by the practices of the former colonial powers, because most of the national archival institutions are based on the records of the former metropolitan entities and are reflective of the latter's administrative structures and systems.

The type of training received by the records managers and archivists, and the institutions giving the training, also have a bearing on the standards used. Almost all countries in Africa have national archives or public records offices. The national archival institutions play the key role in the organisation, management and preservation of records and archives at the national level. Their mandate tends to be allembracing because of the absence of similar facilities at the local government and parastatal levels and in the private sector, as is the case in other regions of the world such as Europe and North America.

In a few countries there are municipal and local government archives, but these are the exception. In quite a number of countries the national archives have established regional offices but the functionality of these in the majority of cases is rather weak. Privatesector archives exist in some countries but these tend to be limited to large multinational corporations. In a number of countries private commercial records centres have been established. Architecture plays an essential role in the preservation and conservation of the archival heritage. The national archives in most countries occupy either purpose-built or converted buildings.

But many archival institutions are housed in buildings which are inadequate. In some cases, such as Cape Verde, Ethiopia, Guinea, Lesotho and Uganda, the archives are temporarily housed in such places as the university library, the basement of a former colonial secretariat building or the national library. Few countries, however, have adequate space for the storage of the archives and most, even those in purposebuilt repositories, are facing severe space shortages in buildings that were filled long ago.

Many of the institutions are unable to receive new accessions because there is no storage space. There are also problems concerning airconditioning. Although most of the purpose built repositories originally included air-conditioning systems, these systems in several cases have broken down or become non-functional for one reason or another. This has created serious difficulties, as often such buildings do not allow for adequate natural ventilation and the archival holdings are therefore at risk. The size of holdings of conventional archives varies enormously from country to country.

These archives can be varied and diverse: diaries and collections of eminent and scholarly individuals, archives of churches, educational institutions and sporting organizations, and business archives recording official transactions such as policies, procedures and meetings. Archival collections are also held by various other institutions and individuals: religious organizations, universities, libraries and some large corporations can contain sizeable archival holdings. In 1987, for example, the National Archives of Mali and Guinea were to be handicapped by insufficient human resources.

The high staff turnover is attributed to a number of factors including low salaries, low grading, lack of attractive career structures and the lure of the private sector. Government registry staff constitute the bulk of the records management staff in all countries. The registry staff, however, are not well trained and of low calibre. The morale of registry staff is quite low in most countries and they operate without recognition and some of the basic necessities. Most national archives in Africa have reprographic and conservation units or laboratories.

These reprographic facilities consist mainly of microfilming equipment but there is also other document-reproduction equipment such as photocopiers and duplicators. Microfilming is used primarily for acquiring copies of documents whose originals cannot be obtained, for preservation purposes when documents are in a fragile condition or are constituted of materials which deteriorate rapidly, such as newspapers, and for the production of multiple copies of documents, as in the case of the records of the former Federation of Rhodesia and Nyasaland, which were microfilmed to provide copies to each of the three successor countries: Malawi, Zambia and Zimbabwe.

Archival Materials and Methods

Document conservation unit have been created to repair and rehabilitate archival materials from depositors that are received in a deteriorated condition. The main method of repair and restoration utilised is lamination, although a limited amount of encapsulation is done in some countries. Most of the countries with conservation units have lamination machines and only in a few countries is the hand method used.

Countries such as Ethiopia and the United Republic of Tanzania do not have conservation units. The need for conservation in a continent with such a harsh climatic environment is self-evident. Unfortunately, in the government ministries and departments of a number of countries in Africa, the condition in which records are being maintained is a cause for great concern. There are numerous detailing situations in which records were exposed to excessive heat, humidity, mould, light, air pollution, insects and rodents.

Records have often been dumped in storerooms and sheds where the roofs leaked, the windows were broken and doors were only partially effective. This grave situation has given rise in the last ten years to international rescue missions which have been used to salvage the situation and avoid total disaster. Such missions have been launched in the Gambia, Uganda and the United Republic of Tanzania. For those countries that do have reprographic and conservation facilities, there are often insurmountable difficulties in maintaining equipment and acquiring adequate and appropriate supplies of chemicals and other materials.

With a few exceptions such as Botswana, Kenya, Namibia, South Africa and Zimbabwe, the national archival institutions only concern themselves with semi-current and non-current records due for transfer to the national archives. And yet by that time, irreparable damage will have been caused to the records. Many countries have established records centres for semi-current records, but in a good number of the cases the records centres have been completely full for many years, making it difficult for new accessions to be received. As a result the records remain in the ministries and departments. The crisis that faces many countries in terms of records management was aptly captured in one consultant's described file index systems that were rudimentary or nonexistent. In several registries records were strewn all over the floors and under shelves; file covers were often torn and crumpled, frequently with large numbers of pages missing; heaps of dirty, tattered and misfiled records could be found in corners and on tops of cupboards; there was a lack of discipline among staff who seemed to be driven more by tradition than by need; and office equipment was in short supply, the few filing cabinets available being rusty and damaged.

This is by no means the scenario in all African countries, and indeed many have well-organized registries, but all the same such situations are a cause for concern. Only in a few countries do national archives carry out regular visits to ministries and departments. While standing instructions for the disposal of time-expired records exist in many countries, these are often outdated and cover only a small proportion of the records produced by the ministries and departments. There are cases where time-expired records are not disposed of because of lack of capacity in the national archives.

In most countries public records become archives and accessible to the public after thirty years. Some countries of huge backlogs in the appraisal of records and the processing of archives, thereby delaying the availability of the archives to the public. There are often finding aids to the collections, and in some cases guides have been published. Unfortunately, in many countries these have not been updated for many years and some predate the attainment of national independence. Many of the archival institutions have search room facilities for researchers and the public. Some of these rooms have facilities for viewing stored cine films and microfilms, but in certain cases these collections are inaccessible because microfilm readers and projection equipment have broken down or become unserviceable. Both static and mobile exhibitions are occasionally mounted by some institutions while a few have educational programmes.

Very few in the private sector have received records management training other than the cursory treatment that it receives in secretarial and office management training courses. The standards of records management in the majority of businesses is therefore very low and no real attempt has been made to mobilize resources and effect improvement. The notable exceptions are the large multinational corporations, which often have elaborate records management procedures developed at their head offices. They also often have established in-house records centres and archives facilities. The availability of unemployed archivists has contributed to the development of archives in banks and large firms in countries like Senegal.

In a few countries, such as Zimbabwe and South Africa, commercial records centres have also been established. In some countries consulting firms are providing services in records and information management. Although increasing numbers of private firms are manufacturing and distributing records management materials, supplies and equipment, a large technology gap remains in comparison with the developed world. South Africa is probably the main exception in this regard. The privatization of public enterprises has also endangered the welfare of large quantities of records. Even when the national archives could cater for the archival collections of former public enterprises such as parastatals, very few of these enterprises made use of this facility or had any relations with the national archives.

When privatizing, little attention has been paid to the fate of the records which in the first instance were public records and archives but now belong to a private entity. The national archives have in any case, by and large, lacked the capacity to intervene in order to ensure that the records are adequately catered for. ICA is by far the most prominent professional archival association in Africa. It has established a network of regional branches: the West African Regional Branch of the International Council on Archives (WARBICA); the Central African Regional Branch of the International Council on Archives (CENARBICA); and the East and Southern African Regional Branch of the International Council on Archives (ESARBICA). Many national archives are also affiliated to such international organizations as the International Association of Sound Archives (IASA) and the International Federation of Library Associations and Institutions (IFLA).

There are other international professional associations in Africa. Archivists from countries in the Commonwealth, for instance, have generally affiliated with the Association of Commonwealth Archivists and Records Managers (ACARM). Some countries such as Benin, Ghana, Mali and Senegal have established national associations of records managers and archivists, but many others find that the number of archivists and records managers is too small for the establishment of viable associations. Africa lacks adequate training facilities for professional and technical staff. Attempts made in the early 1970s to establish regional training schools were only partially successful.

While the school at Dakar, Senegal, for French-speaking Africa seems to have fared better with its two degrees (technical and professional), the school for English-speaking Africa in Ghana has now become no more than a national centre. A number of countries have as a result established their own educational facilities at the national level. Countries such as Botswana and Kenya have graduate schools in archives and information science. Training facilities have been established also at the paraprofessional level, but technical training facilities in conservation and reprography are virtually unavailable.

In the absence of such facilities, it is not surprising that most archives staff have to be educated or trained overseas. For English-speaking Africa, this has mostly been done by University College London (United Kingdom) which runs a Master's programme. France has provided much of the training for French-speaking Africa, and Germany and Portugal have provided training for their former colonies. India has also done a lot of training, especially in conservation. A number of countries, such as South Africa, run their own national programmes within the national archives or through longdistance training, as in the case of the South African Higher Diploma in Archives Studies run by Technikon SA. Other countries with their own training programmes include Senegal and Mauritius. Continuing training in Africa is provided at the national, regional and international levels through workshops and seminars that are organized from time to time

The curriculum being developed within Africa is beginning to put more and more emphasis on the management of current and semi-current records and on automation. While traditional archives principles and practices are still being taught, some elements which are less relevant to the African continent, such as palaeography and sigillography, are now being dropped.

The historical bias and orientation is also becoming less pronounced in accordance with a changing professional perception of the role of archivists and the demands of information technology that are requiring a different breed of archivist. Archives are recognized as the primary instrument through which a nation's historical heritage is preserved. African nations by and large recognize the importance of archives in the preservation of the nation's history, and African scholars make extensive use of archival sources.

A large part of the written archival sources, however, relate to the period after colonization of the continent, and this has forced African nations to mount programmes for the collection and preservation of oral historical sources which narrate and chronicle the lives of the indigenous people. Many countries have developed active programmes for oral history and oral tradition. Some are based at universities and special institutions while others are run by national archives. The latter has resulted in soul-searching by some African archivists, who feel that national archives should not dissipate scarce resources by indulging in activities for which they are neither well equipped nor trained. Archives in Africa have long been viewed as a cultural heritage. There are many instances where there has been conflict with museums who do not view favourably the retention by national archives of museum artefacts.

Archivists hold the view that these constitute an integral component of archives collections bestowed on them. There is an increasing perception, though, that while archives cannot be divorced from the national cultural heritage, nevertheless national archives must pay more attention to information management operations, especially the management of current and non-current records.

This view is strongly supported and promulgated by the United Kingdom based International Records Management Trust (IRMT), which has conducted several rescue missions in Africa and has concentrated on overhauling registry systems in those countries. IRMT currently in several countries including the Gambia, Ghana, Uganda and the United Republic of Tanzania.

The increasing emphasis on records management has also refocused archival activities on the administrative structures of government. Whereas in the past archivists viewed administrative history in relation to those records and archives received and registered, they are now being encouraged to be proactive and to be involved in the current operations of the record-generating agencies. France, Germany, Portugal and the United Kingdom were the major colonial powers in Africa.

On the attainment of independence and nationhood by the African countries, some records were transferred to the metropolitan countries while other natural accumulations of administrative records remained in situ. The new nations laid claim to some of the transferred records, and a limited amount of repatriation was done. By and large, however, the former colonial powers remained steadfast in their claims on the records and instead encouraged the copying of these records to give the new nations access.

In many countries government requirements for automated data processing are fulfilled by central computing departments which usually have mainframe computers. Little has been done by national archives in Africa to deal with electronic media and the electronic records being generated by various agencies. In a few cases, such as Namibia, South Africa and Zimbabwe, special facilities have been put in place, but still the services provided are limited and do not embrace control back to the point of electronic record creation in the agencies.

South Africa began automation in 1974 and today has a database of almost 6 million records. The information technology revolution has provided both an opportunity and a challenge for archives. On the one hand, the availability of such mass storage devices as optical disks creates an opportunity for archives, and computerization can enhance the national archives' capacity to process, manipulate and make information accessible.

On the other hand, this opportunity has not been grasped, and this failure of archival institutions has been accompanied by a failure generally to cope with the challenges that the multimedia society poses as record-creating agencies adopt new technologies. Most African archivists feel that it is inevitable that the disciplines of archives, records management and library science, hitherto seen as separate and distinct, will merge.

African archivists nevertheless caution against failure to recognize the unique nature of archives or to discard the time-immemorial principles of 'provenance' and 'sanctity of the record group'. The major problems facing archives in Africa are as much archives-specific as they are reflections of the general malaise afflicting the continent. Many parts of the continent have been ravaged by wars, droughts and other man-made as well as natural disasters which have inflicted untold misery and suffering.

Infrastructures and technical facilities established in the 1960s and early 1970s have disintegrated in some countries. Government ministries and departments operate without functional registry systems, with untrained and sometimes uncaring staff and without manuals to give guidance. The overall archival situation is one of severe crisis requiring urgent remedial measures.

This must not detract, however, from the achievements of those African nations that have established viable and vibrant archival systems, and which in some respects have pioneered significant breakthroughs in archives development and are at par with similar institutions worldwide.

This sharp contrast gives hope to African archives; the need is for international support to those nations and institutions which already have achieved excellence and international help to foster development in those less fortunate and facing catastrophe. The capacity for classification—for seeing patterns in practices—is an essential characteristic of archivists. Characterizing the state of archives in the countries of Europe, together with Canada and the United States, requires identifying the faultlines that divide the region as well as the considerable bonds that bind it together.

Archives have three universal purposes: to select the records of institutions, the papers of individuals and families and the artificial collections of documentary materials that have enduring value; to preserve them; and to make them available for use. Individual nations and archival institutions accomplish these purposes through programmes which vary in emphasis and administration. Identifying the varieties of archival practice in Europe and North America requires assembling and analysing a sizeable quantity of data. All European archives owe a debt to the Greco-Roman archival tradition. There are, however, several obvious groupings of archives, either by virtue of the legislative structure of the nation or by tradition.

All archives, however, whether in governments, businesses or private organizations, must soon manage electronic records. At the European Summit on Archives in 1996, delegates agreed that the three principal issues for European archivists are the management of electronic records, training for personnel and preservation of the European archival heritage.

Consequently, the critical issue for most European archives is providing guidance to the records creators, in particular in the area of electronic records, not in finding ever larger storage facilities for semi-current records. The electronic records issue binds Europe together. Although the development of the computerized office generally occurred earlier in Western Europe, the computerization of Central and Eastern Europe has occurred at lightning speed, as external donors put computers in parliaments and courts and as businesses snapped them up for commercial ventures. This means that the intensity of the computer question, particularly for the very latest systems, is at least as pervasive in Eastern Europe as in the West.

Archival Education

Archival education increasingly is challenged to provide the new skills needed to manage archives in the current information age. Two shifts are occurring simultaneously: first, records are created and maintained electronically in the entities that are the sources of archival holdings, requiring archives to move aggressively to protect the archival information in the complex environment of modern management systems; second, archives are themselves introducing and adapting automation to facilitate work in the archives. Recent graduates from academic archival programmes emphasizing digital, processrelated information are entering European archival institutions and challenging with their enthusiasm the staff already employed there.

Effective in-service training programmes are urgently needed throughout the European archival world in order to ensure that serious divisions of competency do not occur within the professional community. The third major concern identified at the archival summit in spring 1996 was preservation. Facilities are a central concern of archivists everywhere.

The nature of archives is that the holdings are continuously expanding, and space utilization is a constant preoccupation.

European archives also 66% of central repositories with temperature and humidity controls, and 49% with microform storage accommodation to international standards. By contrast, state archives in the United States, 92% with purpose-built repositories and 92% with climate controls. All this suggests that European archives have major problems of adaptive re-use of older buildings, and consequently must struggle to maintain adequate preservation conditions for the materials stored within them. The average European national archives had 93,000 square metres of holdings in 1993.

In any event, the apparent lack of reformatting capacities in most European archives suggests that original records are made available to users, even those records that are extremely popular, setting up a future need for expensive conservation treatments. Preserving electronic records requires both physical facilities and the management of the physical and logical structures of the item. The technical facilities available in archives to handle electronic records are not as yet widespread. The techniques for preserving electronic records have evolved with the changes in the information industry; the preservation of flat files is well understood, the preservation of relational databases is fast becoming a standard practice and the preservation of electronic mail is rapidly emerging as a basic technique.

The fast advances in imaging technology are currently causing very serious problems for European archives, both because their popularity means that more and more images are created, and because the hardware and software dependency of imaging systems is extremely high and the rate of innovation extremely fast, leaving orphaned systems littering the way. Add to this the developments in the television industry, linking sound, image and text, and the problems mount. At present the only means of preservation is duplication to a current system, assuming that the system on which the image was generated is still operating (or can be made to operate). And yet it is essential that archives grapple with these issues, for in the long term this is the way records will be created, maintained, and used. The purpose of an archives is both preservation and use. One of the most significant developments for archives around the world has been the adoption of international standards for archival description, based on traditional archival practices but adapted for using computers to describe the holdings.

This is particularly important, because European archivists estimated in 1993 that only about 50% of their holdings were adequately described but 83% were using computers to describe holdings. There is considerable variation between Eastern and Central Europe on the one hand, and the rest of Europe on the other; in the former 55% of the institutions use computers for description while in the latter the figure is 91%.

As computers are rapidly introduced, adopting a standard format that can be shared electronically through the Internet will revolutionize archival use. No longer will users be tied to opening hours or transcontinental mail deliveries for service; neither will they have to consider wide variations in national descriptive practice. The day is approaching when the information about holdings can be searched in compatible versions worldwide.

The use of archives is increasing everywhere in Europe, but with particular ferocity in Central and Eastern Europe. As holdings long unavailable are now released for use, scholars and genealogists (to name only two user groups) are streaming into research rooms. The 1993 figures, based as they are on 1992 data, capture only the beginning of this wave.

Archives from Estonia to the Republic of Moldova faced new archival legislation; in addition, legislatures proposed other laws that had a vital impact on archival practices. In 1993, 63% of archives in Europe were operating under legislation passed or revised in the preceding ten years. While avoidance of obsolescence is all to the good, this means that the archivists must learn to interpret these laws, develop a body of practice that accords with them, and consider what further revisions are necessary.

Archivists unite in mourning the actual destruction of documents, but the problems of restitution and division have separated as much as they have united archivists. The break-up of the Ottoman and Habsburg Empires, and the fragmentation of the Soviet Union and the Yugoslavia of Tito, to name only a few examples in this century, caused documents of signal importance to one people to be lodged in the archives of another.

The European Summit on Archives, held in March 1996 in Munich, reaffirmed the desire for this continued, co-operative archival enterprise in Europe. The Council of Europe, UNESCO and the European Commission are major partners for the European Board. At the same meeting, UNESCO gave support to archives through the Memory of the World Programme and the Records and Archives Management Programme (RAMP), and an emphasis on access to archives as a basis for democratic societies.

World Wide Web and Challenges of Archivists

The development of the Internet and the World Wide Web is bringing unprecedented changes to the archival enterprise. In describing and making available holdings, archivists have long developed finding aids, printed them and distributed them in person or by mail. Records have most often been used in research rooms; sometimes records are used through photocopies ordered after consultation with an archivist; sometimes records are used on microform ordered by an archivist and accompanied by some form of description. The general pattern, however, has been of direct communication, one-to-one, between archivist and user, with the archivist able to answer questions, clarify the structure of the holdings and in general mediate the research use.

The World Wide Web and the Internet have changed that. The new pattern is unmediated communication in multiples. Archivists place descriptions on a Web site, and users from all over the world have simultaneous access without intervention of the archivist. Copies of documents placed on the Web site may be used in the order the archivist envisions, or may be used in random sequences over the course of the research. These four great engines of change are reflected in the work of the European archival profession at large.

Ethical and legal issues are now more visible than at any time since the start of the Cold War, resulting in the development of an international Code of Ethics for Archivists, the above-mentioned statement of principles on replevin, the development of a model for archival legislation and a statement on the management of records of former repressive regimes. Bilateral efforts, particularly within the framework of a multilateral body such as ICA or the Council of Europe, have a renewed vigour. But perhaps the most striking feature is the growing importance of professional associations. In North America, professional archival associations have a long, strong history. In both Canada and the United States the majority of archives are outside the administrative control of the national archives, and therefore the professional associations have played a critical role in fostering uniquely important bonds among individual archivists employed in widely divergent institutional settings. Many of these archivists are employed within a library, particularly a university library, and library practice has often influenced the archival tradition in the United States.

Standards for archival education, codes of ethics, statements of best practices, publication of the major journals and newsletters, and a host of other initiatives have come from these societies of professionals organized in their own self-interest, rather than from the central archival institution. In Western Europe, the tradition of professional associations is also strong. The German archival association, the Netherlands association (now well over 100 years old) and the Society of Archivists in the United Kingdom, among others, are influential in shaping archival practice in their countries.

In Central and Eastern Europe the pattern is different. A few strong national associations, such as in Poland, do exist, but in most countries the association is weak and in some countries does not yet exist. What are emerging are regional groups, led by national archivists. European archivists are beginning to have new means of professional development at hand. Co-operative networks, not all dependent upon the intervention of national archives and national governments, are developing. A healthy, vital profession, with no fundamental barriers to professional conversations or to shared competencies, has emerged over the last decade. The archival profession as we know it is largely an invention of the twentieth century. It is now ready for the challenges of the twenty-first. The task of assessing the current situation affecting archives in Latin America and making valid generalizations about it is certainly not an easy one.

Although it is true that many shortcomings in the region's archives still exist and that in some countries there has been scant improvement, in others a sustained process of change has been taking place since the 1980s that allows us to claim a qualitative leap forward in the history of archives. All kinds of limitations have traditionally affected Latin American archives: administrative neglect, a lack of definition of their legal and administrative status, organizational weaknesses, inadequate and insufficient buildings and facilities, budget constraints, obsolete technical working methods, non-professionalized staff, and poor theoretical and methodological development of record-keeping. Most national archives in Latin America were created back in the nineteenth century once the process of achieving independence from the colonizing nations had been completed in the region.

The archives were set up with the twofold aim of collecting and preserving the documentary heritage corresponding to the colonial period and, at the same time, of receiving new records as they were created by the bodies and institutions in the new states. For a variety of different reasons, however, this latter function tended to be overlooked. Thus, by the second half of the twentieth century, many of the national archives had long since ceased to receive transfers from government departments. The overall image they presented was one of inward-looking institutions that devoted all their energy to research and were poorly represented within the wider administrative organization to which they belonged.

Moreover, their internal organization was oldfashioned, making them inoperative. This shortcoming was never corrected despite the attempts that were made to that effect by the different countries. Likewise, the second-rank position they held within the administrative structure made them, as a general rule, subordinate to other higher bodies, and that considerably reduced their capacity for action. However, recent years have seen an intensive overhaul take place in many national archives. This aims, on the one hand, at restoring their link with the government's archives in order to return the flow of documents to normal and, on the other, at reinforcing their institutional position within the national archive structure. In several countries this process has been further consolidated by the recent enactment of legislative provisions that place national archives at the head of the respective national archive systems and significantly extend their previous tasks.

The responsibilities conferred on the national archives by their new status include: drawing up, coordinating and overseeing national archive policy; organizing and managing the national archive system; setting technical standards and guidelines with a view to modernizing public records management; training the human resources required for the smooth running of the archives; guaranteeing and improving access to the information in the archives; and so on. In parallel with this process, and with a view to making it feasible for the national archives to perform these wide-ranging functions, in some countries they have been granted a higher-ranking position in the administrative hierarchy as well as the autonomy needed to develop and finance their own working programmes.

Take, for instance, the 24th International Conference of the Round Table on Archives (CITRA), the first of its kind to be held in Latin America, the various seminars on archival description that have been held, the International Seminar on Construction of Archive Buildings, the Preventive Conservation Course, the Seminar on Restoration, the Seminar on Appraisal or the International Seminar on Archive Policy in Central America. Another patent example of the dynamism of these archives can be found in their activity within ALA, whose working programme is the most far-reaching of all the regional branches of the International Council on Archives (ICA).

Nevertheless, it must also be acknowledged that in a handful of countries the limited support lent by the public authorities to their national archives makes it impossible for these structures to overcome their backward and poverty-stricken situation and become modern institutions. The oldest records held in Latin American archives date back to the time of the Spanish and Portuguese conquest and colonization in the sixteenth century, and many are of extraordinary value.

Most of the holdings in Latin American archives are conventional archives. Cartographic material is also common and some repositories—not just the national ones—boast rich collections of maps and plans. Many of the national archives also hold documents on new media, particularly collections of photographs. At present, however, the existence of records held on computerized media is practically nil. The conservation of the vast documentary heritage held in their archives throws up enormous challenges to countries and its survival is sometimes under serious threat. The administrative archives of bodies attached to the central or federal administration rarely have any professional-level staff, since the people who are responsible for them are administrative public officials who have not been required to undergo any specific training.

Most archives have no other source of income than the budget allocated to them by the state. The possibility of obtaining additional outside resources through the sale of publications, reproductions, etc., is practically non-existent as the budget they are given is not enough to develop this type of activity. Other national archives, whose position within the administrative organizational hierarchy leaves them under the responsibility of a higher body do not have this financial autonomy.

Archiving Audiovisual Heritage

The audiovisual heritage is an important element within the cultural heritage and has achieved prominence in the twentieth century, the first to have been recorded on audiovisual formats. Audiovisuals are not new but have become of increasing importance as art, entertainment and information carriers. In some cases the transmission of sound and visual data has greater value and impact than the printed document - where, for example, there is a literacy or language barrier. Audiovisuals may also be the only suitable records for the oral or sonic transmission of culture and the arts, news and other current items. The spread and development of modern technologies mean an increase in the role of audiovisual data carriers for communication, information and culture.

Today's radio and television rely heavily on archive material and it is estimated that more than 60% of radio and television programmes use archival or stock material for programming. The definitions are still being formulated, but audiovisual materials are to be understood as visual recordings and sound recordings irrespective of their physical base or recording process. The carrier usually requires a playback device. This definition is meant to cover the maximum number of forms and formats.

Audiovisual materials should not be confused with multimedia; the former provide source material for the latter, and multimedia as such are not archival material. Two features of audiovisual materials add an extra dimension to the principles of collection and preservation: a proliferation both of formats and of systems of production and playback. These cause incompatibility problems between formats and systems. Archives have to maintain original playback devices and employ technical staff who know how to use and maintain the machinery. Audiovisual archives are storehouses for a large proportion of the social and cultural heritage of the twentieth century.

An audiovisual archive is defined as an organization or department of an organization which is focused on collecting, managing, preserving and providing access to a collection of audiovisual media and the audiovisual heritage, applying archival principles. Such archives contain huge treasures of unique material. Archives of audiovisual materials are relatively new, but they have proliferated in the past few decades. Television was originally recorded on film, but video has been the principal material since the later 1960s.

Although audiovisual materials have appeared so recently, time is not on their side and the longer we delay in gathering, conserving and preserving the materials, the less we shall be able to retain. It is vital that steps are taken now to collect and manage audiovisual materials properly before their fragile nature takes a further toll. Already much has been lost owing to ignorance, lack of awareness of the dangers and careless handling. Audiovisual archives vary in type, purpose and function, and until recently most of them were singlematerial archives: moving image, sound and still-image archives, the latter frequently housed in more conventional archives of print materials.

As the technologies converge so do the archives, to unite effort and conserve resources. Some archives take responsibility for all recorded materials, others take smaller bites and combine one or two of the materials. The larger archives cannot always combine materials in one department; the physical techniques required to deal with each material from the point of view of storage, handling and restoration need different expertise and materials are therefore separated by this parameter alone. Other functions of collection management can be applied to all the materials: documentation and information retrieval, and selection.

Storage vaults may have to accommodate more than one material and the resulting environmental considerations will be different from those more stringently applied to individual materials. Alternatively, an archive may decide that it must apply the optimum storage and environmental values which apply to each material: single-material archives are more fortunate in these cases. Academic archives also house audiovisual materials, many in universities for research, and latterly educational materials for distance learning. These may be small and specialized, or have substantial collections and preservation programmes. Specialized or thematic archives concentrate on a particular format, subject-matter or locality, or relate to specific cultural groups. Many of these archives have developed within larger organizations.

Film companies, broadcasting companies and record companies maintain archives primarily for use and exploitation by the parent company. Many of these preserve and restore their materials for re-use, but the archives' main obligation is to the parent organization rather than to preserving the cultural heritage. This may be left to a national archive, which obtains a selection of the production company's material by deposit. Other institutions with archival responsibility include museums, cinematheques, videotheques and national libraries.

Most of these are more concerned with maintaining stock for exhibition purposes, and originals may be deposited for long-term preservation in a national archive. There are also collections of last resort which attempt to conserve copies of material in usable condition, but seldom retain archival originals or masters. Audiovisual materials result from a huge level of investment.

Archives in organizations such as broadcast associations or film production companies have commercial backing and motivation, and meet costs from their revenue. Once that commercial motive is fulfilled, however, it is generally acknowledged that, as with other records of the national cultural creativity, the cost of maintaining the collection reverts to government and granting bodies. Many valuable collections have disappeared for ever as a result of production company closures or changes in franchise when materials are not taken over by already overstretched archives. The basic tasks of an audiovisual archive are collection, preservation, documentation and access provision.

Methods of collection and acquisition vary, and include the legal or voluntary deposit of collections or individual items, the deposit of in-house productions, donations, special agreements for copying nationally produced materials, and purchase. Other archives collect their own materials in the form of oral or video history programmes, with the purpose of recording cultures, languages and music before they disappear. Closely allied to acquisition are evaluation, selection and appraisal.

The audiovisual archive acquires materials according to a particular remit, balancing new acquisitions against existing stock and the purpose and function of the archive. Storage space and resources being what they are, archives have to select material for preservation on the basis of relevance, uniqueness and quality. Wherever possible an archive should be dealing with original materials, but originals are hard to come by. There is strictly only one original film, video or master sound recording. Such originals seldom survive and there are various forms of tampering with the products - cut/uncut versions, director's/producer's cut, censored and unexpurgated versions. Owners of original material may be reluctant to deposit their master material in an archive until they have no further use for it, by which time the technical quality has deteriorated. Three elements in audiovisual documents have to be considered in the selection process: the artefact or carrier, the information content and the aesthetic content, particularly with film and sound recordings. The artefact or carrier will designate the form of the audiovisual and influence selection for technical reasons. Audiovisual archives, therefore, do not have a huge selection of material, but most of it has unique value, and such archives retain more material than many other archives.

Some audiovisual collections will include several interpretations of the same work—for example, music recordings—or several records of the same event carried in different documents: a film, video or sound version. Guidelines for archival selection exist, but they are usually those of organizations with their own parameters. Selection of material is dependent upon the function of the archive, the quality of the material and the uniqueness or rarity of the content.

Audiovisual archives should concentrate on recordings of national origin. To avoid duplication of effort, material should be offered back to the country of original production or to archives with a more relevant collection remit. The main function of any archive is to preserve the heritage and the artefacts which make up that heritage.

Organisation of Archives

In a well-designed archival network, institutions can share the burden of archiving journals, and libraries and researchers needing to use archival materials can locate and retrieve appropriate copies from a participant in the network. However an archival system is set up, though, it must be clear who takes responsibility for the material being archived and how this responsibility is enforced.

Self-archiving

Some authors and organizations may attempt to archive their own material. A publisher may declare that it will archive its own back issues indefinitely, for instance. Many authors have also provided preprints of their papers and journal articles on their Web sites for years. This informal practice is now encouraged by manifestos like the Budapest Open Access Initiative."Self-archiving" can also be done by authors' institutions. For instance, MIT's Dspace repository promises stable long-term storage for the scholarly work of its faculty.

Self-archiving, however, will not suffice to preserve scholarly journals, let alone scholarly communication as a whole. It essentially relies on the self-interest of the original creators and publishers to keep the archive viable, but Web sites often disappear when an individual changes institutions or careers. Copies of papers on individual sites are often preprints, so they may lack important revisions and supplementary information that appeared in the journal version.

Publisher-run archives may disappear without warning if they are no longer cost-effective to the publisher, or if the journal or the publisher fails or is acquired by another company. Contents of archives may be changed, corrupted, or withdrawn, either by accident or intentionally. As holders of copyrights to the content they archive, publishers and authors have exclusive rights to disseminate this content unless they grant rights to archives run by disinterested third parties. With exclusive rights comes near-exclusive responsibility for their material.

Without very strong certification and backup strategies, self-archiving with this level of exclusivity is not likely to be widely trusted to preserve scholarly information for the time spans researchers and libraries have come to expect. This does not mean that self-archiving is useless, however. Self-archiving can be a backup to trusted archives run by other parties.

Integrated Responsibility

Whether run by content creators and publishers or by third parties, archives have traditionally taken full responsibility for the content they archive. They are responsible for quality control, continued preservation, and providing appropriate access. If they themselves cannot maintain the content in perpetuity, they are responsible for finding someone else who can. While they may delegate some of their functions, such as ingestion or migration, to outside service providers, they are ultimately responsible to their clients for making sure these functions are carried out correctly and that the content is preserved for future access.

This "integrated" responsibility for preserving and providing access to content may earn the trust of users, since the buck stops, as it were, with a definite party. Publishers, too, may be more willing to grant rights to a specific agent who takes responsibility for their work. Of course, the archive must live up to this responsibility, with its attendant certification and sustainability requirements.

Distributed responsibility

The LOCKSS (Lots of Copies Keep Stuff Safe) project at Stanford suggests a more distributed form of responsibility, similar to the distributed responsibility for print journals discussed earlier. With LOCKSS, no one institution takes responsibility for a journal. Instead, many institutions maintain sites that cache copies of journal content published on Web sites.

Content can be accessed from the cache if it is no longer available on the original publisher's Web site. Cache contents are automatically checked against each other on a regular basis, and corrupted or lost copies of items replaced with other copies.

The cache correction protocol is slow and relies on records of past holdings. These features make it highly unlikely, given enough participants, that a copy of an object will be completely lost, be corrupted, or become unavailable to any site that originally cached the content. Because the protocol also checks what content a site has previously demonstrated that it owned, the protocol does not "leak" content to sites that were not authorized to see it.

LOCKSS is designed to run on low-cost machines with as little maintenance as possible, making it attractive for libraries to set up LOCKSS caches. If enough libraries continue to cache the same content, that content (at least in its original format) can be preserved reliably even if no single institution takes final responsibility for it. The system can be queried to see how many sites are caching content. Institutions that see a need for greater reliability, can arrange to put additional copies on caches run at their own site or other sites.

In its original form, LOCKSS makes a number of simplifying assumptions about what is being cached, that may not be applicable to all journal archives. For instance, LOCKSS obtains publishers' content by automatically polling their Web sites for HTML and image files, but while those sites may include presentation forms of journals they typically do not include source forms. However, the basic LOCKSS model can be generalized to cover a broader range of journal archiving strategies, especially if caching sites can individually decide what to cache and how.

Useful generalizations of the model include:

— *Introducing an explicit representation of trusted sources for journal content.* The basic LOCKSS model assumes the publisher's Web site is the trusted source for journal content. However, other trusted sources might be needed to provide content not available on the Web site such as source forms for journal content, metadata, and updates and migrated versions of journal content.

— *Caching Archival Information Packages (AIPs).* If AIPs and not just Web pages and images are cached, then a distributed archive can reliably cache both source and presentation forms of content, as well as appropriate metadata and migrated forms. These AIPs would need to come from a trusted source.

— I*dentifiers for AIPs and other journal content.* A distributed archiving system requires a consistent way of identifying content so that different servers can check consistency between different copies of the same material. As originally designed, LOCKSS simply uses URLs as identifiers, but this only works for material pulled directly from the Web at static URLs. A distributed archiving system could use AIP identifiers to identify content, but would have to settle on a suitable global scheme for assigning such identifiers. Other globally addressable entities, such as directories, will need globally unique identifiers as well.

— *Metadata.* A distributed archiving system should agree on a common core set of metadata to maintain for journal content, including descriptive and technical metadata, to support searching and browsing and maintenance of particular journal content.

— *Directory services.* Once the metadata above is in place it should be possible for archive users to be able to see what content is in the system, even if they cannot actually view all the content. They should also be able to search and browse it in customary ways, such as looking up an article by its citation, or browsing tables of contents for a particular journal volume. Directory information needs to be updateable as more journal content is added.

— V*ersioning.* LOCKSS' cache consistency protocol works well for objects that do not change once they are imported into the system, but a general-purpose distributed archiving system includes several types of changing objects. AIPs for particular journal articles may change as new manifestations of the articles are added (such as through migration) or if publishers issue a corrected version of an article after its original publication. Directories change as new articles, issues, and journals are added to the system. A versioning discipline would allow LOCKSS-like consistency checks for updates and new manifestations of these objects. A new version could be identified as an update of an existing version of an object in the system, and distributed archive sites could decide whether or not to accept the version. The sites could use acceptance criteria of their choosing, such as the trustworthiness of the source and the nature of the differences between the new version and the older version. Some types of updates may be expected to be monotonic: new data gets added, but old data does not get taken away. Sites could also decide whether or not to retain older versions. Most legitimate updates to journals would not occur more frequently than issues of journals are published, a pace which is compatible with the deliberately slow coherency protocol that LOCKSS uses.

— *Controlled expansion of access*. LOCKSS' access control model is also monotonic: if a site has had a copy of some content in the past, it can be given a copy again, if its old copy has been lost or corrupted. Trusted sources could also grant new copies to sites that previously did not have copies of particular content, when this is permitted, without any further changes in the access control model. It would also be useful to be able to designate that certain content could be given to a wider set of sites. The simplest approach would be to include an "open access" flag that could be given to journal content or metadata that can be distributed freely. Trusted sources could set this flag, either on original distribution, or when previously arranged "triggers" applied that opened access to content.

In making these extensions, one must avoid introducing so much overhead into the system that the primary advantages of LOCKSS — reliable distributed archiving with minimal cost and maintenance — are lost. Each of the enhancements mentioned above should not be overly burdensome in itself, but designers of a distributed archiving system should make sure the enhancements are kept as simple as possible.

Service providers

Service providers perform specific functions on behalf of the archival system. In an "integrated responsibility" model, service providers are essentially subcontractors for the main archive. In the "distributed responsibility" model, service providers are trusted sources, as defined above. Service providers help scale up an archival system by spreading out responsibility for archival tasks. They can be useful when an archival function requires specialized expertise or resources. For instance, if a company provides low-cost, highly replicated reliable data storage, an archive might out-source backups to that company rather than maintain backups itself. Or, if content is submitted or stored in a variety of protocols and formats, ingestion and migration of this content might be usefully parceled out to service providers, each specializing in a particular format or data provider, instead of trying to have one organization handle everything.

Service providers often do not need to make the same sort of long-term commitments as archives themselves do, unless their service includes long term information storage. However, they still need to be visible in the design and operations of an archiving system. Archive users may want to make sure they are certified for carrying out their service correctly. Publisher agreements may need to allow them to access copyrighted material, and publishers may want to be assured that they do not distribute or alter this material without authorization. The business model for the archive or archival system also needs to include some sort of compensation for the services of the providers.

Registries. Several organizations, including JSTOR, Highwire, PubMedCentral, and various publishers and national libraries, are currently archiving journal material. As the population of archives and archived materials grows, it will be increasingly important for archive maintainers and users to be able to keep track of who is doing what and with what content. A registry of journal archiving activity would make this possible. It would allow users to find content they needed, and allow archive maintainers to find service providers, look up technical information on archiving formats and practices, and track redundant archiving of journal content.

Several architectures are possible for such a registry. A centralized knowledge base could be set up to accept information about archival activities. The Jointly Administered Knowledge Environment (Jake) is already set up to record journal information in this manner, though it does not currently record archiving information for journals. Peer-to-peer systems can also act as decentralized "registries." The Typed Object Model, for instance, propagates information about data formats and their conversions between peer "type brokers."

The Open Archives Initiative (OAI) suggests a particularly promising architecture for a registry. Using OAI, repositories can expose metadata about their contents which can then be harvested incrementally by any interested service. The OAI protocol is lightweight and easy to implement and add on to existing systems.

One or more archival information sites could harvest information from appropriately certified archives, and allow archive users and maintainers to search and browse the aggregated metadata. Setting up such a system would require some agreements on "core" metadata that the archives would export, but it would be in the interest of most archives to agree on such metadata. The aggregated information site would not need to be particularly expensive to maintain. It would be automatically updated from the certified archives, and the software to browse and search its records would only need to handle the common "core" metadata format.

A journal archive registry should include at least the following information:

- Information on journals being archived including
  - their names and identifiers
  - the archives or archival systems preserving them, the scope of the issues and articles preserved by these archives, and the formats being archived
  - who is authorized to access the content
- Information on the archives and service providers themselves
  - For "integrated responsibility" archives, information on their certification including how they are certified, when they were last certified, and relevant reports from the certifiers
  - For "distributed responsibility" archival systems, information on how to find out the archival status of journal content, including how to locate and check the reliability and redundancy of the storage of particular journal content.

Rights and Responsibilities of Archives

An electronic journal archive has responsibilities to scholars and their institutions and to publishers. The archive is responsible for ensuring scholars can access journal content for as long as it is of scholarly value in a form that allows it to be used effectively for research, teaching, and learning. The archive is responsible for respecting the copyrights of authors and publishers in its stewardship of electronic journal content. It is also responsible for helping maintain a healthy climate of scholarship and scholarly communication. It should neither hinder publishers or libraries with overly burdensome procedural and economic constraints, nor hinder scholars themselves with overly restrictive policies for access or deposit. Archives need to be granted sufficient rights to carry out these responsibilities.

Selection Responsibilities

The archive is responsible for identifying journals it wishes to archive and making these selections known to a publisher for the publisher's approval. The selection does not have to be enumerated. For instance, archives that plan to include all electronic journals of particular publishers, could agree that any newly added journal will be included in the selection unless either the publisher or the archive notifies the other that the new journal should be excluded. In such cases, the publisher should also inform the archive about newly added electronic journals or of journals that it no longer publishes.

Of course, this notification, and other provisions of information given in this section, can be made simply by publishing the information in an agreed-upon location, such as a Web page or a mailing list. The archive and publisher also need to agree on what content in the journals is being selected. Normally, the archive should collect at least all issues published from the time the agreement is made. Back issues, where feasible, are also desirable to include.

The archive and the publisher also have to agree on a set of formats that will be collected, and protocols for collecting content and metadata. Either the archive or the publisher should be able to request, with sufficient advance notice, that archiving for a journal be cut off: that is, no further issues will be deposited into the archive. The archive is responsible for notifying its clients, including appropriate registries, of its selections.

Ingestion Responsibilities

The publisher is responsible for providing content and metadata for the journal issues being archived. Content should include the journal content as provided to subscribers in presentation forms such as PDF and HTML. Even if an archive does not store presentation forms, it is helpful for an archive to be able to compare any source forms it receives against what the publisher actually supplied to subscribers in the electronic journal. This provision may simply consist of allowing the archive access to the online journal for testing.

When the archive is preserving source forms of content, the publisher is responsible for providing them and for ensuring they are correctly formatted; the publisher is also responsible for ensuring the source forms correspond appropriately to the published presentation forms. The publisher should likewise be responsible for providing metadata for the journal content in sufficient detail to allow standard scholarly citations to be built for all articles and other citable contributions. This includes title, authors, issue information, page numbers or other section delimiters where applicable, and other standard identifiers for the content such as ISSNs and DOIs. Abstracts and keywords would also be useful, when available.

The archive is responsible for collecting content and metadata in a timely fashion, checking it for consistency and proper formatting, and either ingesting it into its repository or informing the publisher of any errors or problems with the data. If the archive reports errors the publisher should remedy them, and the archive should then reingest content. Generally, the archive should try to ingest an issue while it is still the current issue. If the archive is harvesting data from the Web or another published source, it should be able to assume the data is in its final form unless the publisher has notified it otherwise. For example, if the publisher posts "draft" or pre-publication material which it then modifies before an issue's "official" publication, the publisher is responsible for telling the archive when and when not to harvest this information.

The archive is responsible for collecting appendices to articles such as datasets, audiovisual clips, program code, and other multimedia when this is within the archive's stated selection criteria. The publisher may need to assist the archive in collecting these appendices. If the appendices have unusual size or format, they might not be required to be migrated as is regular content. "Appendices" external to the journal itself — a Web site referred to by a URL in a journal article, for example — need not be collected.

If content is to be collected by harvesting from the publisher's site, the publisher is responsible for allowing access by the archive's harvesters, while the archive is responsible for ensuring the harvesters do not unduly load the archive's servers.

Rights and responsibilities for storage and maintenance. The archive is responsible for ensuring the long-term persistence and stability of the archived content. It is also responsible for making sure the content does not become unusable due to technological obsolescence. Therefore, the publisher should give the archive the right to store copies of the journal content and metadata, make and store backup copies, and create derivative works based on the original data for the purpose of maintaining their suitability for research and scholarship. Such derivative works could include migrations to new formats, indexing for searching and browsing, and transformations required for emulation. Ideally, the right to create derivative works would also allow enhancements to the content, at least when the enhancements are for services that researchers come to expect in online journals. Such enhancements, for instance, could include converting static images to wavelet-based forms that allow panning and zooming, or inserting hyperlinks to make it possible for readers to go to referenced articles.

Users expect that reliable, persistent electronic archives will not lose content. Therefore, the rights above and other intellectual property rights given to the archive should be irrevocable by the publisher, provided that the archive fulfills its responsibilities. Publishers can retain copyright; they just need to assign appropriate rights for the archive to do its job.

Rights and responsibilities for access and distribution. The archive is responsible to its clients for providing authorized users with its content and metadata, and it is responsible to publishers for providing content only to authorized users. Content provided to authorized users should include:

— Copies of the journal content as originally published (byte-for-byte copy, in original formats) for journals archived in presentation form.

— Images of the journal pages in formats commonly readable at the time of access for journals archived in presentation form. This may require migration if common data formats change.

— The text of the journal content in formats commonly readable at the time of access. This may also require migration.

— Where feasible and cost-effective, other journal content, such as data sets and audiovisual materials, in formats commonly readable at the time of access.

Metadata should include at least citation information for the journals and their articles. The archive should also provide reasonable facilities for locating an article or journal with a known citation.

It seems relatively uncontroversial to allow general access at least to citation-level descriptive metadata. This allows users to know what is in an archive. Richer descriptions, such as abstracts, may be more controversial, but if they encourage a user to seek out the full content and become more interested in the journal as a whole, providing such detailed metadata can benefit both archive and publisher.

Likewise, allowing access to content by the publisher and by the archive maintainers seems uncontroversial. Widening access further, though, proved more problematic. Even providing access to subscribers to the journal for content that was also available on the publisher's Web site raised concerns that the archive would compete with the publisher's own offerings.

The concerns here seemed to be not just possible loss of marketing opportunities on the publisher's own Web site, but also possible degradation of image. The look, the services, and the authority that the publisher took pains to establish on their Web site could be lost on the archive site, thus weakening the "brand" or reputation of the publisher. This seemed to be less of a concern if the archive just offered material that was no longer available on the publisher's own Web site. Concerns about image may also be alleviated if appropriate links are made between the archive site and the publisher's site.

Even more controversial is allowing access to archived journal content to those who are not subscribers to the journal. JSTOR and Highwire, two established projects that archive journal content, allow such access after a certain time has passed from publication. The point at which access is opened is referred to as the "moving wall." There are several advantages to this sort of access:

— It satisfies, at least in part, the desire of many scholars that scholarly information should be generally accessible to all for little or no cost, whenever feasible.

— It provides an electronic counterpart to the long-standing custom of researchers obtaining older journal articles by interlibrary loan if their institution did not subscribe to the journal or retain their volumes.

— It avoids the overhead of the archive having to keep track of exactly what users should be allowed to access each item in the archive.

— It allows a wide audience of readers and third-party automated programs to examine the archived content and verify that it is being accurately preserved or report problems if it is not, thus enhancing trust in the archive. This may be especially important when material needs to be migrated to a new format, a process that may risk losing information or usability in unexpected ways.

— It may make it easier for mirror sites and other service providers to access the content.

— It provides an ongoing service of document delivery to the scholarly community, instead of just being an unseen "insurance" policy as an inaccessible or "dark" archive would be. This strengthens support for the archive in that community.

These are all benefits for the archive and its users, but they are not direct benefits to publishers. Of greatest concern was the possibility that libraries would cancel subscriptions to their journals or not sign up for them in the first place if they could have access to the archive without a journal subscription. Martin Richardson of Oxford University Press, for instance, reported that institutional subscriptions to eleven journals made available via Highwire had declined by three percent per year in the three years since they had been placed online, even though they had been increasing prior to that time.

Faced with such declines in subscriptions, publishers might have to raise prices for the subscribers that are left, or cut the budgets to produce the journals. As an alternative to general free access Richardson recommended free access to readers in developing countries and low article pricing for infrequent users of journals.

Richardson's report does not prove that opening access caused the drop in subscriptions or that a more distant moving wall, such as the three to five years that is common for JSTOR journals, would not solve the problem. Both Oxford and Cambridge have been willing to experiment with allowing some of their journal content to be accessible to nonsubscribers through JSTOR and Highwire as well as PubMedCentral.

Some may argue that copyright law already specifies a moving wall when works enter the public domain and are available to anyone. However, this moving wall has been extended repeatedly in the United States and is now up to ninety-five years after publication for older publications and works for hire, and to seventy years after the death of the last surviving author for other works. The distance and uncertainty of copyright expiration in these circumstances makes an archive that requires public domain verification before providing access to electronic journal content equivalent to a "dark" archive for most practical purposes.

Other "trigger" events besides a fixed moving wall are also worth considering. For example, opening up access when migration is required would ease user concerns that migration might not be successful. It might also benefit publishers if they found migration too expensive or troublesome to carry out themselves. It is also reasonable for archives to be able to provide general access to content that is no longer being offered online by the publisher or the publisher's agents.

The archiving agreement should not abridge the traditional rights recognized by copyright law. These rights include fair use, first-sale rights, and unrestricted use of public domain material. All of these rights play important roles in scholarship, so archives whose purpose is to support scholarship should avoid restricting them. Some publishers digitizing older material may want to make an exception to this rule for new digitizations of public domain content from early in a journal's run. An archive should weigh this proposed exception carefully.

In some cases, a short-term embargo on unrestricted use of this material may be necessary if the only likely digitizer of the content is worried about the investment going to waste, but there is little justification for extending this embargo beyond the same moving wall term that is given to copyrighted content. On the whole, the copyrighted content of most electronic journal archives will usually be much more valuable than recently-digitized public domain content. Users are also much more likely to trust and support a comprehensive and authorized archive of a journal's run than an unauthorized provider of part of the journal's run.

Rights and responsibilities for certification and evaluation. The archive is responsible for specifying a process for certification of its content and procedures, and for reporting the results of this certification to its clients, including its publisher partners. The RLG-OCLC Trusted Repositories paper notes two basic approaches to certification: an approach based on auditing and an approach based on standards and usage.

For a "dark" archive, or an archival system that uses software that is not available for public inspection, certification will generally need to involve auditing, to satisfy the concerns of constituents who cannot examine the content or the software themselves. In a more open system, such as LOCKSS, each site can examine its own contents and the software it is using. In such cases, separate auditing is less important though it may be desirable for the designers of the system to have the code reviewed and certified by an outside party.

Publishers may want to know how the content they publish is being used in an archive as well as the cost of the archiving processes. It is reasonable for an archive to share aggregated usage information with publishers as long as the form of the information sharing protects the privacy of individual readers. If publishers are subsidizing the archiving they also have a right to be informed of the costs involved. Archives and publishers should agree in advance on the data an archive will collect, what an archive can be expected to provide, and for how long an archive should retain usage data.

Responsibilities for sustainability. The archive is responsible for ensuring it has appropriate technology, procedures, and funding for it to continue archiving activities for as long as needed. Responsibility for funding, however, is related to the other rights and responsibilities of an archive.

Funding for an archive can come from various sources including:

— The organization running the archive (self-funding)

— External sponsors (e.g., private foundations, government grants, marketers)

— The publishers of the journals in the archive

— Users of the archive materials (e.g., individual researchers and libraries)

Self-funding is viable for most academic libraries if the archival system is sufficiently lightweight and inexpensive to run and provides commensurate benefits. We can run a LOCKSS server on a commodity PC, for example, and in its current form it requires very little maintenance. Even a more ambitious system, such as the distributed archiving system described earlier, could easily pay for itself if its cost were similar to the original LOCKSS system and it made it easier for us to move older journals to inexpensive remote storage.

Full-service "integrated responsibility" archives are much more heavyweight. According to discussions with its maintainers, PubMedCentral, run by the National Center for Biotechn0logy Information (NCBI) of the National Institutes of Health (NIH), requires seven full-time employees to run on an ongoing basis. The project archives fewer than thirty externally published journals, plus a few dozen very low volume journals published by NCBI, and makes extensive use of automation. PubMedCentral staff represent only a small fraction of the staff of the NCBI, itself a small division of NIH. Organizations like this, which have national mandates as collectors and providers of research information, should find it a relatively small stretch to maintain an archive of online scholarly journals in-house and to justify it in their budgets.

Many publishers can fund an archive if the archive provides them sufficient benefit. The costs of funding will ultimately be passed on to someone else. For subscription-based journals, the price of subscriptions may account for the cost of funding the archive. Journals that charge authors for publication might build charges for preservation of the article into the author's fee. Journals published by scholarly societies may have those societies fund their preservation.

Costs for preserving journal material are ongoing but publishers may be unwilling or unable to pay for archiving the material indefinitely. One solution to this problem is to structure publisher funding as an endowment. When a publisher deposits a journal volume or issue in an archive, it would also include a one-time payment to endow the future archive needs of the deposited content. Income from this endowment would fund ongoing archiving, backup, mirroring, maintenance, and migration of that journal content in perpetuity. If the archive decided to transfer responsibility for the content to another institution or back to the publisher, the content's endowment would be transferred as well. If a publisher stopped supporting an archive, the endowments associated with previously deposited content could still fund the preservation of that content.

For the publisher and journal subscribers, the endowment would provide a guaranteed source of funds to ensure the ongoing availability of journal content. Funding would not be dependent on an archive's ongoing revenue stream. By guaranteeing long-term availability of journal content, an endowment-funded archive could ultimately save money both for the publisher and subscribers to the journal. Subscribers who can rely on preserved electronic copies may be willing to forgo print versions or keep them in less expensive storage, thereby lowering their costs. Hence, they may be willing to contribute to an endowment fund via their subscription fees. If the archive is sufficiently trustworthy and accessible, it may even be possible to discontinue print production which would lower costs and subscription fees for the publisher.

For the endowment model to work, however, costs have to be well-understood and kept under control. If the costs can be kept down to a small percentage of subscription revenue, the endowment model may be financially viable. For instance, a journal that costs $350 per volume, with 300 annual subscribers, brings in about $100,000 of subscription revenue. If endowment income were five percent per year, then each one percent surcharge for archiving would pay $50 per year of archiving costs for that volume. So if the true costs to the archive were $150 per year per volume, three percent of subscription revenues would need to go towards archiving.

Unfortunately, this may be an optimistic estimate of archiving costs, which are still uncertain and likely to change as archives develop and as technology changes. Long-term costs may be difficult to measure in the early stages of an archiving project, especially since it may be unclear what costs are startup costs and what costs are ongoing or recurrent, given the fluid nature of technology and archiving standards. Automation of as many tasks as possible may help, as long as the cost of computers continues to decrease while the cost of labor increases. The endowment model also works best when an archive's fixed costs of operation are low compared to costs that vary with the size of the archive, favoring larger archives. For similar reasons, high endowment requirements may also favor larger publishers which might be an undesirable side-effect for libraries already worried about over-consolidation of scholarly journal publishing in for-profit conglomerates. If scholarly archives are ultimately designed to meet the needs of scholars and scholarly institutions, a funding model that relies on publishers may produce a less useful archive than one that is funded more directly by scholars and their libraries.

Funding by users appears to be a viable alternative to endowments by publishers. JSTOR has found success through funding from libraries and other journal users. Libraries pay a one-time capital development fee and an annual subscription fee to access JSTOR content. Publishers are not charged for deposits into the archive. JSTOR has proven highly popular with libraries and their patrons.

JSTOR's convenient access is the carrot that encourages libraries to pay for subscriptions that cover both access services and archiving. JSTOR's success with libraries, scholars, and publishers makes a powerful case for this type of funding model. Of course, it is possible for journal archives to have multiple funding sources, but complicated funding models may produce more problems than they solve.

An archive faced with high ingestion costs could depend on users to fund its general operations and development, as JSTOR does, but charge publishers for ingesting their content unless their content came in a prepackaged, easily-validated form prescribed by the archive. In effect, the archive would offer to sell publishers a packaging service for their content. The publisher could pay for the archive to package their content, or pay some other service provider to do it, or do it on its own and avoid having to pay. In any case, the archive's own costs for ingestion would be reduced and publishers would have an incentive to provide their content in accordance with archival standards. Both of these developments would make the archive more reliable and sustainable.

Funding and control of access rights represent a tradeoff. Publishers can provide funds or they can provide access rights to users after a suitable delay. They are reluctant to provide both. Libraries and scholars, on the other hand, may be disinclined to fund an archive that does not give them access except in some far-distant or unforeseeable circumstances. Thus, archives funded primarily by publishers may tend to be "dark," whereas archives funded primarily by libraries and archives should be more open to access by their funders.

Responsibilities and rights for transfer and delegation. Archives must be ready for unforeseen changes in the scholarly or online community that may render the archive unsustainable or make it far preferable to archive content elsewhere. Therefore, agreements with the publisher should allow the transfer, if necessary, of the archival material and its associated rights to another party that agrees to assume the archive's responsibilities. The publisher, if it is still in existence, may want to stipulate some additional qualities of the new party, for instance, that it not be a commercial competitor.

Similarly, the agreement should allow third parties to act as service providers for delegated archival functions as long as the third parties do not distribute archival material or use it for any purpose other than to carry out legitimate archival functions on the archive's behalf. For example, integrated archives may need to have a third-party off-site mirror of the archive's contents in case of a disaster at the main archival site.

Archival Life Cycle

The OAIS model breaks down the archiving process into distinct functional modules which manage archival information packages throughout their life cycles. The key modules defined by OAIS and some of their functions are:

— *Ingest*. This includes the archive's acquisition of journal content and metadata, validation of the content, and packaging for archival storage as Archive Information Packages (AIPs).

— *Archival storage*. This includes maintaining AIP data and ensuring the continued survival and integrity of binary representations of archival data.

— *Data management*. This includes, among other things, maintaining metadata on archived content, managing storage, and handling queries on stored data.

— *Administration*. Among other things, this includes migration.

— *Preservation planning*. This includes planning and implementing further development of the archival system, including migration planning.

— *Access*. This includes delivery of content both to end users and to other archives under appropriate access controls.

— *Ingestion*. Ingestion of presentation content and metadata from Web sites helps to construct a modular prototype harvester that could collect metadata and links to content from different publisher Web sites, then deposit the metadata and links into a common data structure that could be browsed and accessed uniformly.

Size of the content varied greatly among journals. For example, PDFs for American Law and Economics Review, a semi-annual journal, took up little more than 2 MB of storage space per year, whereas PDFs for Brain, a monthly medical journal, took up closer to 100 MB of storage space per year.

Articles in PDF form were generally easy to harvest, usually as one PDF file per article, although in some instances the PDFs were page-oriented instead and included content from multiple or adjacent items in the same file.

Correctly harvesting HTML presentation forms was considerably more problematic. Many of the HTML-formatted articles were clearly generated from source files and included numerous automatically generated links, some of which led to content that was important to the article, such as high-resolution versions of illustrations, while others led to related material that was not part of the article itself. Many of these HTML articles were produced by the same organization, Highwire Press.

Ingesting material into an archive, whether manually or automatically, is far from foolproof. When publishers manually send a journal issue to an archive they may accidentally leave out articles, send misformatted files, or even send the wrong files altogether.

Occasionally, articles published on Web sites included mistakes. An early spot-check of one mathematics journal article revealed a PDF file in which the last pages could not be read as the file was initially posted. Human checks may turn up some of these errors but can be expensive to perform.

Migration. Left alone, archived content and metadata are not likely to stay usable forever. Preserving the integrity of the original digital forms of archived electronic journals is not difficult with proper planning and the right to make copies as needed for archiving. The strategies of generating checksums, making backups and offsite mirrors, regularly refreshing media, and conducting regularly scheduled consistency checks and disaster drills are well-known in digital preservation and data security circles. However, more uncertainty exists about whether the digital forms can continue to be understood and used effectively as technologies and expectations change.

Data structures and formats based on simple, openly-specified, and widely-used standards are the easiest to preserve, and journal archives should encourage their use. The definition of XML, for instance, is straightforward and widely publicized. Even if XML is eventually replaced by some other standard for structured data, it would not be difficult to migrate XML files to the new standard or to maintain programs that continue to parse XML in its original form.

To understand and use archival files formatted in XML or SGML, though, it is not sufficient to be able to parse the markup; it is also necessary to know what the markup represents. In addition, we need to preserve the DTDs or schemas used, as well as the documentation for defining DTDs, schemas, or whatever syntactic convention next comes along to describe markup formats. And, above the level of DTDs or schemas, we need to document and preserve the semantics of the schemas: the meaning of the markup elements and how their composition turns a set of angle-bracketed words and sentences into a journal that speaks from mind to mind.

The semantics may be expressed in English-language descriptions, stylesheets, a program that renders markup as a visual display like that of a Web browser, or all of these. Particularly since some of the syntax and semantics may be specific to the world of electronic journal publishing and archiving, the archival system will need to include a preservation mechanism for both the syntax and semantics of its data.

Preserving format information is not a new idea. The Multipurpose Internet Mail Extensions (MIME) registry maintained by the Internet Assigned Numbers Authority (IANA) preserves descriptions of data formats commonly used on the Internet, as well as standard methods for encoding, packaging, and transmitting them. The Typed Object Model (TOM), adds semantic capabilities to a distributed format registry mechanism, supporting automated services like migration, format identification, and interpretation of data formats by remote servers.

An ideal registry for journal archiving data structures would allow the combination of the prose descriptions and canonical authority of IANA's MIME registry, the computational power of TOM, and the expertise of digital librarians, archivists, and publishers.

Preserving presentation forms presents some special problems: they are often complicated, defined by vendors, and dependent on external information in unexpected ways. Fortunately, the presentation forms of most electronic journals are designed to be viewable by ordinary Web browsers without esoteric plugins. The capabilities of Web browsers are well-documented, for the most part, so it should be possible to deal with the formats they handle.

Archival Collections

In 1990s, a wide variety of digital collections have emerged on the Internet. While digital collections may differ in content or structure, they all share one commonality—the need for metadata. Frequently described as "data about data," metadata is a critical component of all digital collections. Metadata facilitates the discovery and retrieval of information, it provides for resource presentation and navigation, and it contains the information needed to preserve digital data files.

While several digital collections of books have been created for the Internet, it is only recently that libraries and archives have begun to digitize archival collections for Web delivery. The Barren Lands project is a full-text online collection of archival material related to two exploratory surveys conducted by the Canadian explorer, geologist, and mining engineer, Joseph Burr Tyrrell. The collection is centred on Tyrrell's 1893 and 1894 explorations of Canada's Barren Lands region west of Hudson Bay, in the area now known as Nunavut. The first major challenge associated with the Barren Lands project centred on how to represent archival material within an online environment.

A search of the Internet for similar archival projects revealed that online archival collections were most often presented in one of two ways: as an online exhibition or as a simple database of independent archival documents. Following the "exhibition" method, institutions presented archival collections online in much the same way as they would present an exhibition of physical materials; narrative descriptions or transcriptions of items were presented with links to digital representations of those items. In these digital repositories, each archival document was treated as a separate entity and basic descriptive metadata elements such as title, author, and date were given for each item. Although the Barren Lands project team found aspects of both methods of delivery appealing, they decided that neither approach was fully compatible with their vision of the project.

While the "exhibition" approach provided an abundance of narrative contextual information, this method was deemed impracticable for the size of the digital collection. Similarly, a strict database approach was also not favoured, as it did not retain the contextual linkages between the documents. Instead, the Barren Lands project team decided to create two levels of descriptive metadata to provide the necessary contextual information for the archival materials and to allow for comprehensive searching. In most digital collections, each book, article, map, etc. is considered to be an independent digital object. The Barren Lands project was different in that the archival collection consisted of many documents that were inter-related with each other.

It was essential that these natural connections be retained within the digital environment. At the same time, it was necessary that each document remain an independent digital object for the purpose of resource discovery and retrieval. The solution to this problem was to adopt a two-tiered approach to the creation of descriptive metadata—one tier to describe the archival materials as a collective unit and another to describe each digital object. Although paper-based finding aids and item listings for some of the materials did exist for the J.B. Tyrrell and James W. Tyrrell collections, the project team was unable to use this information in the construction of the online collection.

Problems with the pre-existing descriptive metadata were three-fold: first, the metadata was not in electronic format; second, the metadata did not contain all of the necessary descriptive information; and third, the archival materials were not described consistently according to archival descriptive standards. Because of these problems, the project team decided to re-describe both collections according to the Canadian descriptive standard, the Rules for Archival Description (RAD). Once the descriptive metadata was complete, it was necessary to encode this information in a standard data structure.

In order to retain the relationships between archival materials, the project team adopted the Encoded Archival Description (EAD) data structure standard, which is jointly administered by the Society of American Archivists and the Library of Congress. EAD is a non-proprietary standard in the form of a Standard Generalized Markup Language (SGML) and Extensible Markup Language (XML) Document Type Definition (DTD). Developed specifically for archival finding aids, the EAD standard has the ability to accurately represent the multilevel nature of archives in a machine-readable format. Consequently, the EAD standard facilitates access by allowing users to "drill down" into an archival finding aid, beginning at the fonds or collection level description down to the descriptions of individual items. In the Barren Lands project, the descriptions of the J.B. Tyrrell and James W. Tyrrell fonds were encoded using the XML version of the EAD DTD. In these multi-level records, users are provided with descriptions of the entire fonds, the various series of documents that make up the fonds, and file level descriptions if they exist.

Within the description of each series or file containing digitized objects, a link is made from the title of the object to a separate item level description. While EAD does provide the capability to describe archival materials down to the item level of description, the project team decided that within the context of the project, the standard was unsuitable for that purpose. The problems associated with multiple media collections do not generally lie in the presentation of various media, but rather in their preparation for online delivery. The Barren Lands project consists of a variety of documentary forms, all of which needed to be handled in a slightly different manner. As a form of structural metadata, the file naming structure was used to distinguish between documentary forms. Directories were created for each type of document, such as letters, diaries, published text, maps, photographs, and so on.

Then, as each archival document was scanned, a unique identifier, containing a letter to identify the documentary form followed by a five-digit number, was recorded in a relational database. The project team felt strongly that no semantic information be included in the file naming system as this type of information would likely become confusing rather than helpful in the long run. This file-naming system not only ensured that we had a simple, well-organized repository for the images, it also allowed the team to quickly identify which image files required OCR and which files needed rekeying.

In the Barren Lands project, structural information such as unique identifiers, page sequence numbers, page numbers as stated on the document, special features such as tables of contents and indexes, and other relevant information was collected in a relational database at the point of scanning. Some descriptive metadata relating to individual pages of the digital object, such as titles of maps or illustrations and content dates were also recorded in the database. In addition to descriptive and structural metadata, the Barren Lands project team also captured administrative or technical metadata during the scanning process. As each image was scanned, information relating to the source type, file format, scanning date, and scanner was captured in a relational database. Adobe Portable Document Format (PDF) is a widely used standard for electronic document distribution worldwide in many institutional settings. Much of its popularity comes from its ability to faithfully encode both the text and the visual appearance of source documents, preserving their fonts, formatting, colors, and graphics.

PDF files can be viewed, navigated, and printed with a free Adobe Acrobat Reader, available on all major computing platforms. PDF has many applications and is commonly used to publish government, public, and academic documents. Many of the electronic journals and other digital resources acquired by libraries are published in PDF format. As libraries grow more dependent on electronic resources, they need to consider how they can preserve these resources for the long term. Many libraries retain back runs of print journals that are over 100 years old, and which are still consulted by researchers.

No digital technology has lasted nearly that long, and many data formats have already become obsolete and not easily readable in a much shorter time period. PDF is a platform-independent document format developed by Adobe as a follow-up to its Postscript language. Although Postscript was designed specifically for printing, PDF is meant to support on-line, secure, interactive use, as well as printing. PDF combines attributes of structured text formats and traditional image formats, so that a document can be used both in terms of its text and in terms of its "look" on-screen or on the page.

A PDF file does not always contain the full glyph specification of characters in the document, but at least includes the name of the fonts used and specifies the space all characters will occupy. PDF includes metadata on the document, specifying things such as page size, page numbering, and a structured table of contents. Add-ons, such as hyperlinks, forms, and even pieces of scripting code in Java or Postscript that control dynamic displays or the user interface, can also be included. Not all PDF documents encode the text of a document directly. It is possible to embed images of a page in PDF, so that a picture of text is encoded but not the text itself. Some scanners, for instance, can output this "uninterpreted" form of PDF.

Such uninterpreted PDF files tend to be much larger than PDF files that encode text directly as characters, and text-oriented operations such as searching and textual copying and pasting are not supported by these files. Some programs also exist that will attempt to recognize whatever text they can in a scanned PDF document, and replace the images of this text with a briefer encoding of the characters and fonts. Such programs tend to produce "hybrid" PDF files where encoded text strings in appropriate fonts are positioned inside page images, and any unrecognized characters are kept on the page in the form of images. Although such PDF files can be smaller than those that consist only of uninterpreted page images, they also often have only partial, and choppy, encoding of their underlying text, because recognition programs typically cannot recognize 100% of the text in a typical page scan.

PDF was originally designed for 8-bit character sets. Some limited support for Unicode also exists, but the format has not yet taken full advantage of Unicode's capabilities. Unlike XML, PDF was not originally designed for arbitrary structural annotations, although the last revision of PDF includes some facilities for user-defined structural markup. PDF is a less efficient format for text analysis than purely text-based formats such as XML or HTML, and readers have noted that searching for words within a PDF viewer can be noticeably slower than searching for words in an HTML viewer. The central role that appearance plays in PDF is both a strength and a weakness; it allows publishers to specify exactly how they want a document to look, but it also makes it difficult for users to reformat or repaginate the document if that would be better for them.

PDF includes facilities for encrypting content, or directing that a document not be printable. It is possible to use encryption so that a document cannot be decrypted without a password. However, once the document is decrypted, it is possible, in theory, to make an unlocked copy that can be freely copied, read, or printed. Adobe is highly invested in the success of PDF, but even if Adobe fails or abruptly changes course, a community of third-party tools for handling PDF has started to emerge. PDF is used widely by many well-funded bodies so there should be widespread support for using and migrating PDF, should Adobe fail to provide adequate support for the format. Even so, it is likely that PDF will one day be superseded by another format. It may be a successor format, or it may be a completely different format that users prefer over PDF. Hence, it is necessary to have migration strategies planned for PDF.

Currently, there is no other format that can encompass all of the features of PDF in a form that standard tools can interpret. Most page image formats are pixel-oriented, where pictures are encoded using a grid with each grid cell (known as a pixel) associated with a particular color (or with no added color). Some image formats, including PDF and Postscript, are stroke-oriented, encoded with instructions about lines to plot, regions to color, and text to place. They can also include instructions to embed pixel-oriented images at specified locations. Pixel-oriented formats have a well-understood mathematical representation, making them easy to migrate.

Stroke-oriented image formats are not so standardized. They can encode information about the structure of a picture, such as the lines that are drawn in it, that can only be approximated to a certain resolution in purely pixel-oriented formats. On the other hand, since pixel-oriented formats can typically accommodate very fine resolutions, an image converted from a stroke-oriented format to a pixel-oriented format at fine enough resolution can be visually indistinguishable from its original. PDF can also be converted into text, at least when the text (rather than pictures of the text) has been directly encoded in PDF files.

Formatting and layout information would be lost in a straight text conversion, and the text conversion of certain pages with complex layout may not always be read in "logical" reading order, without human intervention. Different PDF-generating programs may be more or less accommodating about rendering PDF text in a logical reading order. A straight text conversion would also lose structural information and other PDF extras, as well non-textual items such as pictures, diagrams, and possibly equations. However, it is possible to write conversions to HTML or XML that would include a "table of contents" header that incorporated the structure of the PDF document, and that would preserve certain types of PDF hyperlinks.

Text in non-European languages may also be difficult to migrate correctly, because of the previously-described limitations of PDF's support for Unicode, unless a standard set of well-defined fonts, with widely available specifications, is used to represent non-European characters. Although it is possible to migrate the appearance of PDF files, or the text, migrating both of them into a single document would be more difficult. The only other formats commonly used to specify both the text and the appearance of documents are word-processor formats, and those tend to be proprietary, system-dependent, and more ephemeral than PDF itself is likely to be.

Converting to these formats may also lead to subtly different appearances, depending on the implementation of the word processing program. RTF (Rich Text Format) may be the best target for word-processor-oriented conversions at this time, though it is far from a perfect choice. Even if it is infeasible to migrate both the text and the look of PDF into a single document, it may still be possible to migrate PDF documents into a presentation that allows one to switch between text-oriented and image-oriented views of the same document. In theory, it is possible to convert all of the information in a PDF file into an XML format with appropriate tags and attributes.

Libraries extend the power of the word over time and over space. The world over, it is emblematic of the largest and most complete collection of written materials. In US, Library of Congress (LC) is incomplete, incomplete in a thousand ways. It holds millions of titles but has no precise idea of how many books in the world it does not hold, although the number is certainly large. The greatness of the Library of Congress since the Second World War lies in the fact that it has developed its own collection at the same time as it has facilitated the growth and interdependency of the worldwide collection of the treasures of human creativity.

It is evidently impossible that copies of everything should ever be found in a single place—it takes an Alexandrian monarch or an Argentinian poet to imagine such things. But it is far from impossible that collections great and small will one day be so tightly interlinked by the exchange of data about their holdings that we will eventually know where and how to find a vastly larger percentage of the materials held in them. The last two generations have already seen huge progress in this regard, going back to LC's epochal agreement to disseminate cataloging information from its holdings and now leveraged to a wider world by such widely accessible catalogs as the Research Library Group's (RLG's) Eureka or the Online Computer Library Center's (OCLC's) WorldCat.

All of these real achievements pale by comparison with what can be imagined for the world of cyberspace. Far more information from far more sources can be brought together in nearly real time. The floods of new, increasingly available electronic information can be drawn together, sorted, filtered, and made usefully accessible. Such a possibility is easy to evoke but difficult to achieve. For a long time, traditional library materials have formed only a part of the collection: beyond books and journals and maps, LC has been collecting advertising materials, motion pictures, and baseball cards.

Today, at least three additional categories of information material challenge LC's traditional practices. The categories of material are as follows:

— *Born-digital*—Under this heading fall materials containing socially valuable and interesting information created in electronic form. Typically, we regard such materials as necessary either because they have no corresponding print form or, if they have one, they possess significant individuality in electronic form to merit inclusion in a serious library collection. Born-digital materials in turn fall into two categories:

— *Artifactual:* These are digital information materials that are published and distributed in ways that depend on particular physical media and artifacts--floppy disks, CD-ROMs, laser video disks, and the like.

— *Nonartifactual:* Increasingly, digital information does not appear in forms that lend themselves to physical collection by libraries. Web sites increase the number of sources where information of the highest social value may be found, but it is often functionally impossible to "acquire" a Web site—even if one copied all the public pages of a site, substantial additional bodies of material that lie behind it (e.g., databases that are accessed by commands issued from the Web pages) would not be publicly available. The quantity and quality of material available in this form can only be expected to grow in the coming years.

— *Turned digital*—By this phrase is meant materials that were originally created in a traditional artifactual form (usually print) but have been converted to digital media for reasons of preservation and/or access. There is already a history of cooperative activity surrounding preservation decisions (that is, decisions to change the media of presentation in order to preserve the content of the original), but this movement must now be accelerated, for two reasons:

  — The use of electronic media for preservation has advantages in cost and accessibility over many other media (though electronic media may introduce new preservation problems of their own).

  — Digital representations of print materials and other physical artifacts are increasingly popular when the purpose is not only preservation but also a concomitant increase in ease of access and use, particularly for rare or fragile materials.

For digital materials, both "born" and "turned," there is a nationwide and worldwide need for coordination and communication so that expensive and time-consuming projects do not duplicate other efforts. Furthermore, the results of digital preservation efforts can and should be widely shared, and for that reason turned-digital materials will quickly begin to behave just as born-digital materials do. A library such as LC will presumably first digitize treasures of its own but will then wish to have access to those of other libraries. In the world of print materials, LC's strategy was straightforward: to leverage its statutory rights of collection (through copyright deposit) to achieve physical collections of unparalleled size and quality.

In the digital realms, LC starts with many fewer advantages. The digitization of its own existing collections can give it, to be sure, tremendously rich and exciting materials for a new digital collection. But no matter how aggressively LC collects digital materials, achieving a truly universal collection will now increasingly mean recognizing that not everything can be collected, because the volume of digital information is so great. Also, many publishers and distributors of material of high value will produce material in a form that must be consulted remotely and cannot be physically added to the working collections of the Library.

When physical possession is not possible or desirable, it will be all the more important that firm and secure links between LC and other stakeholders in the information community are established. If LC possesses a physical book, it can take its own steps to ensure preservation and accessibility—or even, if appropriate, to practice relative neglect—thereby making it possible for a book to be usable generations after its creation. Where LC possesses the original source files or identical copies, preservation will be a demanding chore. Where LC does not possess the digital source files, assurance of preservation and access will require coordination of a complicated social, legal, and economic strategy.

No library in the world has the prestige or the influence of the Library of Congress, if LC will only use it. Over the last two decades, the Library has been too little visible on the national and international stage, particularly in the digital arena. Too many of the stunning achievements of LC leadership and collaboration are now receding into the hallowed past. Moreover, it has been the case that projects and/or exhibitions of great significance have not always been consistently institutionalized as ongoing services.

At the same time, it is important to be clear about the kind of role that LC can and should take. The vast size of its collections and its national importance to the United States do not elevate it—or any other player—above the rest of the library community. The Library should see itself as a particularly privileged, and therefore particularly responsible, partner in a wide range of conversations. The important role LC could play in establishing standards for a wide variety of infrastructural elements of the library of the future, just as it did in the past when it created the MARC record. But LC cannot dictate the outcomes of such a process to others. Rather, its true value would be to bring stakeholders together in a collaborative process that begins by identifying issues and needs that cut across broad swathes of the information community.

While LC and all of the other stakeholders are sobered by the realization that the outcomes of high-level summits are always debatable and never last forever, they can take heart from knowing that LC would participate in such conversations not as one of several hostile parties seeking influence but rather as the genuine representative of a common public good that can advance the interests of other participants in the process. A genuinely broad vision and a determined insistence on turning that vision into reality must be accompanied by a collegial, humble manner that seeks the broadest possible common good for both the users and the producers of information.

The Library must recognize and genuinely respect other senior partners in these undertakings. Over the last three decades, both RLG and OCLC have emerged as serious and respected players in advancing broad and reliable access to library materials. Relations among these three organizations have at times been no better than cool. RLG's and OCLC's joint representations to the committee suggested that they see the value and necessity of working with each other in productive ways and with LC.

Collaboration of this sort may not prove easy for LC, because decisions taken two decades ago led to the creation of a highly successful system whereby OCLC distributes catalog records to a wide variety of libraries, and these records include the very substantial body of cataloging created by LC. The results for users have been overwhelmingly positive, however, and the cost savings to the library community extraordinary. Great things have been achieved by LC, OCLC, and RLG, and it is time to look to the future in a trusting and collaborative spirit.

The experience of installing the new Integrated Library System in 1999 shows that even when the Library waits until a technology is well established and in use at other libraries, its size and scope make it hard to tailor the technology to the Library's needs. The Library should look for ways to influence the technologies it will use earlier in their development cycle, ensuring that both library technology research and product development address issues of scale early on. In order to succeed, it is necessary for LC and its leaders to be seen and heard widely in the library community in the United States and abroad. It is unfortunate, although understandable, that none of the three senior officers of the Library has chosen to dedicate time to becoming heavily involved with the library community.

In US, the National Science Foundation distributed funds through the 1990s for its Digital Libraries Initiative (DLI). The inclusion of LC as a partner of DLI is a promising step in the right direction, but more substantive involvement in the DLI and engagement in other, comparable initiatives need to be pursued aggressively. The Library is at a disadvantage owing to its lack of a research capability and its inability to provide significant funding for research by others, for even when it sees an opportunity it has only modest means to exert influence. Still, LC could provide small research grants to be used for cooperative efforts with others, or it could develop other means to support the needed research (e.g., sponsor visiting research fellows at LC, if such a program were in place).

The Library of Congress must seek out, generate, and empower leaders who will be visible and influential as spokespersons for the library community and the interests of a broad range of information users. Such leadership could be credible and effective at creating the connections that the future of libraries requires. By U.S. law, the Library of Congress is only Congress's library, not the nation's. The Library's role and function thus differ significantly from those of counterpart libraries in other countries. It is important, however, to understand that a number of the Library's functions are characteristic of the functions of a national library. These include but are not limited to the following:

— It serves as the national (copyright) depository library with a mission to assemble a comprehensive national collection.

— It is the authoritative national source of cataloging information.

— It de facto represents the United States in bodies and organizations where the other participants represent the national libraries of their countries.

There is today no easy replacement of paper with digital materials, and comparatively few cost-saving benefits will be reaped from automation per se: those days are largely over. We live in a time when libraries will see their missions expanded as they continue to collect and preserve analog materials while at the same time participating wholeheartedly in the digital revolution. The users of libraries—from senators to ordinary citizens to research scholars—will demand (and deserve) no less.

The Library owns precious content that many publishers and entertainment industry producers would be happy to develop. It has reservations, however, for it has had some negative experiences with such partners. These reservations are understandable, but they should transmute not into suspicion but into a strategy for partnership. Insofar as LC remains committed to the business of disseminating its collections to a broad public, and in particular to schoolchildren, it should look for neither a core congressional allocation nor charitable contributions to support that commitment. Rather, LC should seek to disseminate its collections to a wider public by means of a mutually beneficial partnership with the private sector—a partnership that goes beyond the contribution of funds or equipment by using the partnership to develop the technical and marketing expertise of the Library (i.e., to effect technology transfer).

To the extent that there are legal and practical restrictions on such partnerships, the committee strongly urges Congress to respond by facilitating the creative exploitation of a cultural treasure. In the end, of course, LC's collections belong to the nation, and that fact sets limits to the rights that LC can assign to its prospective partners and thus, inevitably, to the degree of exploitation that is possible.

Traditional processes can also be facilitated through the use of information technology to improve access for clients and to increase revenue. For example, the Photoduplication Service might sell its products through the Web. There are surely other strategic opportunities of a nontraditional kind, for example, with "portals" that would let the portals' customers link more effectively to LC, while LC would find in such (presumably nonexclusive) arrangements an effective and essentially cost-free marketing strategy.

E-JOURNAL ARCHIVING

E-journals may publish articles as they are ready, without waiting for a whole issue's worth of articles, but this change is sequential addition. Dynamic e-journals can be defined as those that contain moving elements or make elements move. Moving elements include, for example, audio and video clips as well as animations. Because moving elements are not printable, libraries can no longer rely on printing the e-journals as a primary preservation strategy. Microfilm and microform are likewise static and cannot accommodate moving elements either. E-journals that can make elements move typically include embedded software that enables movement, or scripts and programs that render content on the fly. Because one cannot print dynamic e-journals to preserve them, the task at hand is to define new ways of preserving content that makes no sense without these constituent, dynamic aspects.

While we know how to catalog, index, and retrieve moving files, we must refine this cataloging since the elements are embedded in more readily cataloged articles. Cataloging, indexing, and retrieving the kind of content that cannot be rendered without interactive functionality are particularly vexing hurdles, especially if the content changes with every user's instantiation of that content. Dynamic electronic journals are a natural outgrowth of Internet and Web technologies. The electronic journals were born in Web environments and are meant to be rendered and displayed in current Web environments. However we preserve them, for the time being they must also be Web accessible.

In the future, it is likely that electronic material will be rendered in other digital (and perhaps even non-digital) environments. Of course, besides dynamic elements and functionalities, dynamic e-journals contain text and other intellectually significant elements.

Information Retrieval

Information retrieval is not a service to be delivered exclusively by publishers. The libraries in particular have an important role as facilitators of the navigation possibilities available to the users. There are several reasons for this. Traditionally, libraries operate in close contact with their users and communicate with them in order to establish specific user needs. The invisible library could offer the following services to its users. Search facilities are subject to a number of basic user requirements, the most important of which can be summarised as follows. Users will want to be able to start the search process immediately, without first having to study complex interfaces and codes.

They are looking for information and cannot be expected to be interested in the technical structure or format of the data involved. Neither are users likely to be interested in the origin of the source (the identity of the publisher or intermediary), or in the location where the information they need is physically stored. They just want to find an answer to a particular question. During the search process, moreover, users will only want to be presented answers that are fully relevant to their question, without being swamped by thousands of articles only marginally related to the subject.

Personal alerting system is vital to provide an easily accessible information universe which the user can enter independently provided he is equipped with the proper IR tools. In addition, the user should be served by his own personal assistant, who offers packages of information tailored to the user's individual reader profile. Such assistants have already been created in self-learning software known as intelligent agents technology. These assistants, or agents, are used in the construction of a personal alerting system.

The set-up and testing of such personal alerting systems is the responsibility of support organisations, for example university libraries; their use requires no additional intermediaries. Researchers, teachers and students will all make use of this tool independently and will only require assistance from the library when they need specific instructions or are confronted with specific problems. The traditional library organisation was characterised by a decentralised structure in which individual libraries were found in the locations where teaching and research activities actually took place (mostly in the university professors' rooms).

In order to improve efficiency, to solve logistic problems and, above all, to cut costs books and magazines were relocated to central or faculty libraries. Double subscriptions were cancelled. While obviously provoking some protest from among faculty members, this operation was in many cases inevitable. Due to the advent of the Internet and electronic sources of information, the physical location of those sources has become irrelevant. From behind a PC in his or her own office, today's scientist has access to a range of sources that is incomparable to the access provided by the traditional library in the professor's lecture room. While the range of sources offers clear and major advantages, its very extensiveness also causes a number of problems.

Some of these can be obviated by IR systems and personal agents, but more tools are required; tools that help the user to create and manage his/her own limited but tailor-made collection. These tools allow the scientist to become a librarian himself, but a librarian who has no other clients. Scientists need tools to perform this role, tools that help them organise their own articles, research data, teaching material, etc.; tools which respect the preferences of their users and can deal with even the most idiosyncratic approach to building up personal collections.

It is one of the library's tasks to make such tools available. They can be described as the creation of facilities, the supply of user instructions for those facilities and the provision of assistance when problems occur, and are all consistent with user demands. Information cannot be separated from the purpose it is used for. At universities, that purpose can be found in the primary processes of education and research. This is why the university library's tasks are focused on the integration of information services in the user's primary processes. Such integration is not achieved automatically, however.

A teacher who is preparing a new online reader will need access not only to all relevant sources and search and selection tools, but also to online publishing facilities. These may be templates provided with conversion programmes which adapt the content (text, image, video) for presentation on the world wide web, or old readers already converted from the old, illegible formats to formats that enable the teacher to cut and paste selected items for use in his new reader. The library consists of information and software and has been fully integrated into the teaching process. The tasks of the library may reach beyond the efficient and effective supply of information. Researchers do not merely consume information, but also communicate intensively with their colleagues. When they read a scientific article, many researchers will want to respond, ask the author questions or give critical comments.

The integration of the library in primary processes can advance to such a degree that the library becomes altogether invisible as a separate institute. The user takes on the role of the librarian. He gains access to a vast amount of information and is provided with a set of tools and aids that will help him extract the data he needs and arrange and process it in the manner that suits him best. Library services in which libraries provide access to as much electronic information as possible and offer additional services that enable users to organise the sources of information they need for personal professional purposes. The future of the library, the "collection' tends to be seen as a concept that will continue to play a prominent role.

The user can arrange the information sources relevant to his own professional needs into a tailor-made collection with the help of the tools presented by the library, organise those sources according to the use he expects to make of them, and integrate them into his own publications or educational programmes. These considerations do not apply to certified sources, such as freely accessible sources on the Internet. In that area, libraries will continue to be responsible for the selection of high-quality scientific material; a selection in the form of pointers, sets of references.

Far-reaching forms of cooperation among the libraries themselves are also quite conceivable. What is known in the physical world as the alignment of collection formation profiles, or priority area formation, is, understandably, only rarely successful. This concept may yield countless advantages for the virtual selection of Internet sources. The task of designating quality sources can be distributed due to the very fact that the physical location of the information is irrelevant and, hence, allows universal access. This is because this task does not involve the development of a central collection, but rather the certification of a sub-collection of information. In part, collection management is limited to measuring the frequency with which the sources are consulted and the type of use that is made of them. Related to, and indeed derived from this is the management not of the collection itself, but of various types of licenses.

Collection management refers to a distributed process of assessment of the quality of freely accessible sources on the Internet. Librarians whose careers spanned the pre- and post-1950s worlds noted a marked expansion in the scope of scholarship in America. Before World War II, academic research in America concentrated on Western culture and classical areas of science. After the war, American research horizons expanded to cover all areas of the world as well as applied and specialized fields of science. Library collections grew rapidly to house the products of this expanded research effort. In the 1950s and 60s many university librarians found themselves in the midst of a "golden age" of collection development when acquisitions funds seemed plentiful, U.S. currency was strong, and there was still room in academic library book stacks. In the mid-1980s many universities and research libraries found themselves in a period of fiscal constraint and even decline. Economic constraints affected all aspects of research library operations.

Librarians now had to balance the demands of print and digital materials, even as they sought to understand the nature and consequences of digital, networked information and the impact a new information system would have on library operations, including the budget. At the same time, scholarly publishing was also experiencing dramatic change. With fewer orders from libraries, university presses had to cut back the number of monograph titles they published, while commercial journal publishers, at least some of the largest science and technology publishers, were expanding and flourishing. Collection management librarians - and library directors - are faced with a new and uncharted environment. Libraries have much less buying power than they had a decade ago.

With fewer staff in collection management full time, many selectors and bibliographers work at collection management part time while handling a much broader range of disciplines and formats. The technical advances in digitization are truly revolutionizing the way scholarly information is published, organized, and maintained, and both the scope and extent of this change are difficult to comprehend and manage. As difficult as it was to manage a print collection, librarians now have two equally formidable formats to consider: print and digital. When digital resources were first introduced in research libraries, there was a good deal of conflict between the old and new format.

Rather than a highly decentralized system as exists today, with duplicative print collections spread across the country, digital technology has the potential to provide more centrally organized information storage and highly distributed, quick, and cost-effective access. Digital technology can also foster the integration of the various components and sources of scholarly publication. Such integration is already happening on the Web platform and through the efforts of library and scientific information services.

References

Bearman, D., "Archival methods", *Archives and Museum Informatics*, 3(1): 17-27, 1989.

Gopal Krishan, *Digital Libraries in Electronic Information Era*, Authorspress, New Delhi, 2000.

Harvery, Ross, *Preservation in Libraries: Principles, Strategies and Practices for Librarians*, London: Bowker-Saur, 1993.

Kahle, B., *Archiving the Internet*, Paper submitted to Scientific American for March 1997 issue, 1997.

Raitt, David, (ed.), *Libraries for the New Millennium: Implication for Managers*, London, Library Association Publishing, 1987.

4

Digital Video Archives

Libraries and archives face increasing pressure to make materials in their collections accessible through digital library systems. While early research on digital libraries has focused primarily on collections of textual and still image material, the growing bandwidth available to both end-users and cultural memory organisations, along with the falling price of disk storage, has meant that the creation of digital libraries of audio/visual materials is increasingly feasible. As a result, many libraries and archives have begun to make parts of their audio/visual collections available online.

As these organisations begin to digitise audio/visual materials, however, some key differences between previous projects, that focused on text and still image works, and new ones focused on time-based materials have emerged. Many early digital library projects focused on materials that are rare, unique, and quite often fragile, but these materials are also to some degree inherently long-lived. One of the justifications for digital library projects such as this, in fact, is that digital images in many cases provide an acceptable surrogate for the original, and hence reduce wear and tear due to handling and help preserve the original artifact. They also do not suffer from technological obsolescence; the media will not become unreadable for lack of a suitable player.

The moving image materials that libraries and archives have begun to digitise are, in many cases, proving to be nowhere near as long-lived, both due to the fragility of the underlying media and the rapid rate of technological change in the field of moving images. This has meant that when libraries and archives begin digitising moving image materials within their collections, they must in many cases consider whether to design these efforts simply as a means to enhance access to materials in their collections, or whether they should also use such projects as an opportunity to engage in reformatting essential to preserve at-risk material. The acceptability of digitisation as a preservation strategy is still a matter of some dispute in the library and archival communities.

Digital Video 101

A video signal consists of a single luma and two chroma components. Luma (Y') provides the brightness value associated with any point in the video signal; the two chroma components, a red color difference value (R'-Y') and a blue color difference (B'-Y'), provide color information for each point independent of the luma value. For those whose experience with video systems has been confined to computer video, where the signal is transmitted as a set of red, green and blue components, this use of luma and chroma may seem peculiar, but historically it has served a valuable function.

The use of luma and chroma meant that broadcasters did not need to produce and transmit two different signals to support black and white and color television; a single signal could be transmitted, and black and white sets would use the luma portion of the signal and disregard the chroma information, while color television sets used all three components to generate the viewable image. The lack of any apparent green component to a standard video signal is also somewhat confusing to those accustomed to computer video color spaces. However, it is possible to reconstruct the value for the green portion of a video display based upon the values of the luma and chroma components. Human beings are somewhat better at perceiving green light than we are at perceiving red light, and better at red light than blue. The value of luma for any point in a video display can therefore be expressed as a weighted sum of the nonlinear red, green and blue components for that point:

$$Y' = 0.299R' + 0.587G' + 0.114B'$$

Given this, the value of green can be expressed as:

$$G' = \frac{Y' - 0.299R' - 0.114B'}{0.587}$$

If then a video signal provides the value of Y', B' - Y', and R' - Y', it is a simple matter to reconstruct the values of B' and R' by adding the value of Y' to the two color difference signals, and then using the values of Y', B' and R' to calculate the value for G'. In effect, green information is encoded in the video signal as a function of the luma and chroma information.

Sampling of the analog values for the luma and chroma components of a video signal during digitisation is typically conducted in a manner rather different from the approach that libraries and archives have used to digitise still image materials. In capturing still images, the usual practice is to sample and record red, blue and green color information for each pixel in the image. The equivalent in video would be to sample and record the luma, red color difference and blue color difference values for each pixel. This is almost never the case in video digitisation. More typically, a digitisation process for video will record luma for every pixel, but will sample the color difference signals less frequently. Some of the more common sampling regimes for digital video are as follows:

— Luma is sampled at every pixel, while the two color difference signals are sampled at every other pixel. This is the standard for most professional digital video equipment.

— Luma is sampled at every pixel. Sampling of the color difference signals is alternated every line, with the R'-Y' sampled line for line, then B'-Y' on the next. For both color difference signals, the samples are taken every other pixel. This regime is used MPEG2, and hence is in common use as the standard format for DVDs.

— Luma is sampled at every pixel, while the color difference signals are sampled every fourth pixel. This regime is used in DV and DVCAM products.

There are other less common sampling regimes, such as 3:1:0 and 3:1:1. As with the use of luma and chroma, the use of subsampling regimes in digital video may appear somewhat unusual to those with experience digitising still image materials. The reason for subsampling in digital video is reasonably simple; without it, the data rates and data storage requirements would present formidable obstacles to implementation. Consider a standard NTSC video frame, with an active display area of 720 x 480 pixels, or a total of 345,600 pixels per frame. If the three channels are each sampled at 10 bits, then sampling a single frame will require 10,368,000 bits.

There are 29.97 frames per second in NTSC video, so with full three channel sampling at 10 bits per sample, the resulting digital stream would consume 310,728,960 bits per second. Storing an hour of video at this rate would require nearly 140 gigabytes. It is only comparatively recently that computing equipment capable of sustained throughput of 310 megabits/second reached a price where libraries and archives might consider its use on digitisation projects. Relatively few institutions are capable of affording large-scale video storage, if such storage requires 140 GB for a single hour of video. 4:2:2 subsampling drops the data rate and storage requirements for digital video by a third, and the resulting video, when displayed, is almost indistinguishable from the original source. 4:2:0 and 4:1:1 subsampling cut the requirements in half, and still provide perfectly acceptable video quality for consumer applications.

It is relatively common within publications and advertisements aimed at the video production community to see the term "4:2:2 uncompressed" to refer to video which uses 4:2:2 chroma subsampling, but otherwise does not compress the video signal. Strictly speaking, this is an oxymoron. Use of chroma subsampling is a form of lossy compression; color information is being discarded to reduce the size of the video stream, in anticipation of the fact that it can be interpolated relatively successfully from the remaining information when the stream must be displayed to the viewer. Such a reconstructed signal, however, will not be a perfect match for the original.

Chroma subsampling is by no means the only form of compression used to reduce the data rate and storage requirements of video. Standards such as MPEG2 and MJPEG2000 employ a variety of techniques, including motion compensation, discrete cosine transformation and wavelet-based compression to further reduce the size of a video stream to a more manageable level. Current video production practice is built upon a foundation of lossless and lossy compression techniques.

Worthy Video vs. Normal Video

While the library and archival world has only limited experience in creating digital libraries of video materials, we have gained a fair amount of experience in digitising text and still image works. Research and experimentation over the past several years has led us to identify several characteristics a digital file must possess if we are to consider it 'preservation-worthy':

— As formats tend to fall out of use over time, the file must be in a format that will enable us to move its content to new formats without loss of information;

— Similarly, as media inevitably decays, the file must be stored on a medium that allows us to move the information to new media without loss;

— The file must be in a format for which the complete technical specifications are publicly documented (preferably in a formal standard), so that we can examine the format's characteristics to be certain that it will not place information at risk of loss, and so that if necessary we can create new software to access information within the file;

— As users' needs may not be as well satisfied by a digital file we consider preservable as they may be by some other format, to the degree possible, a preservation file should be in a format chosen with an eye towards insuring the easy production of derivative files for distribution to end users;

— Preservation is an expensive activity, and in order to insure the preservation of the largest quantity of material possible, files should be stored in a format that minimises our costs of digital production, distribution and migration.

In practice, these requirements have tended to favor standards-based file formats over proprietary ones, as standards insure the availability of the technical information needed to evaluate a particular file format. They also require avoiding the use of lossy compression techniques, as migrating from one form of lossy compression into a new form is almost certain to introduce artifacts into the digital file.

Unfortunately, use of lossy compression is the normal practice in almost every piece of video production equipment employed today. All video processing involving chroma subsampling, even that advertising itself as 'uncompressed', is actually using lossy compression. Because of this, we can anticipate that video streams stored using chroma subsamplin, will be apt to experience artifacting when moved to new formats.

In normal video production, a video stream would not be subject to ten successive encoding runs, and artifacting of the severity seen above would not occur. If we are digitising video with an eye towards its long-term preservation however, we must consider the possibility that digital video streams in our care may be migrated far more often than ten times if we are to keep them accessible to our users. The artifacting seen above is produced by a codec where the software engineers went to a great deal of effort to insure that the compression and decompression operations were, to the extent possible, inverse operations.

We can expect more extensive degradation if we subject a video stream to successively different compression and decompression operations with different assumptions regarding treatment of the video stream's colorspace. It is possible to produce digital video today that is not subject to the degradation demonstrated above by 4:2:2 video. By using 4:4:4 sampling. Using a 4:4:4 sampling regime eliminates one of the problems faced in trying to produce a digital video stream capable of being preserved in the long term, however it raises additional problems. The first of these is the choice of media on which to store the stream.

Standard digital video production equipment and digital videotape formats all employ some form of chroma subsampling; even the highest quality equipment and tape formats use 4:2:2 sampling. If you wish to store and retain 4:4:4 video, then, you cannot use videotape systems. You must store the video stream as a file in data repository system of some kind, whether on magnetic disk or using a hierarchical storage management (HSM) system to take advantage of the lower cost of magnetic tape as a storage medium.

Given the tremendous storage requirements for uncompressed 4:4:4 video, most institutions choosing a storage architecture will probably lean towards an HSM system due to the significant cost savings over an entirely disk-based architecture. For longterm preservation, however, there are at least a few considerations that libraries and archives should bear in mind in deciding upon a storage architecture.

First, files on any storage media can become corrupt, and in any video archive of significant size, you will need to automate the process of examining video assets to determine whether they have become corrupted and need to be restored from a backup copy. Software for this purpose is readily available, but the constant checking of all the files in your repository required by this sort of application will place an additional strain on the tape robotics used in most HSM systems, and may hamper performance for your users.

Second, any storage architecture you might choose to implement will eventually become antiquated and need to be replaced, and all of your assets migrated to a new system. At that point, the ability to quickly move terabytes or petabytes of information from one system to another will be a paramount concern. While there are tape storage library systems that can sustain the necessary throughput to accomplish this type of migration in a timely fashion, they tend to be on the higher end of the price range for these systems. Those implementing HSM for long-term archival video storage should take care to insure that there is a technologically feasible escape path from whatever storage system they choose to put in place.

A final consideration for any storage mechanism is the maximum allowable file size under the operating system used. An hour of standard NTSC 4:4:4 video stored uncompressed will consume 140 GB; for HDTV, an hour will consume over 840 GB. While modern file systems can accommodate files of that size, care must be taken in selecting and configuring a storage system to insure that it can handle the size of files to be generated.

Choosing a file format for storing a 4:4:4 digital stream presents another challenge. While there are several file formats that can store 4:4:4 video, real world production depends on not only the existence of a suitable format, but software capable of supporting it. At the moment, finding a file format that supports 4:4:4 uncompressed video, is publicly documented, and for which software support is readily available is somewhat difficult. The QuickTime format fulfills the basic technical requirement of supporting 4:4:4 uncompressed video and software support is readily available. While it is a publicly documented format, it is also a proprietary one. It provides what is probably the easiest to use format capable of supporting 4:4:4 video today, but archivists employing it may wish to track the availability of public documentation for the format and consider abandoning it if documentation ceases to be available.

Motion JPEG 2000 is another alternative, supporting 4:4:4 uncompressed video and also being documented in an official standard. However, software support for Motion JPEG is not as widely available as support for QuickTime. Another possibility that has recently emerged is the Material Exchange Format (MXF), developed by the Pro-MPEG Forum and aimed at the interchange of audio/visual information, along with associated data and metadata, between systems.

It is an XML-based format, and is agnostic with regards to the video coding and compression algorithms used to store video 'essence'. It has also been submitted to SMPTE for standardisation. It has support from several of the major corporations involved in the video production industry, and some early test software is available for working with the format, but the SMPTE version of MXF has not been finalised, and anyone adopting MXF at the moment must be ready to deal with some changes to the official file format when it is standardised. It is theoretically conceivable to establish a video archive today using 4:4:4 video in a data repository using QuickTime or MJPEG2000 as a file format. However, to do so presents cost issues that will probably be insurmountable for most archives.

Metadata for Digital Video Archives

We are faced with a great opportunity as analog video resources are digitized and new video is produced digitally from the outset. The video itself, once encoded as bits, can be copied without loss in quality and distributed cheaply and broadly over the ever-growing communication channels set up for facilitating transfer of computer data.

The great opportunity is that these video bits can be described digitally as well, so that producers' identities and rights can be tracked and consumers' information needs can be efficiently, effectively addressed. Without metadata, a thousand-hour digital video archive is reduced to a terabyte or greater jumble of bits; with metadata, those thousand hours can become a valuable information resource. Metadata for video are crucial when one considers the huge volume of bits within digital video representations.

When digitizing an analog signal for video, the signal needs to be sampled a number of times per second, and those samples quantized into numeric values that can then be represented as bits. Only with infinite sampling and quantization could the digital representation exactly reproduce the analog signal. However, human physiology provides some upper bounds on differences that can actually be distinguished. For example, the human eye can typically differentiate at most 16 million colours, and so representing color with 24 bits provides as much color resolution as is needed for the human viewer. Similar visual physiological factors on critical viewing distance and persistence of vision establish other guidelines on pixel resolution per image and images per second playback rate.

For a given screen size and viewer distance, 640 pixels per line and 480 lines per image provide adequate resolution, with 30 images per second resulting in no visible flicker or break in motion. Digital video at these rates requires 640 x 480 x 30 x (24 bits per pixel) = 221 megabits per second, or 100 gigabytes per hour.

The number of bits increases if higher resolution (such as high-density TV [HDTV] resolution of 1920 by 1080) is desired (for example, to allow for larger displays viewed at closer distances without distinguishing the individual pixels). Hence, even a single hour of video can result in 100 gigabytes of data. Associating metadata with the video makes these gigabytes of data more manageable. Numerous strategies exist to reduce the number of bits required for digital video, from relaxed resolution requirements to lossy compression in which some information is sacrificed in order to reduce significantly the number of bits used to encode the video. Motion Picture Experts Group-1 (MPEG-1) and MPEG-2 are two such lossy compression formats; MPEG-2 allows higher resolution than MPEG-1 does.

Because preservationists want to maintain the highest-quality representation of artifacts in their archives, they are predisposed against lossy compression. However, the only way to fit more than a few seconds of HDTV video onto a CD-ROM is through lossy compression. The introduction to scanning by the Preservation Resources Division of OCLC Online Computer Library Center, Inc., reflects this tension between quality and accessibility.

Although traditional preservation methods have ensured the longevity of endangered research materials, it has sometimes been at the cost of reduced access. With digital technology, images are used to reproduce rare items, allowing for virtually universal copying, distribution, and access.

The technology also makes it possible to bring collections of disparate holdings together in digital form, making resource sharing more feasible. Hence, for long-term preservation, digital video presents a number of challenges. What should the sampling and quantization rates be? What compression strategies should be used-lossy or lossless? What media should be used to store the resulting digital files-optical (such as digital video disc [DVD]) or magnetic? What is the shelf life for such media, i.e., how often should the digital records be transferred to new media? What are the environmental factors for long-term media storage? What decompression software needs to exist for subsequent extraction of video recordings?

These challenges are not discussed further here, as they warrant their own separate treatments. Regardless of how these challenges are addressed, digital video has huge size, but also huge potential, for facilitating access to video archive material. Digital technology has the potential to improve access to research material, allowing access to precisely the content sought by an end user. This implies full content search and retrieval, so that users can get to precisely the page they are interested in for text, or precisely the sound or video clip for audio or video productions. Creating such metadata by hand is prohibitively expensive and inappropriate for digital video, where much of the metadata is a by-product of the way in which the artifact is generated. Current research will extend the automated techniques for contemporaneous metadata creation.

To realize this potential, video must be described so that its production attributes are preserved and so users can navigate to the content meeting their needs. Video has a temporal aspect, in which its contents are revealed over time, i.e., it is isochronal. Finding a nugget of information within an hour of video could take a user an hour of viewing time.

Delivering this hour of video over the Internet, or perhaps over wireless networks to a personal digital assistant (PDA) user, would require the transfer of megabytes or gigabytes of data. Isochronal media are therefore expensive both in terms of network bandwidth as well as user attention. If, however, metadata enabled surrogates to be produced or extracted that either were nonisochronal or significantly shorter in duration, then both bandwidth and the user's attention could be used more efficiently. After checking the surrogate, the user could decide whether access to the video was really necessary. A surrogate can also pinpoint the region of interest within a large video file or video archive. As video archives grow, metadata become increasingly important: "In spite of the fact that users have increasing access to these resources, identifying and managing them efficiently is becoming more difficult, because of the sheer volume".

The capability of metadata to enrich video archives has not been overlooked by research communities and industry. Digital asset management refers to the improved storage, tracking, and retrieval of digital assets in general. Metadata for digital information objects, including video, can be assigned to one of three categories:

1. Descriptive: facilitating resource identification and exploration

2. Administrative: supporting resource management within a collection
3. Structural: binding together the components of more complex information objects

Various communities involved in the production, distribution, and use of video have addressed the need for metadata to supplement and describe video archives. Librarians are very concerned about interoperability and having standardized access to descriptors for archives. Producers and content rights owners are greatly interested in intellectual property rights (IPR) management and in compliance with regulations concerning content ratings and access controls.

The World Wide Web Consortium (W3C) produces recommendations on XML, XPath, XML-Schema, and related efforts for metadata formatting and semantics. Special interest groups such as trainers and educators have specific needs within particular domains, e.g., tagging video by curriculum or grade level.

The Dublin Core Metadata Initiative provides a 15-element set for describing a wide range of resources. While the Dublin Core "favours document-like objects (because traditional text resources are fairly well understood)", it has been tested against moving-image resources and found to be generally adequate.

The Dublin Core is also extensible, and has been used as the basis for other metadata frameworks, such as an ongoing effort to develop interoperable metadata for learning, education, and training, which could then describe the resources available in libraries such as the Digital Library for Earth System Education (DLESE).

Hence, Dublin Core is an ideal candidate for a high-level (i.e., very general) metadata scheme for video archives. An outside library service, with likely support for Dublin Core, would then be able to make use of information drawn from video archives expressed in the Dublin Core element set.

Professional video producers are interested in tagging data with IPR, production and talent credits, and other information commonly found in film or television credits. In addition, metadata descriptors from the basic Dublin Core set are too general to adequately describe the complexity of a video. For example, one of the Dublin Core elements is the instantiation date, but for a video, date can refer to copyright date, first broadcast date, last broadcast date, allowable broadcast period, date of production, or the setting date for the subject matter.

Producers are especially interested in defining metadata standards because video production is becoming a digital process, with new equipment such as digital cameras supporting the capture of metadata such as date, time, and location at recording time. The Society of Motion Picture and Television Engineers (SMPTE) has been working on a universal preservation format for videos, the SMPTE Metadata Dictionary.

For born-digital material, many of the metadata elements can be filled in during the media creation process. The SMPTE Metadata Dictionary has slots for time and place, further resolved into elements such as time of production and time of setting, place of production and place setting, where place is described both in terms of country codes and place names as well as through latitude and longitude. The SMPTE effort is often cited by other video metadata efforts as a comprehensive complement to the minimalist Dublin Core element set.

In 1999, the European Broadcasting Union (EBU) launched a two-year project named "EBU Project P/Meta" designed to develop a common approach to standardizing and exchanging program-related information and embedded metadata throughout the production and distribution life cycle of audiovisual material.

A number of professional industry and consortia standardization efforts are in progress to provide more detailed video descriptors. The new member of the MPEG family, Multimedia Content Description Interface, or MPEG-7, aims at providing standardized core technologies allowing description of audiovisual data content in multimedia environments. It will extend the limited capabilities of proprietary solutions in identifying content that exist today, notably by including more data types.

MPEG-7 addresses many different applications in many different environments, which means that it needs to provide a flexible and extensible framework for describing audiovisual data. Therefore, MPEG-7 does not define a monolithic system for content description but rather a set of methods and tools for the different viewpoints of the description of audiovisual content. Having this in mind, MPEG-7 is designed to take into account all the viewpoints under consideration by other leading standards such as, among others, SMPTE Metadata Dictionary, Dublin Core, EBU P/Meta, and TV Anytime.

These standardization activities are focused to more specific applications or application domains, whilst MPEG-7 tries to be as generic as possible. MPEG-7 uses also XML Schema as the language of choice for the textual representation of content description and for allowing extensibility of description tools. Considering the popularity of XML, usage of it will facilitate interoperability in the future.

Because the descriptive features must be meaningful in the context of the application, they will be different for different user domains and different applications. This implies that the same material may be described using different types of features, tuned to the area of application. To take the example of visual material, a lower abstraction level would be a description of shape, size, texture, color, movement (trajectory), and position (where in the scene can the object be found?).

For audio, a description at this level would include key, mood, tempo, tempo changes, and point of origin. The highest level would give semantic information, e.g., "This is a scene with a barking brown dog on the left and a blue ball that falls down on the right, with the sound of passing cars in the background." Intermediate levels of abstraction may also exist.

The level of abstraction is related to the way in which the features can be extracted: many low-level features can be extracted in fully automatic ways, whereas high-level features need human interaction. Next to having a continuous description of the content, it is also required to include other types of information about the multimedia data. It is important to note that these metadata may also relate to the entire production, segments of it (e.g., as defined by time codes), or single frames.

This enables granularity that can describe a single scene's action, limit that scene's redistribution because of its source, or classify that scene as inappropriate for child viewing because of its content. Therefore, MPEG-7 description tools will allow a user to create, at will, descriptions (that is, a set of instantiated description schemes and their corresponding descriptors) of content that may include the following:

— information describing the creation and production processes of the content (director, title, short feature movie)
— information related to the usage of the content (copyright pointers, usage history, broadcast schedule)
— information about the storage features of the content (storage format, encoding)

— structural information on spatial, temporal, or spatio-temporal components of the content (scene cuts, segmentation in regions, region motion tracking)

— information about low-level features in the content (colors, textures, timbres, melody description)

— conceptual information of the reality captured by the content (objects and events, interactions among objects)

— information about how to browse the content in an efficient way (summaries, variations, spatial and frequency subbands)

— information about collections of objects

— information about the interaction of the user with the content (user preferences, usage history)

There is room for domain specialization within the metadata architectures, whether by audience and function (education vs. entertainment), genre (documentary, travelogue), or content (news vs. lecture), but there is also a risk of overspecificity. Because the technology continues to evolve, MPEG-7 is intended to be flexible.

The scope of MPEG-21 could be described as the integration of the critical technologies enabling transparent and augmented use of multimedia resources across a wide range of networks and devices to support functions such as content creation, content production, content distribution, content consumption and usage, content packaging, intellectual property management and protection, content identification and description, financial management, user privacy, terminals and network resource abstraction, content representation, and event reporting.

References

Bailey, C.W., 'Public-Access Computer Systems', *Information Technology and Libraries*, 12, March 1993.

Barker, P., *Electronic Books and Libraries of the Future*, Electronic Library, 10, 3, 1992.

Fox, E. A., *Source Book on Digital Libraries*, Virginia Tech, Department of Computer Science, TR 93-35, 1993.

Lynn, M.S., "Digital Preservation and Access", *Collection Management* 22, nos. 1998.

Moy, Naomi, *CyberSpace Reference Library: the Virtual Reference Collection*. Carson, CA: CA State University at Dominguez Hills, 1997.

5

Role of ICTs in Information Environment

There are many thousands of digital library projects currently underway, in all sectors of the library community. These projects have taken widely varying approaches, dependent on the needs of the different libraries, the sector in which they are based, and, in part, the definition of digital library that has been applied.

This has led to a variety of digital libraries being developed, with no common model being available. The many existing digital library studies can give a useful pointer to the general development of digital libraries. However, the majority of published digital library research has occurred in the academic and public library sectors.

Watson and Streatfield were concerned that there has been a major focus on digital library developments in recent years, yet there has been relatively little attention paid to special libraries, especially those outside the "commercial" arena. Missingham concurred with this view, noting that the use of new technology in special libraries has been quite different to that of academic and public libraries. Government libraries usually fill a quite different role within their agency than their academic and public library counterparts.

The basic concept underlying the digital library is not new. In 1945, Dr Vannevar Bush of the U.S. Office of Scientific Research and Development discussed a device called a "memex". He envisioned this device being used by individuals as "a sort of mechanised private file and library". It would be able to store large amounts of books, pictures, periodicals, newspapers, correspondence, and so on, with material being indexed for easy retrieval. According to Saffady, the Bush vision is "one of the most influential and frequently cited precursors" of the modern digital library concept. He continued to note that although the digital library seems a revolutionary development, the concepts and technologies involved are more accurately described as evolutionary.

Although not a recent concept, in terms of actual development, digital libraries are still relatively new. Because of this, there is as yet no universally agreed terminology in place. In the literature, the digital library may also be called the library without walls, virtual library, electronic library, e-library, desktop library, online library, future library, library of the future, logical library, networked library, hybrid library, gateway library, extended library or information superhighway.

Of these many terms, digital library, virtual library, hybrid library and electronic (or e-) library are most common. Just as there is no universally agreed upon terminology for digital libraries, neither is there a common definition for this concept. In the 1990s, terms such as digital library, virtual library and electronic library became widely used, but considerable uncertainty remains about what they actually mean.

The term digital library has been defined both broadly and narrowly. In the narrower form, a digital library is construed as a mainly, if not wholly, digital entity, although this fully digital scenario is dependent on the necessary materials being available in an appropriate format. In the broader construction, the digital library is defined as a hybrid of traditional library services and new electronic sources and methods.

One of the more comprehensive definitions by Gapen, who defined digital libraries as:

> ...the concept of remote access to the contents and services of libraries and other information resources, combining an on-site collection of current and heavily used materials in both print and electronic form, with an electronic network which provides access to, and delivery from, external worldwide library and commercial information and knowledge sources. In essence, the user is provided the effect of a library which is a synergy created by bringing together technologically the resources of many, many libraries and information services.

The broader definition of digital libraries offered by Gapen was adopted. No distinction was made in defining the various terms used to describe the digital library concept, and for the sake of clarity, the term digital library has been used throughout..

Regardless of the wide variety of terms used to describe the digital library concept, it is clear from the literature that there are certain common elements, regardless of the terminology applied. There must be, in some sense, a collection, to which clients must be linked in an efficient and satisfying manner. There is also a set of services, either human or electronic, which link clients to the collections.

The technologies involved in providing digital library services should support document creation, retrieval, transfer, dissemination, manipulation and management. Finally, there must be an institution in which the digital library collections and services are embedded. A major study, conducted by the Association of Research Libraries (ARL) in 1992, identified series of different activities considered essential to the formation of digital libraries. These included:

— Use of, or development of electronic document delivery services;

— Policies, services, or reallocations that emphasise access [to information] over ownership;

— Participation in cooperative development or purchase of electronic files;

— Participation in the development of a campus-wide information system;

— A written plan that states its goal as access to information from a single workstation;

— Enhancement of the online public access catalogue (OPAC) to include the holdings of other libraries besides those held locally;

— Providing a gateway from the OPAC to other databases or networks, such as the Internet;

— End-user access to online files from on or off campus;

— Connection with the Internet;

— Training faculty and students:

— in the use of Internet sources; and,

— in end-user searching;

— Subscribing to electronic journals;

— Digitisation of text for electronic storage, retrieval and/or dissemination.

These elements, then, may be considered the basic building blocks of the digital library, although the nature and extent of the application of each component will depend upon the circumstances and needs of the library and/ or organisation to which the digital library is attached.

There are number of activities that together make up digital libraries, so too does it show that the development of digital libraries is heavily dependent on a number of inter-related enabling (or hindering) factors. These include such issues as copyright, client attitudes, changes to funding and financial structures, the need for new organisational structures, technological issues, staff training, and so on.

A study of Commonwealth library digital library developments was conducted in 1998-1999, with one of its objects to determine if the model developed from the general literature on digital libraries was appropriate to digital library development in the Commonwealth library sector. Libraries included in the study were libraries within those agencies, statutory and non-statutory authorities administered by the Commonwealth Government. Where an agency had more than one library, only those libraries that had policy and budgetary control over their individual library or network was included.

The National Library of Australia was excluded from this study as, although it is a Commonwealth library, it is also a national library, and as such, has different foci, programs and priorities than special libraries delivering information services to public sector organisations. An examination of the digital library activities undertaken in Commonwealth libraries showed that some activities were undertaken by far more libraries than were others.

This suggests that the various issues that impact on the digital library environment have relatively equal importance, with none assuming much greater significance than another.

Content Management in Web Environment

The idea of "content management" is multifaceted. One's choice of a perspective on the idea carries with it distinctive terminology, particular alliances with facets of a complex information technology infrastructure, specific limits on what content is and is not, and implied commitments to organizational and administrative priorities. Each of the three perspectives outlined below attempts to deal with various aspects of the content management issue, ranging from digital content (as objects or assets), to the people who add value to the content, to the tools one uses to add support or manage the process of adding value.

For many people in the IT community, content management simply means WEB content. The key concept in Web content management is the creation of value through a reduction in "time to web." In practice, this concept translates into more dynamic web delivery systems built on the back of a relational database tied to a template-driven workflow process that allows fewer people to create and deliver more web content.

A database-driven approach to web content management opens up new possibilities within an organization to share content across units and to share in the costs of creating and maintaining digital content. Some writers on content management have chosen to focus almost exclusively on protecting the asset value of digital objects, without regard to the purposes to which the objects may be put. From an asset management perspective, the organization of digital objects in well structured and well-documented databases is the most critical activity.

The digital preservation community in libraries has tended to emphasize asset management as a key value. The present movement to specify preservation metadata requirements within the construct of the Open Archival Information System reference model is the most dramatic example of efforts define content management in terms of the archival repository.

Knowledge management has traditionally suffered from the hubris of modernism: the belief that we can discover ultimate truths and organize the world according to rational principles using clever code. The idea was that we should capture and organize bits of "knowledge" in central databases. The people involved were relevant only as donors to the common ontology or as empty vessels into which knowledge could be poured.

Therefore, postmodern KM can't be about management at all, because management implies external control of some definable resource. Its goal is simpler yet deeper: leveraging people. Postmodern KM operates within and on the basis of existing behavior patterns, mining conversation streams and relationships automatically to incorporate structure and context into the information human users already manipulate. It fosters human intelligence and interaction rather than trying to replace them.

This vision of content management suggests that librarians must reconcile the tensions between the structured and the dynamic, between "control zones" and empowerment, and between the Web that we access and the digital content that we provide. These tensions are not new or particularly interesting, except in so far as they help to extend the concept of "content" to encompass a much wider range of management responsibilities for digital content than we have heretofore chosen to consider appropriate.

Increasingly, libraries are being asked or expected to step up to the challenge of acquiring, organizing, and protecting digital content that they have neither created themselves (digitization) or licensed from publishers. Examples of new generations of digital content that are just beginning to flow into and through libraries include digital products produced and distributed or otherwise published by faculty, the output of research collaboratives, graduate student theses, the electronic records or the university's administrative offices, courseware content, and streaming audio and video resources generated from courses, conferences, and other campus activities.

In the Web environment, the business community has adopted the term "knowledge management" to refer to processes that use technology to leverage human expertise and know-how to create new value for the organization. In the higher education context, knowledge management constructs are most closely tied to scholarly communication processes. A critical issue for libraries is tension between possibly competing commitments to the process of scholarship as a discipline-based enterprise and the product of the process as an institutional imperative.

Another critical aspect of considering "content management" to be an important but limited component of the scholarly communication process is the relationship of librarians and libraries to content creators, whether those creators are faculty/authors or publishers/owners. Today's library is "all digital" in the sense that all services and content (digital and non-digital) are mediated via web gateways. Users begin and end their scholarly work with digital information, even if there is a considerable amount of paper in between.

Without some form of digital accessibility, library resources in any format are invisible and therefore unusable. Physical browsing for all but a vocal few has become a chimera. Libraries are already in the new business of digital product development by nature of their creation of digital resources, regardless of whether creation encompasses only digitization or extends to the development of specialized aggregations of digital resources.

Libraries and archives cannot possibly assume full responsibility for preserving digital information, but rather must participate in a marketplace that itself has not come to terms with the idea of lost value. Librarians are critical players in the conception of the IT marketplace but have neither exclusive claim on content management concepts or a particularly strong share of the marketplace that is driving the development of content management tools.

Content management in the "all digital" environment within higher education can only function effectively at the corporate (i.e., university) level, even when the digital content itself is created and managed to support disciplinary or interdisciplinary scholarship.

Digital Repositories

The development of institutional repositories emerged as a new strategy that allows universities to apply serious, systematic leverage to accelerate changes taking place in scholarship and scholarly communication, both moving beyond their historic relatively passive role of supporting established publishers in modernizing scholarly publishing through the licensing of digital content, and also scaling up beyond ad-hoc alliances, partnerships, and support arrangements with a few select faculty pioneers exploring more transformative new uses of the digital medium.

Many technology trends and development efforts came together to make this strategy possible. Online storage costs have dropped significantly; repositories are now affordable. Standards like the open archives metadata harvesting protocol are now in place; some progress has also been made on the standards for the underlying metadata itself. The thinking about digital preservation over the past five years has advanced to the point where the needs are widely recognized and well defined, the technical approaches at least superficially mapped out, and the need for action is now clear.

The development of free, publicly accessible journal article collections in disciplines such as high-energy physics has demonstrated ways in which the network can change scholarly communication by altering dissemination and access patterns; separately, the development of a series of extraordinary digital works had at least suggested the potential of creative authorship specifically for the digital medium to transform the presentation and transmission of scholarship.

A university-based institutional repository is a set of services that a university offers to the members of its community for the management and dissemination of digital materials created by the institution and its community members. It is most essentially an organizational commitment to the stewardship of these digital materials, including long-term preservation where appropriate, as well as organization and access or distribution.

While operational responsibility for these services may reasonably be situated in different organizational units at different universities, an effective institutional repository of necessity represents a collaboration among librarians, information technologists, archives and records mangers, faculty, and university administrators and policymakers. At any given point in time, an institutional repository will be supported by a set of information technologies, but a key part of the services that comprise an institutional repository is the management of technological changes, and the migration of digital content from one set of technologies to the next as part of the organizational commitment to providing repository services.

An institutional repository is not simply a fixed set of software and hardware. While early implementers of institutional repositories have chosen different paths to begin populating their repositories and to build campus community acceptance, support, and participation, that a mature and fully realized institutional repository will contain the intellectual works of faculty and students—both research and teaching materials—and also documentation of the activities of the institution itself in the form of records of events and performance and of the ongoing intellectual life of the institution. It will also house experimental and observational data captured by members of the institution that support their scholarly activities.

At the most basic and fundamental level, an institutional repository is a recognition that the intellectual life and scholarship of our universities will increasingly be represented, documented, and shared in digital form, and that a primary responsibility of our universities is to exercise stewardship over these riches: both to make them available and to preserve them.

An institutional repository is the means by which our universities will address this responsibility both to the members of their communities and to the public. It is a new channel for structuring the university's contribution to the broader world, and as such invites policy and cultural reassessment of this relationship.

Global Resource Program

A globally oriented program is by definition ambitious, especially when it is focused on information and its dissemination. Despite an increasing reliance on electronic information, print book and journal publishing worldwide continues to expand dramatically. Accordingly, the strategies adopted to tackle the goals of the Global Resources Program are multiple and varied:

— providing seed money for an initial set of six diverse regional projects (on Africa, Germany, Japan, Latin America, South Asia, Southeast Asia);

— gathering information into a clearinghouse on ARL libraries' linkages with institutions abroad;

— building bridges to scholars who use international materials, and to the scholarly associations to which they belong, in order to develop a better understanding of the research resources they need and how libraries can facilitate access to them; and

— helping to create new models for recruiting and training future area specialists who have strong subject knowledge, initiative, and the right skill set.

The systematic identification of collection strengths of North American libraries will be another important step toward the Program's full implementation, and the launching of other area- and subject-specific projects as they are designed is an ongoing objective. The overarching strategy for the Program is to scale up from the projects by selecting, from among the models they are testing, the elements that will contribute to a comprehensive, cooperative, distributed program of access to international resources, regardless of their format or location.

The eventual goal is to move beyond a set of discrete, area-specific projects to an interconnected, globally oriented program in which "lead institutions" provide users throughout North America with both physical collections and access points to diverse resources published in or relating to a given world area. Another long-term goal of the Program–essential for making the vision into reality–is to develop a system of financial incentives that will benefit a broad range of institutions, as well as sustain the Program well into the future.

The six regional projects currently underway offer an impressive array of approaches to addressing some of the most urgent information needs of scholars researching individual world regions. These approaches range from the creation of a web-based union list of sub-Saharan African newspapers to an international document delivery service between North American and German research libraries, from a Latin American table-of-contents database with direct, user-initiated article requesting capability to the digitization, in India, of South Asian reference works and periodicals, and the creation of an image database of Thai journal literature.

The full impact of the Program, however, extends beyond this set of projects. For example, awareness of the factors that negatively affect the ability of libraries to provide the materials that users need, that litany of pressures with which librarians are all too familiar, has been heightened among faculty and within scholarly associations.

Librarians with responsibility for one region of the world are finding common ground with those whose principal focus is another. The Overseas Offices of the Library of Congress are key participants in many of the projects and are uniquely prepared to address directly the key issue of access through the expansion of the services they provide in Cairo, Islamabad, Nairobi, New Delhi, Jakarta, and Rio de Janeiro.

The Center for Research Libraries has launched the International Coalition on Newspapers (ICON), an ambitious and much-needed effort to identify, preserve, and make accessible as wide a range of foreign newspapers as possible. Collaboration with institutions outside North America, both formal and informal, has been stimulated by the identification of reciprocal relationships for collection development, interlibrary lending and borrowing, and document delivery.

In short, the AAU/ARL Global Resources Program has been a catalyst in stimulating interest and action to strengthen international library resources. This new Department of Education program has stimulated the development of projects that bring together librarians and faculty in creative joint undertakings whose goal is exactly consistent with that of the Global Resources Program: to expand access to international resources through the use of new technologies.

The initial focus of the Global Resources Program was on cooperative collection development. This is arguably the necessary first step toward a distributed network of interdependent collections, and yet the Program has since shifted focus within some of the regional projects to concentrate on document delivery. At first glance, this would seem to be a major change; however, they are part and parcel of the same theme.

For years, at meetings of collection development librarians and other conferences, inadequate document delivery and interlibrary loan capability has been pinpointed as a major obstacle to successful cooperative collection development, whether it be on a relatively small, regional scale, or at the national or North American level. Certainly, to gain faculty acceptance of a distributed collection it is critical to guarantee rapid access to needed materials that are not held locally.

And since engaging faculty as supporters of the premises of the Global Resources Program and illustrating for them the potential of structured interdependence are among the Program's original goals, a focus on rapid delivery of the resources they need seems logical. It is important to demonstrate to faculty that the Program and other cooperative collection-building structures will expand access, not decrease it. They are gaining, not losing.

An acute awareness of the importance of building collections cooperatively still characterizes the Program, although several current efforts focus on disseminating information about what is held where rather than on orchestrating firm cooperative agreements. In order to distribute responsibility for collecting, it is important to know who has what, a need that has promoted the development of projects to establish union lists of journals and newspapers, or periodical indexes, for example.

Nevertheless, the Program will only achieve its goals and realize its full potential when participants take the difficult steps of redefining collecting policies to focus on local strengths and reallocating resources accordingly, while simultaneously moving toward a more inter-reliant network of research libraries. An emphasis on cataloging and preservation is inherent in all of the activities of the Global Resources Program.

The American Council of Learned Societies (ACLS) featured a special session on the AAU/ARL Global Resources Program. Executive directors of area studies scholarly associations and delegates to each organization, along with other interested participants, responded to a presentation about the Program and expressed their views on its future development. The environment, human rights, migration, popular culture, ethnic studies–these are examples of areas of scholarship with a significant international dimension, in which research requires access to a multiplicity of resources that may be ephemeral, difficult to locate, poorly preserved, and undercollected in North America.

A Global Resources project that takes a topical rather than a regional approach would encourage links among library collections that are not based on the traditional area studies model, that span national boundaries, and yet still address the core challenges of the Reed-Scott book and the studies that preceded it.

There are many nonaffiliated projects underway that bear a relationship to the Global Resources Program. Similarly, any distributed collection development structure will take advantage of existing consortia and work in progress. Links among libraries and scholars, and the active involvement of faculty in helping to imagine and anticipate future needs, will be critical to the Program's continued success. Just as important will be a practical vision of a new interdependence among libraries.

Although it has focused on projects that expand access to international research materials, in many cases vernacular resources, the lessons of the Global Resources Program are not limited to the acquisition and distribution of foreign materials. The Program is also raising issues with broader, more general implications. In this way, the Program contains a microcosm of the newest challenges and concerns for research libraries, issues that are not peculiar to area studies.

These include, of course, the creation of cooperative structures for collection development and document delivery services that are rapid, efficient, and international. The Program is built on the need to discover ways to stretch budgets so that libraries collectively can offer access to more than they currently do individually. The Program has stimulated new thinking about service to users, especially those who are remote but rely on specialized collections held in our libraries, and has shifted focus to a user-based model of distributed collection development and away from an emphasis on amassing collections locally.

Participation in large-scale collaborative endeavors requires a significant commitment of staff time and energy, and this in turn requires a re-thinking of the collection development librarian's job description. The success of the Global Resources regional projects would have been impossible without the ideas, initiative, and action of a number of area studies librarians. Such energy and creativity will continue to be prerequisites for achieving the goals of multi-institutional collaboration, whether international or not.

To achieve the goals of the Global Resources Program, and any program based on cooperative collection development, we must view "collections" as a wide array of resources, some held locally but many found elsewhere–even outside North America–and not necessarily in libraries, or in print form. We do not need to own the physical object to consider it part of our "collection."

Technology makes it feasible to consider remote collections to be local resources as long as it is reasonably straightforward for users to gain access to these materials. It is apparent that university administrators, faculty, library administrators, and collection development librarians need a new vision for their local library collection, and new ways of measuring its strength as part of a shared North American collection.

The Global Resources Program forces a redefinition of "collections" if we are to meet the needs of current users of our libraries and anticipate those of future generations. Bringing about the change in perspective that is necessary for distributed collecting to succeed will require progress in several interconnected areas:

— an understanding on the part of faculty that it is in their long-term interest for their university's library to have an interdependent relationship with other institutions, so that someone, somewhere, is collecting the materials that they, and their colleagues within North America, need;

— the autonomy for collection development librarians to craft cooperative policies that share responsibility for collecting and commit their institutions to a particular set of areas, the will and authority to cancel journals that are widely held elsewhere in favor of more specialized acquisitions in their areas of collecting responsibility, and the political sensitivity to explain these decisions to library users in compelling and convincing terms;

— an acknowledgment of the critical role of document delivery and interlibrary loan in making distributed collections feasible, and a commitment to invest in the redesign of systems of access;

— the necessary determination and support for rapid cataloging of international materials, which will not only make these resources more accessible to users but will also provide bibliographers with important information on holdings that may influence their acquisitions decisions; and

— a firm commitment on the part of library and university administrators to a new vision of interdependent collections, acknowledgment of the benefits of the strategy, and adequate, long-term financial support to continue building and preserving the collections for which their institution has accepted responsibility.

The Latin Americanist Research Resources Project is experimenting with distributed collecting responsibilities through its "Distributed Resources" component, in which each participating institution commits to redirecting a minimum of either $3,000 or 7% of its monographic budget for Latin American materials towards an area of locally established collection strength. By implication, they will rely on other Project libraries for materials they will no longer be acquiring.

Participating bibliographers have confirmed that, through reallocation, they have been able to acquire items that enrich their local collections in areas of emphasis while also providing access to these materials for users anywhere. In the division of responsibilities among the participating libraries, based on local strengths and local choice, nearly all countries are represented. Thus, the Project is demonstrating broad coverage and balance.

This element of the Latin American project is a significant step towards strengthening North American collections of Latin American publications. The Project has succeeded in large part because it is allowing individual institutions to emphasize local strengths (thereby eliminating the tension between local program needs and national-level commitments) and because it is focusing on materials that do not generally receive high use.

Redefining the Role of Librarians

An expansion and redefinition of the role of the collection development librarian, or bibliographer, has been underway for some time as the job has required more contact with the public and advanced technological skills. In the Global Resources arena, bibliographers have the opportunity to serve as intellectual leaders in crafting new models for access and new structures for cooperative collection building.

Rather than being marginalized, bibliographers have become even more central to the success of complex international projects. They play a visible role in fund raising, including drafting proposals and administering grants. Designing area- and subject-specific projects to address the goals of the Global Resources Program also brings bibliographers together with faculty to think strategically about the variety of future scholarly resource needs.

Working with a much broader definition of "collections" than ever before, bibliographers are collaborating with colleagues at other libraries and in other countries to ensure that research libraries are together providing access to the widest range of resources possible. The creation and maintenance of web pages with detailed collection descriptions and links to many other carefully selected and vetted resources is increasingly part of the bibliographer's job.

As the Global Resources Program moves toward the identification of a network of lead institutions, bibliographers' knowledge and experience will become even more important. The Global Resources Program has opened positive new lines of communication within individual libraries as well. The implementation of the regional projects, particularly those with significant document delivery components, encourages a closer relationship between collection development librarians and interlibrary loan staff.

ILL librarians are in an excellent position to help identify where there may be gaps in local collections coverage. They are also key players in determining the nature and usefulness of new document delivery mechanisms that are at the core of enhanced access. Additional intra-institutional collaboration will flourish as cross-regional projects are developed, and subject and area studies bibliographers begin to work together to implement and publicize the projects and to evaluate their effectiveness.

Creation of a new limitation on liability for online service providers (OSPs) was perhaps the most complex task of the DMCA legislators. The new rules establish certain procedures and conditions that grant OSPs, including libraries and educational institutions, an exclusion from monetary liability for copyright infringement by a user of the service.

Balancing a myriad of interests and fashioning legislation for technology that is arcane and evolving are no simple tasks. Thus, the OSP limitation of liability represents a very important contribution of the DMCA to copyright law. Also, the process used to develop this statutory limitation-congressional committee supervised negotiations-may also serve as a model for preparing legislation on other issues that require discreet balancing of concerns of contentious but politically powerful interests.

For libraries, the initial issue is whether to assert status as a "service provider" and register with the Copyright Office. This is not an easy question to resolve. Certainly, the definition of "service provider" is broad enough to encompass many of the libraries' online activities. However, the legislation's complex rules will require very careful compliance practices, including the use of sophisticated software and systems and the development of notification and termination policies.

Although monitoring of sites is not required, once a service provider receives notice of an infringement, actions such as "notice and take down" or "counter notice and put back" must also be taken. In weighing the benefits of coming within the statutory limitation terms, libraries should appreciate the reduction of potential damages for innocent, but contributory, infringements.

For libraries that are part of larger, educational institutions, exposure to money damages from cyberspace violations by patrons, students, and faculty-as well as third parties-must be deemed a real threat. It should be understood that online copyright infringements are a "hot button" issue for publishers. It should also be anticipated that a test case or two would be brought in the near future.

Further, it must be underscored that even though monetary damages may be avoided, all service providers are subject to all other copyright legal remedies, including injunctive relief. It is not known whether content owners will use the website list of service providers maintained by the Copyright Office as the "go-to group" that receives all the infringement notifications.

Since each OSP is an online ramp to the cyber-violations, whether more than a limited group will receive infringement notices is not yet known. If many owners adopt an approach that blankets the potential universe of OSPs, then those identified OSPs could be flooded with requests for take down. Such a situation could render operations at small- to medium-sized libraries into an immediate state of chaos. Then, too, how much technological support in terms of advanced software and personnel is required to satisfy the legal strictures is unknown.

Although DMCA did not include explicit expanded protection for educational activities involving the Internet, the creation of a congressionally-mandated study of the subject by the Copyright Office is important and deserves immediate and active attention by the library community. From its inception, copyright law has balanced owners' rights with users' rights.

Despite copyright owners proclaiming the need for fair return on their creative works and the importance of securing economic rewards in a global economy, principles like fair use and exemptions for classroom teaching and library preservation survive. Distance education is the latest major battleground in the effort to balance educational interests in a federal law that increasingly emphasizes the commerce of copyright.

Extending the face-to-face and transmission exemptions to Internet education will not happen without aggressive and active participation by the library and educational communities. In the initial hearings held in January 1999 by the Copyright Office, owners have already asserted there is no need to change the law. They argue licensing and other permissive approaches to incorporating works into course content will suffice.

Moreover, they claim to be the primary producers of course texts and thus any exemption hurts their markets and damages them competitively. Unless educators are energized by the opportunity to create a new and important expansion of principles embodied in the current classroom and closed circuit transmission limitations, no change will occur. The central points to be made include the following:

— Obtaining clearances for spontaneous use of copyrighted works in online courses is virtually impossible.
— Identifying copyright owners of certain works, like photographs, is so daunting as to make it a task not worth pursuing.
— Licensing is not an acceptable alternative because, when offered, the price is often far too high to justify the use.
— Unless the copyright law is modified, the playing field for parties negotiating licenses is out of balance. Libraries and educators will find

they have less leverage to negotiate fair terms for digital use within their communities.

— The transaction costs associated with clearances and licensing requirements threatens to perpetuate or exacerbate the traditional disparities between "have" and "have-not" communities that distance education and the Internet could otherwise help to mitigate.

But if the library and educational communities are unified in their desire to update copyright law exemptions so that online education is treated on a par with classroom learning, then there is a chance that reform can be accomplished in the near future. With congressional and presidential elections coming in the next year, education will be a very important electoral issue and distance education should be a central topic in all races.

The DMCA provides the most significant updating of library and archival preservation rules since procedures to cope with photocopy machines were established in 1976. The changes permit preservation and storage of a copyrighted work in a digitized format and describe a mechanism for handling preservation of works originating in outmoded formats.

The updating of Section 108 to enable libraries to work in digital preservation was surprisingly hard fought. Even with the endorsement of the authors of the White Paper3, it required extensive negotiations in the House and Senate. The content community is very nervous about allowing digital copies of works to exist anywhere without explicit authorization. In the end, this update is a modest, yet important, change for libraries that will make their task of maintaining collections easier in a technologically advanced environment.

Moving in tandem to the DMCA legislation was another copyright reform bill-term extension. For the past three years, there was a drumbeat by certain copyright proprietors, especially those owning movies and musical works, for extension of the copyright term. Although the legislation had strong support, it was held hostage to a debate over the demand of certain groups-notably restaurants, bars, and religious broadcasters-to be entitled to relief from the high charges for use of music on their premises and in their broadcasts.

For the library community, concern about extension of the copyright term was expressed early in the debate. It was posited that the overwhelming majority of works are neither commercially exploited nor readily accessible in the marketplace after several decades, much less 75 years. Yet, for researchers and scholars, access to such works from the library's collection are important and no limitation should be made on such noncommercial uses. Moreover, with regard to already-existing works, no "extra incentive" is needed to spur creativity.

In an effort to resolve the concerns expressed by library interests, an understanding was reached regarding the ability of nonprofit libraries, archives, and educational institutions to exploit older works during what constitutes the extended copyright term. Suggesting that libraries should be able to exploit works that have lain fallow for decades should not strike one as an explosive proposal.

The Copyright Office, through the vehicle of regulations, will help determine the reach of the new exception that permits libraries to continue to freely use old works in the last 20 years of the extended term, just like public domain works. This is a vital concern for the library and education community, because maintenance of the public domain assures the role of libraries as archivists of history, not licensees of commerce.

Participation in the regulatory process that will define the terms and establish rules is a relatively efficient way to get one's key points across. Just as was noted with regard to the anti-circumvention rulemaking and the distance education study, active participation in these administrative proceedings assures that the library and education community's voice will be heard at the opportune time and its views not ignored.

ICT Infrastructure and Connectivity

Connectivity comprises at least three elements: telecommunications infrastructure; the availability of adequate compatible hardware and software; and access to needed technical support. Levels of investment in ICT infrastructure and hardware prior to the launch of the People's Network varied greatly from one library authority to another, as well as from one home country to another, resulting in wide disparities in public library connectivity and services. A main goal in connecting all public libraries to the internet was thus about 'levelling the playing field'.

The universality of physical access and consistency in standards represents both a remarkable technical achievement as well as an organisational feat in implementing such a large scale infrastructure initiative within the scheduled timescale and budget. At a programme level as well as at the level of the individual library service, it has involved entering into partnerships, and managing relationships, with a number of different stakeholders, including telecom providers, local authorities and corporate IT.

The People's Network has been successfully rolled-out across the UK, connecting all library authorities to the internet. Over 4,000 public libraries provide broadband access to the internet and other online services. This amounts to a huge leap in connectivity from just 1% in 1995 to almost 100% of branch library coverage in just short of a decade. At the start of the People's Network in 1999, only a minority of library authorities could be described as 'early adopters' of ICT. Three lacked even the most basic of electronic management systems and were using old card indexes.

The People's Network has added in excess of 30,000 computer terminals to the public library system. The central libraries of some large metropolitan library authorities now have as many as 100 terminals, whilst at the other extreme some small branch libraries have just two terminals because of limited space. This expansion in hardware capacity, coupled with increased opening hours in many libraries to make ICT more accessible, is now providing over 68.5 million hours of potential internet use a year, across the UK. Hardware includes more than terminals.

The People's Network has provided a cluster of networked technology and facilities that include principally scanners and printers. In many library authorities, videoconferencing facilities were also incorporated into the technology package. Other hardware found in around half the library authorities includes assistive and adaptive technology appropriate to older users and those with disabilities. These include keyboard and trackball mouse alternatives, height adjustable workstations and lap trays, sound cards and headphones and large 22" screens.

Monitoring returns indicate that adaptive technologies are commonly restricted to one workstation/terminal point within a library and not all branch libraries are kitted out. Specific hardware is also found in individual library services, reflecting local population characteristics and requirements. An example is multi-language keyboards and software. The technical requirements for the People's Network specified a minimum 2MB connection. Although small libraries were not expected to need this capacity in the short term, the infrastructure allowed for the likelihood that web-based resources would become increasingly broadband dependent. Bandwidth is now impressive: while averages do not tell the whole story, libraries reported a mean of 23MB connections.

Nearly all People's Network terminals are providing access to a suite of applications, including Microsoft Explorer, Word, Excel, Access and PowerPoint. There was no requirement on libraries to extend this basic package, although some library authorities have done so in response to demand from their more sophisticated ICT users, or as library staff have themselves increased their knowledge and skills of what software is on offer. Proprietary software available across the network of some library services includes desk-top publishing packages, desk-top digital imaging such as Photoshop, web page design programmes such as Dreamweaver or FrontPage.

For people who have particular disabilities which inhibit their use of ICT, access to adaptive software is especially important, and particularly so if income levels are low. The same is true of those with low levels of literacy. A good proportion of libraries have catered for users whose access to ICT is impaired by a physical or learning disability, although, as with the hardware, software may only be available in one library or on one terminal per library. Different software packages have been installed to support blind or partially sighted users, people with learning difficulties such as dyslexia or low levels of literacy.

Library services have traditionally used mobile libraries as a way of reaching users remote from library service points or physically unable to access the library. Many of the case study libraries had mobile libraries, but not all offered access to PN services. CALL PN funding was for static library access points only and so any equipment available in mobile libraries was funded from other sources. Just one or two had equipped the mobile library van with full ICT access, including disability access to the vehicle. Another, serving remote communities in Scotland where internet access is not possible, was looking at packages that would enable staff to download complete websites on a non-networked PC.

Other libraries similarly provided access to a PC, but no network access. Laptops were the other way of reaching physically and socially isolated groups, although again these did not always provide real time access to the internet or networked resources. Library services with advanced library management systems were better placed to provide users in community settings with access to on-line catalogues and services, using high spec lap tops. Physical access involves more than rolling out the technology. Once in place, it is important that the system works reliably, that the hardware and software are relatively trouble free, and that back up technical support is readily available when needed. Case studies provide a window for looking at the realities on the ground of the internet access afforded by PN.

In the first round of field visits, libraries had many tales about hiccoughs in rolling out the infrastructure and problems with bedding down the hardware and setting up appropriate management systems for PN to ensure its smooth running. By the time of the second round visit, these had mainly dissipated. Not surprisingly though, given the scale of PN, individual libraries have encountered various obstacles to keeping systems running and providing reliable open access to the terminals and the internet for library users. Here, give a flavour of these:

— A major source of technical difficulty was the peripheral hardware (printers and scanners) rather than the computers, which for the most part were technically robust. One county library service described its decision to go for low-end scanners as a mistake - the PN coordinator had come round to the view that photocopying was a more cost-effective alternative. Several libraries reported systemic failures with print management software. Because printing is networked, a local problem on one printer often impacted on other printers, clogging up the entire system. Such problems could be exacerbated by lack of inter-operability between hardware and software in different libraries.

—Viruses were a problem for several libraries, occasionally requiring the whole system to be closed down, in one case for several weeks during the busy summer period. This caused the staff endless problems, but made them realise how embedded PN had become and what a useful asset it is.

— Systems failure was a periodic occurrence, in one library service taking all PN terminals out of action for five weeks. This particular library service also had a high failure rate on its computers, eventually dealt with by the supplier replacing the hardware.

— Not all library services had fully installed PN hardware and software. In one case, the terminals only provided access to email and internet.

The computers didn't come with MS Office already installed and the library service had waited more than a year for corporate IT to load them and give them a common 'cyber café' look. Delays were also experienced in installing video-conferencing hardware.

— Providing free internet access for all in a public space raised particular concerns about information abuse and the censorship of illegal or inappropriate material which could be displayed and downloaded by users. Open information access also created potential issues of liability, culpability and accountability for the local authority and library service. Firewalling and filtering were the common ways of dealing with these issues, although a heavy hand could restrict users from accessing legitimate sites and was a common cause of user complaint. Several libraries had installed software that allowed them to reboot the machines clean.

— Securing adequate bandwidth was a problem for two library services.

— For many libraries, the main software deficiency was the lack of an automated booking system. Instead, staff were spending many hours manually logging users into the system or using a paper based system.

ICTs and Technical Support in Library Services

The experience of technical support varied widely across library services, reflecting such things as relations with corporate IT, the appointment of staff to dedicated posts for frontline ICT support and the existence of service level agreements with suppliers. Some libraries had no funding for frontline support and were dependent on a central ICT support desk; others could call on the services of an in-library ICT support team or officer. One county library service had included a high level support agreement as part of its PFI contract, with a rapid response time and penalties for failure to deliver within targets.

An aspect of physical access to PN computers and online services is the way they are grouped and located within the library setting, and the social and cultural ambience of the library more generally. Some libraries had located PN terminals in a separate learning centre or suite, away from book stacks and other services; others distributed small banks of computers in different parts of the library, often zoned areas for particular user groups such as teenagers; still others integrated them with the physical stock wherever space allowed.

Physical space could sometimes dictate the arrangement; other times the library made a conscious choice about location. In one library for example, a conscious decision had been made about where to locate the terminals as a result of earlier experience of working alongside adult education. In this particular case, the PCs were integrated with the physical stock, in groupings that were sufficient to ensure viable numbers for adult education courses. Another library which had chosen to locate all its computers in a large learning centre alongside the reference section of the library was reconsidering the appropriateness of this choice.

User Perspective

The users of ICT in public libraries represent the ultimate test-bed or litmus-test of the connectivity afforded by PN, and their experiences of its accessibility, reliability and comparative advantage over other modes of ICT access. Focus groups with users explored some of these aspects, and users' experience and overall satisfaction with the 'hard' end of PN. Functioning effectively in the information age of the 21st century is not just a matter of computer or technological competence. It also calls for a new kind of information literacy or intelligence attuned to the digital world and the changing nature of what counts for knowledge, and for what have termed civic literacy.

The 'C' in ICT represents a new communitarian capability of technology that can strengthen a host of civic purposes and can be harnessed to other kinds of learning. Today's citizens thus need to be competent and confident in at least three different facets of Information and Communication Technology:

— The technical side of handling technology and exploiting its multiple uses

— The information side of dealing with the chaotic nature of the internet, including discovering, evaluating and making sense of information encountered in a web environment

— The civic side of familiarity with ICT as a tool for participative citizenship

The main thrust of the efforts of public libraries in developing citizens' capability and confidence in using ICT has been on the first facet. Some library services have paid attention to the second, but the third remains a largely neglected area. A main purpose of the People's Network was to reach out to citizens whose lack of awareness and familiarity with ICT placed them at risk of being disenfranchised from the mainstream of society. Beyond helping citizens to achieve a basic threshold in ICT competence, public libraries were also expected to play an important role in helping learners along a 'learning pathway', developing and building on their basic level ICT skills to take advantage of the full range of learning opportunities on offer. Public libraries have taken on this new area of work with enthusiasm, generally in partnership with other agencies.

Building Blocks of ICT Competence

Library staff have generally viewed technical competence as cumulative hierarchy, with four main building blocks. A novice user needs to master one before moving on to the next. So awareness and familiarisation are followed by simple use of online and computer applications, and lead on to more structured basic, intermediate and advanced training. Many libraries have provided opportunities for ICT skill development at these different levels, in partnership with other agencies. These have commonly included the adult education service of the local authority, local colleges or other ICT training providers. Libraries funded as UK online centres were in a position to fund one or more training positions which were filled by nonlibrarians with ICT training expertise. Other libraries, especially some of the smaller branch libraries, offered training and support at the lower levels only.

The citizens or users who were attracted to the library as an environment where they felt comfortable either to explore ICT for the first time or to develop their ICT competence and confidence, were not a homogenous group: they varied widely in terms of awareness, motivation, purpose and confidence. A substantial proportion of ICT learners had no specific purpose in mind and were only vaguely aware of its potential uses. Thus, the kinds of support, guidance and ICT training provided by the library or learning centre could be very important in shaping users' experiences, expectations and ultimate use of the technology.

In one community based library, for example, a survey was undertaken to gather information on the interests of local people in ICT. It was framed only in training terms, asking respondents to indicate what level of training they would like the library to provide. The majority of libraries however, offered a more limited repertoire of ICT training and support focused on awareness and familiarisation, with more tenuous links to advanced training through signposting to other providers.

Complementary Strategies

There are two main strategies taken by libraries: one, a skill based or vertical strategy, the other a use based or horizontal strategy. The skill based vertical strategy was aimed at moving people up the technical competence hierarchy through a deliberate programme of instruction and development. Success was measured by progression from novice to basic to intermediate to advanced levels, and often reflected in numbers completing certificated courses. Developing ICT capability was very much its own end, or a route to other organised learning, or into employment. The emphasis here was on generic ICT competences, developed outside their immediate context of use.

The use based horizontal strategy was aimed more at helping people put their newly acquired computer skills to good use, and to extend the number of activities or purposes involving the use of ICT. In the process of 'learning by doing' in themed sessions, assisted by various kinds of tutor and peer support, individuals were also able to develop their ICT competence and confidence, but in less formalised ways. It might involve developing a higher level of skill on a particular piece of software to accomplish some learning project or task, or extending beyond a text activity such as email to learning how to scan, download and send photos to family and friends; or finding out more about online family history resources and how to use search tools to locate specific information.

In this strategy, ICT was primarily seen as a means or a tool to add value to some other activity or to accomplish a learner's purpose. Number of drivers or pressures on libraries towards a skill based strategy. A key one was the preoccupation with measurable outputs and evidence of ICT progression, reinforced by funding agencies. The targets commonly included completion of formal training, or numbers of formal training sessions. Another driver was a consequence of the close partnership between the library service and the adult education service, local college or Workers' Educational Association (WEA) in the provision of ICT training. These agencies tended to have a strong preference for instructional modes of teaching ICT, leading to formal qualifications and tied into progression routes. Other pressures came from the external environment.

One library service, with a strong commitment to an informal learning and community learning approach, found little support from its regional Learning and Skills Council: "The Learning and Skills Council have not been a good partner, in terms of starting up any new initiatives or furthering existing projects. They were not interested in informal learning or community based learning initiatives for older members - basically not interested in working with libraries period. They were only interested in accredited or formal learning and not even interested in developing links, which lead to pathway development in libraries - from informal to formal learning. A community based outcomes approach is anathema to the LSC."

Learner Progression

The idea of learner progression was nearly always construed as progressing up the technical competence hierarchy and along a formal learning pathway. In a few library services, staff were thinking about progression along horizontal lines, for example where libraries were providing building blocks along an informal learning pathway. In both cases, the conception was of progression from one kind of learning onto another, whether formal or informal, or of building cumulatively on different layers of skill.

Progression could be seen as an individual learner responsibility, or as an appropriate area where library or other agency staff might play a role. Approaches to facilitating learner progressions took weak and strong forms. Many of the library staff interviewed saw advice and guidance beyond their remit or level of professional competence. The micro-case studies included twelve examples of ICT training and development activities. They showed that: Tutor-led instruction, based on standardised courses at taster, basic and intermediate levels, was the sole or predominant mode in two-thirds of the libraries. Four of these libraries were externally funded centres with target numbers for course completions.

Training was generally supplemented by other kinds of coaching and support, either as an additional form of available support or as a kind of 'bootstrap' to move people back onto the instructional track, or as an alternative mode for certain groups of users/learners. In one-third of cases, the preferred approach was to provide structured or informal coaching and support, either because the library had no facilities for training, or it was delivered in outreach settings via laptops and was more suited to informal methods, or the tutor/librarian judged a less formal approach as more appropriate to the profile of the learners/users.

Peer and mutual support was a strong feature of four of the twelve examples. Volunteers and peers were given training or coaching for their roles. In two libraries, a peer support group had been set up to take the pressure off staff and as a more sustainable model for the longer term. The following are the main findings and observations about the different approaches libraries took to develop user ICT competence and confidence that were derived from the 16 case study library services:

— The tutor-led instructional mode was best suited to moving individuals up the ICT competence hierarchy, with progression along a well sign-posted route leading to recognised achievements along the way.

— Training of this formal kind was in all cases performed by staff from other agencies, mostly adult education services or the local college.

— Library staff almost uniformly felt a formal training role was beyond their level of ICT competence as well as outside their remit. This was reinforced by external agency staff who saw ICT training as their own domain.

— A high proportion of the staff spoke to were also reluctant to offer structured coaching sessions, and in some libraries, staff at some levels were uncomfortable with an informal coaching role as well. They were more likely to offer just-in-time support if there was a fall-back position: i.e. they could refer a user on to some other person or service if the query or help needed was beyond their competence.

— Although a needs analysis or assessment was sometimes undertaken prior to provision of ICT skills training and development to ascertain the kinds of training and support users wanted, this was generally framed within a training paradigm or approach. A survey in one learning centre, for example, asked users of the community library learning centre whether they wanted training at taster, basic or intermediate levels, and what applications they were interested in. The priority group for this centre was people aged 50+.

— The valuing of formal learning over informal learning, and the visibility of progression into formal courses compared with the more invisible journey of the informal learner. This too pushes library staff towards encouraging individuals along the course based route.

— The situated or context based approach to ICT skills development and use was a new development for most library services, and except for very small number. Some library staff saw it as a more effective method of developing ICT competence - learning through using ICT in a real or authentic activity - or as more appropriate to some kinds of learners than formal training, for example older people or retirees. In other places, 'themed sessions' such as ICT for local history or family learning, were introduced as horizontal building blocks, leading people on from basic taster and awareness sessions to using ICT for some wider purpose.

— Many examples of ICT 'dead-ending'. That is to say, where computer novices completed a taster course or developed their ICT skills to a very basic level, but were not given any guidance as to how they might use them. Many library staff seemed not to see it as their role to open up new learning and lifeskill possibilities for the user/learner.

— On the other hand, it was clear from conversations with library managers that they saw libraries as having a role to play in helping people move on from limited ICT use such as email and the internet to other kinds of learning. The themed approach offered one set of learning possibilities, but the choice was usually quite narrow. What is currently missing in nearly all public libraries is a well designed and extensive range of online courseware with content that is relevant to people's needs and interests as well as being fun and enjoyable.

Information Literacy Skills

Technical competences are required to participate fully in the digital environment. In addition, there is a separate set of attributes around the ability to solve information and learning problems, more or less independent of the form in which that information is provided. This is commonly referred to as 'information literacy'. It involves an ability to recognise when information is needed and to locate, evaluate, and use effectively the needed information, whether it comes from a computer, a book, a government report or any number of other possible resources.

Locating, evaluating and assessing the utility of the information for a particular purpose in a web environment is not simple. The sheer volume of material in digital form makes it vital to have an appropriate array of skills for locating needed information. Not only is the amount of information constantly growing, which makes it difficult to locate, but much of it is constantly changing. Indeed, much information is dynamically generated at the time of the enquiry and is created specifically in response to a search enquiry. Knowledge is seen as provisional and evanescent. Increasingly, people will need to be able to deal with a shifting mixture of words, images and sounds. The normal cues one uses in an offline environment to evaluate information are often not available, so that different ways of assessing currency, truthfulness and trustworthiness of various knowledge claims may need to be re-learned.

Digital Citizenship

The different ways in which libraries are enabling citizens to access networked information resources and to exploit the communication potential of the new technologies. These relate to:

— Helping users discover and retrieve electronic information relevant to their needs and interests.

— Organising, presenting and creating new online content, especially local content.

— Facilitating interactive learning environments and creating virtual learning communities.

There are four examples of an ICT service, as illustrations of how ICT has been used to enhance, improve or add significant new value for the user. Next, look at ICT-enabled services generally and look at the different ways in which libraries have incorporated ICT information resources and tools into services and service delivery, as well as the different organisational and social support mechanisms which have emerged to support the service and the user.

In keeping with the democratising intent of the public library service, see the conditions for effective use as involving users not only as consumers but also as producers of information and knowledge, and as active participants in dialogue about what applications or uses would be most beneficial in particular local contexts. Libraries were providing or developing different discovery tools or navigational and finding aids intended to help users more easily discover, locate and retrieve networked information and other knowledge resources. These were of two main kinds:

— Those to do with the content, organisation or accessibility of websites.

— Those relating to online catalogues and advanced search and retrieval functions.

In many case study libraries, but by no means all, library staff were placing finding aids which were to do with content, organisation or accessibility on the library's website, signposting users to information and other resources. Examples of these included:

— Signposts or hyperlinks from the library home page to useful, new and interesting websites. These might be sites of general or specific interest, sites with top-rating hits or sites hosting databases of interest to particular user groups.

— Web pages with content or links relevant to a particular group stored in a database. For example, legal rights materials relevant to asylum seekers, or family and local history sources and resources.

— A 'walled garden' of sites and resources suitable for children and linked to the curriculum, available via the library's portal. A homework club might sometimes have it's own dedicated site or web pages.

— Portals to authenticated or validated information resources in specific topic areas such as health and well-being, with browsing and retrieval functions.

— Websites with a specialist interface, providing a range of information content and interactive services aimed at different client groups such as children, businesses, teenagers, readers.

— Advanced search and browsing facilities on the council interface for finding information about council services, including library services.

Libraries were at different stages in creating an electronic portal or gateway to all library services and catalogues, with links to other services of interest to library users. A few had interactive online catalogues with advanced service functions up and running; others were in the process of implementing or changing over to an advanced library management system; and a few were still in the throes of mounting a static version of the library catalogue onto the PN network, accessible from any Internet-PC. The more advanced systems allow users to:

— Remotely access the full range of library services, including the ability to renew or reserve books and other stock, and to check the user's own borrower record.

— Hire a meeting room or book internet sessions and classes.

— Access an electronic database of community information, tailored to the library.

— Post an inquiry to the 'Ask a Librarian' service.

— Use the electronic portal to access the digital resources of the library and partner organisations.

— Find information helpful to selecting reading material e.g. 'top ten reads' of the month.

There were instances of library authorities providing additional services on the back of catalogue-based resource discovery. Kent Library Service, for example, was piloting a revenue-based online document search and delivery service based on its genealogy and local history resources, using an online secure payment system. Its service attracted worldwide usage. In Northern Ireland, library services acting together are exploring the feasibility of a genealogy related service based on library resources, involving a partnership between the Service Provider and other complementary bodies on a revenue-sharing basis.

Effectiveness of ICT Service

There are many criteria one might use for assessing the effectiveness of the ICT services developed by libraries. Usability is often singled out as the most important one. With the People's Network, the ultimate test of effectiveness of the many different tools and products being developed is whether people are using them, whether they find them easy to use and useful, and whether they result in the hoped for benefits or outcomes.

The key to usability is 'user centred design'. That is to say, an approach which begins with the user's needs and a concern with how the tool or application is to be used, rather than with the technology or the provider's view of what users want or need. And it involves users, either directly or indirectly, in the ongoing design and development process in ways that foster their ownership of the end product or service. In any service development, users can be involved in a variety of ways and at one or more stages of the development process.

— Users can be simply the end consumers or recipients of a service, or they can be consulted, involved as collaborators or take a more active role as co-creators or co-producers of a service

— Users can be involved at the stages of needs analysis, design and development of the service, delivery and implementation or throughout the whole process.

Although there were many instances of user involvement at different stages, on the whole user involvement was not a strong feature of the micro-case studies. Indeed, almost a third of projects or activities had no element of user involvement and where it existed it took the weaker forms of consultation and collaboration, although there were some good examples of each of these. There was no example of user-centred design, in which users were involved throughout the process from original inception through to ongoing feedback and evaluation.

A study support club for young people at risk of social exclusion involves young people in making decisions about the service in a variety of ways:

— Young people set the ground rules for the club, in discussion with library and project staff.
— A youth group, drawn from volunteers, meets monthly to plan the programme, organise different activities and talk though any behaviour problems.
— Young people have the 'freedom of the library' in a closed weekly session which gives them ownership of the whole library space.

A homework club involves the community in its running. A committee, with members drawn from the agency partners, library members and community volunteers meets once a term to monitor and evaluate what the homework club is doing and how to develop it further. A learning centre with an ICT training suite is setting up a learners' pool and a community focus group. The learners' pool will provide feedback from local users about the services they would like to see provided.

The community focus group will take a more active role in organising, providing peer support, community advocacy and publicity. A peer support group is already in place, providing ICT novices with one-on-one help. In another community learning centre, users came up with the idea of a computer club. Although librarian led in its current form, the intention is for the group to become self-sufficient. The computer club invites guest speakers, provides peer support, and a forum for making suggestions about how to improve the service.

The different kinds of networked information and ICT training and support services offered by libraries. In these sections, we can see the domains where libraries have been most active in developing and delivering these services and the issues which have arisen from them. These are:

— Education and lifelong learning
— Social inclusion
— Access to information
— Citizen's information
— Business and the economy
— Community history and identity
— National digital library

Within each domain, identified one or more specific ICT service activities. The assessment is based on three nominal levels of activity, derived from reports of service activities in interviews with library staff at all levels:

— minor activity - five or fewer library services
— moderate activity - between six and ten library services
— significant activity - eleven or more library services

Issues in ICT Services

Some level of activity across all domain areas, the development of ICT-enabled services has been very uneven. Lifelong learning for example has been an area of significant activity, whilst initiatives around the egovernment agenda have been slow to develop. Using ICT to support local economic development has similarly had a low profile in the case study library services, with one or two exceptions.

The unevenness is also marked between library services. Setting aside activities in the making and future plans, there were two library services who were not able to point to any ICT information management or development initiative that was up and running, and several more where only one or two were identified. Moreover, their activities were often spread across different domain areas, reflecting broadly spread staff interests and capabilities.

References

Bawden, D., *User-oriented Evaluation of Information Systems and Services,* Aldershot: Gower, 1990.

Brandt, D. Scott, "Evaluating Information on the Internet", *Computers in Libraries* 16(5), May 1996: 44-46, 1996.

Chen, C., "Global Digital Library Development," *Knowledge-based Data Management for Digital Libraries,* Tsinghua University Press, pp. 197-204, 2001.

Conway, Paul , *Preservation in the Digital World,* Washington, D.C.: Commission on Preservation and Access, 1996.

Kelleher, J., E. Sommerlad, and E. Stern, *Evalution of the Electronic Libraries Programmes: Guidelines for e-Lib Project Evaluation*, London: Tavistock Institute, 1996.

Lee H W., Networked, electronic and virtual library: Libraries of the 1990s, *Jl. of Educational Media and Library Sciences,* 32 (2), 1995.

Malwad N. M., *et al* (ed.), *Digital Libraries: Dynamics storehouse of digitised information,* New Delhi, New Age International, 1996.

Sproull, L., and S. Kiesler, *Connections: New Ways of Working in the Networked Organisation*, MIT Press, Cambridge, MA, 1991.

6

Features of Changing Library

An informal definition of a digital library is a managed collection of information, with associated services, where the information is stored in digital formats and accessible over a network. A key part of this definition is that the information is managed. A stream of data sent to earth from a satellite is not a library. The same data, when organised systematically, becomes a digital library collection. Most people would not consider a database containing financial records of one company to be a digital library, but would accept a collection of such information from many companies as part of a library.

Digital libraries contain diverse collections of information for use by many different users. Digital libraries range in size from tiny to huge. They can use any type of computing equipment and any suitable software. The unifying theme is that information is organised on computers and available over a network, with procedures to select the material in the collections, to organise it, to make it available to users, and to archive it.

In some ways, digital libraries are very different from traditional libraries, yet in others they are remarkably similar. People do not change because new technology is invented. They still create information that has to be organised, stored, and distributed. They still need to find information that others have created, and use it for study, reference, or entertainment. However, the form in which the information is expressed and the methods that are used to manage it are greatly influenced by technology and this creates change. Every year, the quantity and variety of collections available in digital form grows, while the supporting technology continues to improve steadily. Cumulatively, these changes are stimulating fundamental alterations in how people create information and how they use it.

To understand these forces requires an understanding of the people who are developing the libraries. Technology has dictated the pace at which digital libraries have been able to develop, but the manner in which the technology is used depends upon people. Two important communities are the source of much of this innovation. One group is the information professionals. They include librarians, publishers, and a wide range of information providers, such as indexing and abstracting services. The other community contains the computer science researchers and their offspring, the Internet developers.

Until recently, these two communities had disappointingly little interaction; even now it is commonplace to find a computer scientist who knows nothing of the basic tools of librarianship, or a librarian whose concepts of information retrieval are years out of date. Over the past few years, however, there has been much more collaboration and understanding. Partly this is a consequence of digital libraries becoming a recognised field for research, but an even more important factor is greater involvement from the users themselves. Low-cost equipment and simple software have made electronic information directly available to everybody. Authors no longer need the services of a publisher to distribute their works. Readers can have direct access to information without going through an intermediary.

Many exciting developments come from academic or professional groups who develop digital libraries for their own needs. Medicine has a long tradition of creative developments; the pioneering legal information systems were developed by lawyers for lawyers; the Web was initially developed by physicists, for their own use.

Technology influences the economic and social aspects of information, and vice versa. The technology of digital libraries is developing fast and so are the financial, organisational, and social frameworks. The various groups that are developing digital libraries bring different social conventions and different attitudes to money. Publishers and libraries have a long tradition of managing physical objects, notably books, but also maps, photographs, sound recordings and other artifacts. They evolved economic and legal frameworks that are based on buying and selling these objects. Their natural instinct is to transfer to digital libraries the concepts that have served them well for physical artifacts.

Computer scientists and scientific users, such as physicists, have a different tradition. Their interest in digital information began in the days when computers were very expensive. Only a few well-funded researchers had computers on the first networks. They exchanged information informally and openly with colleagues, without payment. The networks have grown, but the tradition of open information remains.

The economic framework that is developing for digital libraries shows a mixture of these two approaches. Some digital libraries mimic traditional publishing by requiring a form of payment before users may access the collections and use the services. Other digital libraries use a different economic model. Their material is provided with open access to everybody. The costs of creating and distributing the information are borne by the producer, not the user of the information.

The fundamental reason for building digital libraries is a belief that they will provide better delivery of information than was possible in the past. Traditional libraries are a fundamental part of society, but they are not perfect. Enthusiasts for digital libraries point out that computers and networks have already changed the ways in which people communicate with each other. In some disciplines, they argue, a professional or scholar is better served by sitting at a personal computer connected to a communications network than by making a visit to a library. Information that was previously available only to the professional is now directly available to all.

From a personal computer, the user is able to consult materials that are stored on computers around the world. Conversely, all but the most diehard enthusiasts recognise that printed documents are so much part of civilisation that their dominant role cannot change except gradually. While some important uses of printing may be replaced by electronic information, not everybody considers a large-scale movement to electronic information desirable, even if it is technically, economically, and legally feasible. Here are some of the potential benefits of digital libraries.

Role of Digital Computers

Digital library brings the ibrary to the user: To use a library requires access. Traditional methods require that the user goes to the library. In a university, the walk to a library takes a few minutes, but not many people are member of universities or have a nearby library. Many engineers or physicians carry out their work with depressingly poor access to the latest information. A digital library brings the information to the user's desk, either at work or at home, making it easier to use and hence increasing its usage. With a digital library on the desk top, a user need never visit a library building. The library is wherever there is a personal computer and a network connection.

Computer power is used for searching and browsing: Computing power can be used to find information. Paper documents are convenient to read, but finding information that is stored on paper can be difficult. Despite the myriad of secondary tools and the skill of reference librarians, using a large library can be a tough challenge. A claim that used to be made for traditional libraries is that they stimulate serendipity, because readers stumble across unexpected items of value. The truth is that libraries are full of useful materials that readers discover only by accident.

In most aspects, computer systems are already better than manual methods for finding information. They are not as good as everybody would like, but they are good and improving steadily. Computers are particularly useful for reference work that involves repeated leaps from one source of information to another.

Information can be shared: Libraries and archives contain much information that is unique. Placing digital information on a network makes it available to everybody. Many digital libraries or electronic publications are maintained at a single central site, perhaps with a few duplicate copies strategically placed around the world. This is a vast improvement over expensive physical duplication of little used material, or the inconvenience of unique material that is inaccessible without traveling to the location where it is stored.

Information is easier to keep current: Much important information needs to be brought up to date continually. Printed materials are awkward to update, since the entire document must be reprinted; all copies of the old version must be tracked down and replaced. Keeping information current is much less of a problem when the definitive version is in digital format and stored on a central computer. Many libraries provide online the text of reference works, such as directories or encyclopedias. Whenever revisions are received from the publisher, they are installed on the library's computer. The new versions are available immediately. The Library of Congress has an online collection, called Thomas, that contains the latest drafts of all legislation currently before the U.S. Congress; it changes continually.

Information is always available: The doors of the digital library never close; a recent study at a British university found that about half the usage of a library's digital collections was at hours when the library buildings were closed. Materials are never checked out to other readers, miss-shelved or stolen; they are never in an off-campus warehouse. The scope of the collections expands beyond the walls of the library. Private papers in an office or the collections of a library on the other side of the world are as easy to use as materials in the local library.

Digital libraries are not perfect. Computer systems can fail and networks may be slow or unreliable, but, compared with a traditional library, information is much more likely to be available when and where the user wants it.

New forms of information become possible: Most of what is stored in a conventional library is printed on paper, yet print is not always the best way to record and disseminate information. A database may be the best way to store census data, so that it can be analysed by computer; satellite data can be rendered in many different ways; a mathematics library can store mathematical expressions, not as ink marks on paper but as computer symbols to be manipulated by programs such as Mathematica or Maple.

Even when the formats are similar, materials that are created explicitly for the digital world are not the same as materials originally designed for paper or other media. Words that are spoken have a different impact from words that are written, and online textual materials are subtly different from either the spoken or printed word. Good authors use words differently when they write for different media and users find new ways to use the information. Materials created for the digital world can have a vitality that is lacking in material that has been mechanically converted to digital formats, just as a feature film never looks quite right when shown on television.

Each of the benefits described above can be seen in existing digital libraries. There is another group of potential benefits, which have not yet been demonstrated, but hold tantalising prospects. The hope is that digital libraries will develop from static repositories of immutable objects to provide a wide range of services that allow collaboration and exchange of ideas. The technology of digital libraries is closely related to the technology used in fields such as electronic mail and teleconferencing, which have historically had little relationship to libraries. The potential for convergence between these fields is exciting.

High-speed Networks

The growth of the Internet over the past few years has been phenomenal. Telecommunications companies compete to provide local and long distance Internet service across the United States; international links reach almost every country in the world; every sizable company has its internal network; universities have built campus networks; individuals can purchase low-cost, dial-up services for their homes.

The coverage is not universal. Even in the U.S. there are many gaps and some countries are not yet connected at all, but in many countries of the world it is easier to receive information over the Internet than to acquire printed books and journals by orthodox methods.

Although digital libraries are based around networks, their utility has been greatly enhanced by the development of portable, laptop computers. By attaching a laptop computer to a network connection, a user combines the digital library resources of the Internet with the personal work that is stored on the laptop. When the user disconnects the laptop, copies of selected library materials can be retained for personal use. During the past few years, laptop computers have increased in power, while the quality of their screens has improved immeasurably. Although batteries remain a problem, laptops are no heavier than a large book, and the cost continues to decline steadily.

Access to Digital Libraries

Traditional libraries usually require that the user be a member of an organisation that maintains expensive physical collections. In the United States, universities and some other organisations have excellent libraries, but most people do not belong to such an organisation. In theory, much of the Library of Congress is open to anybody over the age of eighteen, and a few cities have excellent public libraries, but in practice, most people are restricted to the small collections held by their local public library. Even scientists often have poor library facilities. Doctors in large medical centers have excellent libraries, but those in remote locations typically have nothing. One of the motives that led the Institute of Electrical and Electronics Engineers (IEEE) to its early interest in electronic publishing was the fact that most engineers do not have access to an engineering library.

Users of digital libraries need a computer attached to the Internet. In the United States, many organisations provide every member of staff with a computer. Some have done so for many years. Across the nation, there are programs to bring computers to schools and to install them in pubic libraries. For individuals who must provide their own computing, adequate access to the Internet requires less than $2,000 worth of equipment, perhaps $20 per month for a dial-up connection, and a modicum of skill. Increase the costs a little and very attractive services can be obtained, with a powerful computer and a dedicated, higher speed connection. These are small investments for a prosperous professional, but can be a barrier for others.

In 1998 it was estimated that 95 percent of people in the United States live in areas where there is reasonable access to the Internet. This percentage is growing rapidly. Outside the United States, the situation varies. In most countries of the world, library services are worse than in the United States. Digital libraries do bring information to many people who lack traditional libraries, but the Internet is far from being conveniently accessible world-wide. A factor that must be considered in planning digital libraries is that the quality of the technology available to users varies greatly. A favored few have the latest personal computers on their desks, high-speed connections to the Internet, and the most recent release of software; they are supported by skilled staff who can configure and tune the equipment, solve problems, and keep the software up to date. Most people, however, have to make do with less. Their equipment may be old, their software out of date, their Internet connection troublesome, and their technical support from staff who are under-trained and over-worked.

One of the great challenges in developing digital libraries is to build systems that take advantage of modern technology, yet perform adequately in less perfect situations. Terminology often proves to be a barrier in discussing digital libraries. The people who build digital libraries come from many disciplines and bring the terminology of those disciplines with them. Some words have such strong social, professional, legal, or technical connotations that they obstruct discussion between people of varying backgrounds. Simple words mean different things to different people. For example, the words "copy" and "publish" have different meanings to computing professionals, publishers, and lawyers.

Common English usage is not the same as professional usage, the versions of English around the world have subtle variations of meaning, and discussions of digital libraries are not restricted to the English language. Some words cause such misunderstandings that it is tempting to ban them from any discussion of digital libraries. In addition to "copy" and "publish", the list includes "document", "object", and "work". At the very least, such words must be used carefully and their exact meaning made clear whenever they are used. Most of the time, however, such precision is mere pedantry. Where the context is clear, the book uses terms informally. Where the majority of the practitioners in the field use a word in certain way, their usage is followed.

Collections

Digital libraries hold any information that can be encoded as sequences of bits. Sometimes these are digitised versions of conventional media, such as text, images, music, sound recordings, specifications and designs, and many, many more. As digital libraries expand, the contents are less often the digital equivalents of physical items and more often items that have no equivalent, such as data from scientific instruments, computer programs, video games, and databases.

Data and metadata

The information stored in a digital library can be divided into data and metadata. Data is a general term to describe information that is encoded in digital form. Whether the word "data" is singular or plural is a source of contention. Metadata is data about other data. Many people dislike the word "metadata", but it is widely used. Common categories of metadata include descriptive metadata, such as bibliographic information, structural metadata about formats and structures, and administrative metadata, which includes, rights, permissions, and other information that is used to manage access. One item of metadata is the identifier, which identifies an item to the outside world.

The distinction between data and metadata often depends upon the context. Catalog records or abstracts are usually considered to be metadata, because they describe other data, but in an online catalog or a database of abstracts they are the data.

Digital library items

No generic term has yet been established for the items that are stored in a digital library. The most general is material, which is anything that might be stored in a library. The word item is essentially synonymous. Neither word implies anything about the content, structure, or the user's view of the information. The word can be used to describe physical objects or information in digital formats. The term digital material is used when needed for emphasis.

A more precise term is digital object. This is used to describe an item as stored in a digital library, typically consisting of data, associated metadata, and an identifier. Some people call every item in a digital library a document.

Library objects

The term library object is useful for the user's view of what is stored in a library. Consider an article in an online periodical. The reader thinks of it as a single entity, a library object, but the article is probably stored on a computer as several separate objects. They contain pages of digitised text, graphics, perhaps even computer programs, or linked items stored on remote computers. From the user's viewpoint, this is one library object made up of several digital objects. This example shows that library objects have internal structure. They usually have both data and associated metadata. Structural metadata is used to describe the formats and the relationship of the parts.

Presentations, disseminations, and the stored form of a digital object

The form in which information is stored in a digital library may be very different from the form in which it is used. A simulator used to train airplane pilots might be stored as several computer programs, data structures, digitised images, and other data. This is called the stored form of the object. The user is provided with a series of images, synthesised sound, and control sequences. Some people use the term presentation for what is presented to the user and in many contexts this is appropriate terminology. A more general term is dissemination, which emphasises that the transformation from the stored form to the user requires the execution of some computer program.

When digital information is received by a user's computer, it must be converted into the form that is provided to the user, typically by displaying on the computer screen, possibly augmented by a sound track or other presentation. This conversion is called rendering.

Finding terminology to describe content is especially complicated. Part of the problem is that the English language is very flexible. Words have varying meanings depending upon the context. Consider, the example, "the song Simple Gifts". Depending on the context, that phrase could refer to the song as a work with words and music, the score of the song, a performance of somebody singing it, a recording of the performance, an edition of music on compact disk, a specific compact disc, the act of playing the music from the recording, the performance encoded in a digital library, and various other aspects of the song.

Such distinctions are important to the music industry, because they determine who receives money that is paid for a musical performance or recording. Several digital library researchers have attempted to define a general hierarchy of terms that can be applied to all works and library objects. This is a bold and useful objective, but fraught with difficulties. The problem is that library materials have so much variety that a classification may match some types of material well but fail to describe others adequately.

Despite these problems, the words work and content are useful words. Most people use the word content loosely. The word is used in any context when the emphasis is on library materials, not as bits and bytes to be processed by a computer but as information that is of interest to a user. To misquote a famous judge, we can not define "content", but we know it when we see it.

While the word content is used as a loosely defined, general term, the word work is used more specifically. The term "literary work" is carefully defined in U. S. copyright law as the abstract content, the sequence of words or music independent of any particular stored representation, presentation, or performance.

A variety of words are used to describe the people who are associated with digital libraries. One group of people are the creators of information in the library. Creators include authors, composers, photographers, map makers, designers, and anybody else who creates intellectual works. Some are professionals; some are amateurs. Some work individually, others in teams. They have many different reasons for creating information. Another group are the users of the digital library.

Depending on the context, users may be described by different terms. In libraries, they are often called "readers" or "patrons"; at other times they may be called the "audience", or the "customers". A characteristic of digital libraries is that creators and users are sometimes the same people. In academia, scholars and researchers use libraries as resources for their research, and publish their findings in forms that become part of digital library collections.

The final group of people is a broad one that includes everybody whose role is to support the creators and the users. They can be called information managers. The group includes computer specialists, librarians, publishers, editors, and many others. The World Wide Web has created a new profession of Webmaster. Frequently a publisher will represent a creator, or a library will act on behalf of users, but publishers should not be confused with creators, or librarians with users. A single individual may be creator, user, and information manager.

Networks in Libraries

The emergence of the Internet as a flexible, low-cost, world-wide network has been one of the key factors that has led to the growth of digital libraries. Figure 1 shows some of the computers that are used in digital libraries. The computers have three main function: to help users interact with the library, to store collections of materials, and to provide services.

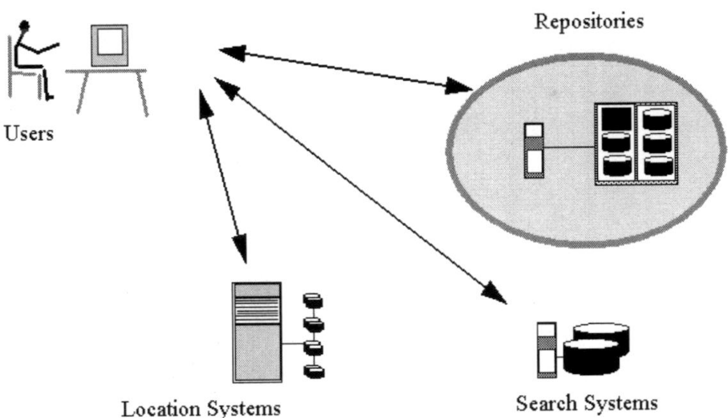

Figure 1. Computers in digital libraries

— In the terminology of computing, anybody who interacts with a computer is called a user or computer user. This is a broad term that covers creators, library users, information professionals, and anybody else who accesses the computer. To access a digital library, users normally use personal computers. These computers are given the general name clients. Sometimes, clients may interact with a digital library without no human user involved, such as the robots that automatically index library collections, and sensors that gather data, such as information about the weather, and supply it to digital libraries.

— The next major group of computers in digital libraries are repositories which store collections of information and provide access to them. An archive is a repository that is organised for long-term preservation of materials.

— The figure shows two typical services which are provided by digital libraries: location systems and search systems. Search systems provide catalogs, indexes, and other services to help users find information. Location systems are used to identify and locate information.

— In some circumstances there may be other computers that sit between the clients and computers that store information. These are not shown in the figure. Mirrors and caches store duplicate copies of information, for faster performance and reliability. The distinction between them is that mirrors replicate large sets of information, while caches store recently used information only. Proxies and gateways provide bridges between different types of computer system. They are particularly useful in reconciling systems that have conflicting technical specifications.

The generic term server is used to describe any computer other than the user's personal computer. A single server may provide several of the functions, perhaps acting as a repository, search system, and location system. Conversely, individual functions can be distributed across many servers. For example, the domain name system, which is a locator system for computers on the Internet, is a single, integrated service that runs on thousands of separate servers. In computing terminology, a distributed system is a group of computers that work as a team to provide services to users.

Digital libraries are some of the most complex and ambitious distributed systems ever built. The personal computers that users have on their desks have to exchange messages with the server computers; these computers are of every known type, managed by thousands of different organisations, running software that ranges from state-of-the art to antiquated. The term interoperability refers to the task of building coherent services for users, when the individual components are technically different and managed by different organisations. Some people argue that all technical problems in digital libraries are aspects of this one problem, interoperability. This is probably an overstatement, but it is certainly true that interoperability is a fundamental challenge in all aspects of digital libraries.

If digital technology is so splendid, what is stopping every library immediately becoming entirely digital? Part of the answer is that the technology of digital libraries is still immature, but the challenge is much more than technology. An equal challenge is the ability of individuals and organisations to devise ways that use technology effectively, to absorb the inevitable changes, and to create the required social frameworks. The world of information is like a huge machine with many participants each contributing their experience, expertise, and resources. To make fundamental changes in the system requires inter-related shifts in the economic, social and legal relationships amongst these parties.

Digital libraries depend on people and can not be introduced faster than people and organisations can adapt. This applies equally to the creators, users, and the professionals who support them. The relationships amongst these groups are changing. With digital libraries, readers are more likely to go directly to information, without visiting a library building or having any contact with a professional intermediary. Authors carry out more of the preparation of a manuscript. Professionals need new skills and new training to support these new relationships.

Some of these skills are absorbed through experience, while others can be taught. Since librarians have a career path based around schools of librarianship, these schools are adapting their curriculum, but it will be many years before the changes work through the system. The traditions of hundreds of years go deep. The general wisdom is that, except in a few specialised areas, digital libraries and conventional collections are going to coexist for the foreseeable future.

Institutional libraries will maintain large collections of traditional materials in parallel with their digital services, while publishers will continue to have large markets for their existing products. This does not imply that the organisations need not change, as new services extend the old. The full deployment of digital libraries will require extensive reallocation of money, with funds moving from the areas where savings are made to the areas that incur increased cost. Within an institution, such reallocations are painful to achieve, though they will eventually take place, but some of the changes are on a larger scale.

When a new and old technology compete, the new technology is never an exact match. Typically, the new has some features that are not in the old, but lacks some basic characteristics of the old. Therefore the old and new usually exist along side. However, the spectacular and continuing decline in the cost of computing with the corresponding increase in capabilities sometimes leads to complete substitution. Word processors were such an improvement that they supplanted typewriters in barely ten years. Card catalogs in libraries are on the same track.

In 1980, only a handful of libraries could afford an online catalog. Twenty years later, a card catalog is becoming a historic curiosity in American libraries. In some specialised areas, digital libraries may completely replace conventional library materials.

Since established organisations have difficulties changing rapidly, many exciting developments in digital libraries have been introduced by new organisations. New organisations can begin afresh, but older organisations are faced with the problems of maintaining old services while introducing the new. The likely effect of digital libraries will be a massive transfer of money from traditional suppliers of information to new information entrepreneurs and to the computing industry.

Naturally, existing organisations will try hard to discourage any change in which their importance diminishes, but the economic relationships between the various parties are already changing. Some important organisations will undoubtedly shrink in size or even go out of business. Predicting these changes is made particularly difficult by uncertainties about the finances of digital libraries and electronic publishing, and by the need for the legal system to adapt. Eventually, the pressures of the marketplace will establish a new order. At some stage, the market will have settled down sufficiently for the legal rules to be clarified. Until then, economic and legal uncertainties are annoying, though they have not proved to be serious barriers to progress. Overall, there appear to be no barriers to digital libraries and electronic publishing. Technical, economic, social, and legal challenges abound, but they are being overcome steadily.

TECHNOLOGICAL CHANGE

The role of library service is to provide access to documents. We could, if we wished, choose to define documents generously to include a range of informative objects that can be stored and retrieve, not only writings and not only published writings. Library service may be concerned with knowledge, but it is so in a fashion that is doubly indirect.

Firstly, library services are concerned with texts and images that are representations of knowledge. Secondly, library services are, in practice, often concerned less with the texts and images themselves than with physical objects that are text-bearing and image-bearing, such as books, journals, manuscripts, and photographs.

Libraries deal with text-bearing and image-bearing objects in vast quantities. Much of libraries' operating budgets and space is devoted not to the use of these materials, but to the assembling, organizing, and describing these materials so that it would become possible to use them. Hence, any significant change in the technology of text-bearing objects or of handling them could have very profound consequences, not on the purpose and mission of library services, but on the means for achieving them.

There is overwhelming consensus concerning trends in unit costs in information technology:

- the cost of computing power will continue to decrease rapidly;
- data storage costs will continue to decrease steadily; and
- the technology of telecommunications indicates strong long-term reductions.

Software, being labor-intensive to develop and maintain, should not be assumed to share in the dramatic improvements in hardware costs. Nevertheless the overall trend is very clear: Computer-based operations are becoming steadily and substantially more affordable. The practical conclusion is easily drawn. To the extent that computer-based procedures can be substituted for pre-computer procedures, they will be. Overall, the amount of computer-based activity will increase.

Information technology may only be a means and not an end, but that does not make it unimportant. We have just noted that in the provision of library service a very large proportion of present budgets is devoted to arranging the means to enable service to be provided.

The substitution of computing power, electronic data storage, and use of telecommunications holds considerable potential, not least because of the expectation that they will continue to become more attractive on cost grounds. The important questions become how and when the substitution of procedures based on new information technology should be adopted. The constraints include our limited ability to determine how to achieve that substitution, when that substitution will become cost-effective, and, at least as important, how to discriminate between substitutions that support improved library service and substitutions that subvert the mission and role of library service.

The initial task can reasonably be to find out how and when to substitute techniques using new information technology in the place of more traditional methods. This, in itself, misjudges the real options. Each technology offers a different set of constraints. Each technology is suited for doing different things.

The automating of manual procedures may well be worthwhile, but, in the longer term, misses the point of technological change. The initial question may be: How could library services be advantageously automated? This is a matter of doing the same things better. The longer term, more interesting question is: How could library service be re-designed with a change in technology? This is a matter of how to do better, different things.

Critical for addressing the second question--which better, different things should be done--is an understanding of past constraints upon library services that are attributable to the constraints of the technology of paper, card, and microform. However, constraints that are familiar tend to be transparent and not easy to recognize.

Paper is a strictly localized medium; a paper document is generally suited for use by only one person at a time; paper copies of paper documents have the same constraints as do the original; paper records are rather inflexible and can become expensively bulky. These constraints, in turn, determine the major limitations of the library service based on paper and paper-like technology:

1. Only documents that are local are usable: In all other cases the document must be fetched or the user must travel. The contents, scale, and suitability of the local collection dominates the quality of library service in the Paper Library and in the Automated Library.

2. Space for storing large local collections can become a significant practical problem.
3. Paper documents can be copied but are otherwise inflexible.
4. Catalogs on card are more flexible (but less moveable) than catalogs in printed book form. In both cases adding points of access becomes very cumbersome. Traditional U.S. practice has been to maintain access by author, by subject heading, and by title. Each requires an additional sequence of cards. Adding sequences to provide access by date, for example, or by language becomes prohibitively expensive. Economical subject access is at the price of using a highly complex pre-coordinate subject heading system, such as the Library of Congress Subject Headings.
5. Users, catalog, documents, and bibliographies are each physically separate from each other. There is inconvenience in getting from any one to any other.
6. Paper Libraries are closed much of the time and are invariably at some distance from the user.
7. Sought documents are commonly unavailable because they are already being used by someone else.
8. Time and patience is often needed to use Paper Libraries.
9. The problems of Paper Libraries are sensitive to size. Small libraries are limited in what they can provide. In large libraries there are diseconomies of scale because unit costs of filing, finding, and re-shelving increase as collections become larger.

Computer-based processing and electronic document storage have been found to have its own distinctive characteristics. The constraints include a greater need for standardization, increased technical complexity, and greater dependence on equipment that is much fragile and much more prone to obsolescence than that of a Paper Library.

Advantages of the new technology are that repetitive, mechanical tasks can be delegated to the machinery; the rate of increase in labor costs can thereby be moderated; electronic records can be modified, rearranged,and combined with each other; and, with telecommunications, distance becomes substantially irrelevant. These factors transform those aspects of library service that derive from the constraints of paper and cardboard.

The location of the user, the catalog record, the bibliography, and of the document cease to be dominating considerations. The user, the catalog, the bibliography, and the document can now be connected in ways that, hitherto, could only be dreamed about. As these changed constraints come to be appreciated it becomes clear that these new circumstances offer the possibility--indeed the inevitability--of new designs for library service. Several major changes are indicated:

1. Since library materials in electronic form lend themselves to remote access and shared use, the assembling of local collections becomes less important. Coordinated collection development and cooperative, shared access to collections become more important.
2. With materials on paper, having copies stored locally is a necessary condition for convenient access. With electronic materials, local storage may be desirable but is no longer necessary. Therefore, a catalog defined as a guide to what is locally stored becomes progressively less complete as a guide to what is conveniently accessible. One might as well catalog books published in odd years but not those published in even years. The answer is to shift from catalogs to union catalogs or linked catalogs and to holdings data linked to bibliographies, reversing our usual perspective on catalogs as bibliographic descriptions attached to a holdings records. Arguably the present day catalog, online or on cards, is a more a product of the limitations of nineteenth century library technology than of present day opportunities.
3. In the meanwhile, those to be served are changing their information-handling habits. Paper and pen are being supplemented by desk-top workstations, capable of using a multiplicity of remote sources. This leads to an entirely different perspective: from a library-centered world view to one that is user-centered.
4. These technological changes also invite reconsideration of the professional orthodoxy of consolidating academic library services. The view that a multiplicity of branch and departmental libraries is inefficient might well change. Under different conditions the decentralization of library service might well be regarded as an effective strategy by administrators as well by as users.
5. The trend is to digitize everything for storage and manipulation: sound, image, moving images, text, and numeric data. Documents of all kinds

are becoming more homogeneous in their physical medium. Limiting libraries to printed documents, or, indeed, written documents, makes less and less sense. If that demarcation dissolves, there is a blurring of boundaries. The functions of the library, the computer center, and the telecommunications office are converging, overlapping, or, at least, more closely related. New patterns are evolving in the relationships between libraries, publishers, and others in the information industry. The roles of archives, libraries, museums, and other information stores seem likely to become less clearly differentiated.

6. There is much greater opportunity to bring service to wherever potential users of library service happen to be.

Catalogs, collections, buildings, and library staff are the familiar means for providing library services. Computers, networks, and electronic documents provide additional means with interesting possibilities.

Hitherto library services have been dominated by local catalogs, local collections, and great inequalities in the geographical distribution of services. The constraints on library service are changing right now. None of this is a argument for abandoning paper and local collections. All of this requires us to think again about the mission of the library, the role of library, and the means of providing service. For the first time in one hundred years we face the grand and difficult challenge of redesigning library services.

Features of Electronic Library

The term "digital" is used to mean text in which individual letters, numbers, and other characters are each separately coded and the term "digitized" is used to denote an image composed of lots of bits. One could well have a digitized image of a page of text, but in that case none of the individual characters would be coded as characters. The term "Electronic Library" to describe the situation in which documents are stored in electronic form, rather than on paper or other localised media.

In some cases where the characters are regularly formed, it may be feasible to use pattern recognition techniques to identify the individual characters within the digitized image and, thereby, to derive a digital version of the text from a digitized image of the text. A digital record is more economical and, ordinarily, more useful. The adoption of computers for libraries' technical operations, the transition from the Paper Library to the

Automated Library, can be viewed as an evolutionary development. The changes have been, at least until the provision of on-line catalogs, mainly for internal efficiency and for the convenience of library employees. In contrast, the rise of the Electronic Library, in which materials are stored in electronic form, may seem more revolutionary than evolutionary because of the implications for the provision and use of library services. But is it really so radical a change? Where are the impacts on the provision of library service.

Nevertheless, the "full text" of documents in machine-readable form has been generally absent from library services until recently, in contrast with the progress made in making bibliographies, catalogs, and numerical data available in electronic form.

Electronic Documents

The characteristics of electronic documents differ greatly from those of paper documents.

- Electronic documents are not localised. Given telecommunications connections, an electronic document can be used from anywhere, without one even knowing where it is stored geographically.
- In practice several people can use the same database or electronic records at the same time.
- Electronic documents are easily copied.
- Documents stored electronically are very flexible. They are easy to revise, rearrange, reformat, and combine with other documents. Hence the popularity of word-processing among people who have to create and, more especially, revise documents.
- Collections of documents stored in electronic form are now less bulky than paper versions. The trend is to even greater compactness.

In each of these five important characteristics, electronic documents are quite different from paper documents.

There is a steady growth of documents in electronic form and access will necessarily have to be provided to them. Databases are increasingly available in machine-readable form. Publishers commonly have or could have the text of their books in machine readable form even if they may not yet choose to publish them in that form.

The most obvious source of electronic documents is new publications issued in electronic form. But what of the older materials on paper that occupy so many miles of libraries' shelves? Libraries have undertaken a major, systematic effort at the retrospective conversion of older catalog records from cards to electronic records. What of the retrospective conversion of the texts of older paper documents themselves? The idea might seem wildly unrealistic, but there are grounds to believe that, over time, significant and increasing amounts of older material will become available as electronic documents.

In selected areas, notably literature, texts have been converted for research purposes: All classical Greek texts and increasing quantities of medieval and modern literary texts are already available in electronic form. Devices have been available for some years that can scan printed material, derive digital versions, and "read" the text out loud for the blind and visually-impaired. The same approach can be used to convert paper texts into electronic form as an alternative to keying them when an electronic form of the text is needed for word processing purposes. These electronic copies are usually discarded or, at least, are not made systematically available. They could be.

The latest fax technology, using the CCITT class IV standards, involves the transmission of pages of documents by means of digitized images of pages. Interlibrary loans sent by CCITT class IV fax could be stored and, probably, whenever feasible, converted to digital form for ease of use and economy of storage. Technology exists for copying microfilmed materials into electronic, digitized form and, most likely, much of this, once digitized, could be also be converted to digital text. Therefore, it is technically feasible that very substantial amounts of older as well as future library material becoming available in electronic form whether or not librarians engage in retrospective conversion. Storage costs for electronic documents are decreasing steadily, while the building costs for storing paper documents are not.

A document on paper, such as a letter or a book, is unquestionably extremely convenient to use compared with other media such as microfilm or floppy disks, at least for most purposes. Paper were the best medium for documents, it is increasingly clear that there are significant exceptions to this rule. Electronic documents, with or without the generation of paper copies, become preferable:

— When documents are highly volatile: For example it is unwise to depend on printed paper versions of highly changeable material such as airplane schedules, stock prices, and currency exchange rates.

— When manipulation of the document is desired: No one would want to have to transcribe printed numerical data for statistical analysis if the data were already available in electronic form. Similarly, when a text is to be modified, a bibliography revised, or the layout rearranged, the availability of an electronic copy in a standard format for word processing can dramatically reduce the work involved compared with having only a typed or handwritten copy.

— When scanning for names or for particular words or phrases in a lengthy document. Trying to find mention of some thing or person in, say, a multi-volume printed work or a run of periodical is very tedious and error-prone. No one now would want to compile a concordance "by hand" anymore: The first step in concordance making now is the creation of an electronic copy of the text.

— When light use of remote material is needed. For a thorough reading of a document that is not available locally, obtaining a paper copy by interlibrary loan would probably be preferred. If, however, use were light – to check here and there in the document or to skim the document superficially to see whether or not a more careful reading would be warranted – rapid access by telecommunications to an electronic copy could be attractive.

— When rapid communication is desired, especially within a dispersed group that is not conveniently available at the same time and place, the use of electronic mail has considerable advantages over ordinary mail and, for some purposes, over telephone.

Note that these examples do not include the usual notion of solid, systematic, consecutive reading. They could be regarded as exceptional cases around the fringes of "normal" use of documents, but in some circumstances, as when geographically separated quantitative researchers collaborate, these exceptions could add up to substantial amounts of activity and a significant proportion of total use. Electronic documents add new possibilities for the use of texts and, in this regard, constitute an enhancement that is valuable in its own right.

Reinventing the Library

There is little choice but to do the same as we do with a paper document or with microfilm document:

— Catalog it and, as with manuscripts, pay careful attention to which version or state of text it is.

— Store it in some accessible place.

— Give it a call number.

— Ensure that pertinent bibliographic and location data are accessible in or through bibliographic databases.

Given that electronic documents exist and are becoming progressively more important, to ignore them would be to provide a progressively less complete library service. A library administration might choose to retain an exclusive concentration on paper, microfilm, and other localised media, but that would mean that access to electronic documents would have to be found through other channels, such as the computer center. The result would be a split in the provision of library service: the "library" providing access to only some kinds of documents; and another organisation providing the balance of the library service—that which involves access to electronic documents.

The significant difference with an electronic document is that if you have the call number it should in principle be possible, from any workstation, to gain access to it remotely, view it, download it, and, in brief, "use" it. Think how much simpler and quicker it would be if librarians and, even better, library users could obtain their own interlibrary "loans" on a self-service basis, requiring the tolerance but not the time or energy of the staff of the library from which it is obtained.

This change would be rather like the change from having closed library stacks, in which library employees had to fetch each book for users, to open stacks in which library users could obtain and examine books by themselves. Similarly, in the Electronic Library, library staff would be mainly concerned with creating and sustaining the system so that users could serve themselves.

Self-service, however, is a mixed blessing. It also assumes standardised, intelligible procedures, presupposes some expertise on the users' part, and may make it less easy for the service providers to know what is going well and what is not going well. Yet it may be the only affordable way to support large-scale library use.

The advent of text in electronic form, the step from the Automated Library to the Electronic Library, has two profound consequences for bibliographic access and catalog design. First, card catalogs are, necessarily, physically separate from the physical (paper) documents that they describe. Given the technology of paper and of cardboard, it could not be otherwise.

Further, use of the documents involves physical handling, often borrowing. However, to the extent that both catalog and text are in machine-readable form, both would be remotely accessed from the same workstation and the former physical separation between catalog and text becomes unnecessary—or, at least, transparent and irrelevant to the library user, who should be able to move effortlessly between catalog and text. The catalog might be searched and one or more catalog records retrieved. Then the user might want to examine the contents of a book. A book on paper is more than a mere string of characters since there is an extensive internal structure of references: from the table of contents to chapters and sometimes sections within chapters; form the index entries to numerous points in the text; and, often, internally from one part of the text to another.

In an on-line world the user could move to the table of contents by depressing a key, then on to examine a chapter. Next the user might want to look for specific terms or names in the index, on-line, then move to specific patches of text, again on-line. Since the text is on-line one could expect a concordance providing access to all of the text. The user might abandon that text, follow up a reference to another text, go back to the catalog records to look for another book, or scan the subject headings with a view to reformulating the search.

There would be a continual changing, "zooming in" and out between a broad view and focus on details. It is not that the familiar data elements of the catalog record will have disappeared or that the identifying and locating functions are any less important, but rather that the catalog will effectively have disappeared as a recognisably separate, physical entity. Instead, the catalog data would be part of a much broader set of data elements and the catalog function would have become one feature in a suite of related functions in on-line library use.

The second consequence for bibliographic access and catalog design in an Electronic Library is that the traditional justification for having a catalog begins to disappear. Historically a library catalog was a guide to local holdings. Yet for a library user what matters is convenient access to texts. With documents on paper, what is locally owned is what is conveniently accessible.

In practice at least in university libraries, users typically cannot find 40 percent of locally owned material on the shelves when they seek it. However, with convenient telecommunications, the physical location of an electronic text is substantially irrelevant. Databases at a distance could be more reliably accessible than paper documents owned by one's local library. What is needed, then, is a bibliography, or union catalog, of what is conveniently accessible rather than the much narrower concept of a catalog of what happens to be locally stored.

Three elements--documents, bibliography, and holdings records--remain the needed elements: Documents becoming available in electronic form will need to be stored somewhere; bibliographies will continue to be published; libraries, as documents stores, have to have their copy-specific inventory and status records.

In the Paper Library and in the Automated Library, conveniently accessible meant, for practical, physical reasons, "locally held." Given some major assumptions about telecommunications and adherence to standards, the close coupling of "conveniently accessible" and "locally held" begins to dissolve with the Electronic Library. Because electronic documents are remotely accessible, it does not matter much to the library user where the documents are located — any more than it matters much to the user of an automated library where the disk drives of the on-line catalog are located.

There are economic, engineering, and security considerations concerning the storage of electronic records but these are technical matters for those who provide the service and of limited concern to the library user. In brief, in the Electronic Library "conveniently accessible" ceases to mean locally held. It becomes as foolish to want to limit library users to locally held documents in the Electronic Library as it would be to want to limit cataloging in the Paper Library to documents published in even years.

To the extent that texts become available in electronic form, the whole view of library collections changes. The location and ownership of copies of texts becomes a technical detail for librarians but irrelevant to the reader: What counts is what is conveniently accessible. Given modern telecommunications, any attempt to restrict users' attention to locally stored electronic documents would be a travesty of long-established traditions of library service.

Architecture of Electronic Library

What would it take to build an Electronic Library and, indeed, to make Electronic Library service common practice?. With electronic documents, even more than with microforms, adherence to standards is important for progress.

Electronic documents should themselves be in standard formats. Standards are needed for cataloging electronic documents. Communications formats are needed for conveying electronic documents. Substantial and compatible telecommunications protocols are of great importance. Much work needs to be done in developing and adopting compatible national and international standards for characters, images, documents, telecommunications, and so on.

Also, of course, the concept of an Electronic Library assumes a substantial and expensive infrastructure of computing capacity, data storage, and telecommunications, which in turn, requires expertise for successful use. These investments are being made anyway in some of the contexts in which library services are being provided.

Although the growth in electronic documents can be expected to be dramatic, the proportion of documents that are available in electronic form will vary greatly from one situation to another. Further, for some purposes paper documents are preferable. Not all documents will be available in electronic form. Paper documents are unlikely to disappear and it is undesirable that they should. So discussion of the Paper Library versus the Electronic Library is likely to be of limited benefit. Just a few basic issues are important for planning:

— Electronic documents are becoming increasingly important and arrangements to provide access to them – the Electronic Library – must be developed and is best viewed as additive. The world is changing and this additional form of library service appears to be not only desirable for library users but also inevitable.

— Library services from now on will have to provide access to paper documents and to electronic documents according to their users' needs. In other words, library planning should be based on the assumption that all libraries will evolve into some combination of an Automated Library and an Electronic Library. The balance between paper documents and electronic documents can be expected to vary widely between libraries and over time. What the balance is at any given place and time matters far less than ensuring that libraries are equipped to provide access to both kinds of document.

— The difference between the Electronic Library and the Automated Library is in the technology of the documents, not in the bibliographic access. Bibliographic records need to include information indicating the physical properties of each document, (e.g. paper, microform, electronic, optical), but a unified bibliographic approach for all documents is most likely to be helpful. The bibliographic apparatus and internal procedures of the Automated Library would not need to change much for the shift from Automated Library to the Electronic Library. (Figure 2.)

— The view of the Electronic Library as an addition to the Automated Library needs to be modified in two ways.

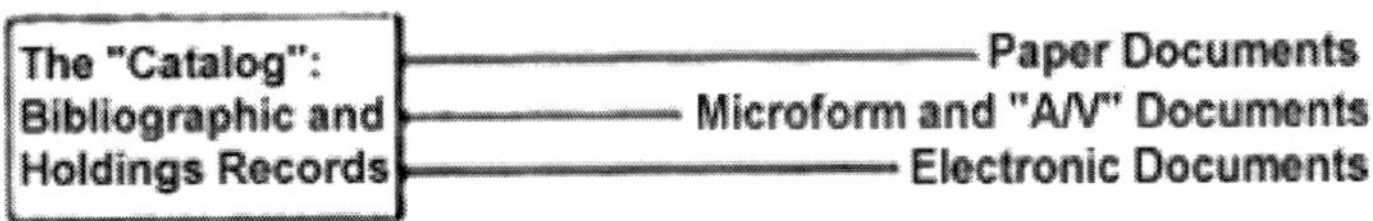

Figure 2. Common bibliographic approach

First, purely additive funding should not be assumed. Even though a plausible argument could be made that, in any given case, funding is insufficient to support the Automated Library, nevertheless it is to be expected that service priorities will increasingly lead to a reallocation of total library resources from the Automated Library to the combination of Automated and Electronic Library.

In this sense the Electronic Library may well be additive since it is a new form of service, but in its claim to resources, subtractive from the Automated Library. It should be a matter of very careful deliberation and consultation to determine when and to what extent, in any given situation, library service should change from only being an Automated Library to being a combination of Automated and Electronic Library service.

Second, in practice there will be some acceptable scope for the substitution of electronic for paper documents, of the Electronic Library for Automated Library. At some point of adequacy and reliability in on-line catalog service, it becomes reasonable to abandon the card catalog with its high maintenance costs.

At some point, in at least some cases, subscription to printed bibliographies cease to be justified when on-line versions can be searched conveniently. In the same way, it is reasonable to expect that in some circumstances where there is a choice, access to electronic documents will be preferred to use of paper documents even when the paper version is conveniently available.

Redesigning Library Services

The elements of the probable form of the electronic library of the twenty-first century were being glimpsed, albeit imperfectly, by the early 1930s by perceptive thinkers. More recently visions of the library of the future have been associated with speculation on the demise of the book, the supposed obsolescence of librarians, and other questionable rhetoric. Discussion of providing "access" to "information" is commonly incomplete or misleading.

The good news is that additional, different means for providing library service are becoming available in a manner unprecedented since the nineteenth century. The challenge for all concerned with libraries, is to determine how, whether, and when these new means should be used. Libraries exist for the benefit of the mind, but they have serious practical problems coping with the acquisition, storage and handling of the documents and records with which they deal.

Major constraints arise from the technology used as a means for providing service. Any change in technology that would have a significant effect on the methods available for acquisition, storage, delivery, or searching procedures could have important consequences for library service. Consequently a continuing quest for technological improvement has been and should continue to be important. Those responsible for providing library service have been more or less conscious of the nature of the underlying problems to be solved and some of the more gifted and farsighted groped towards radical solutions based on a deep understanding of the nature of the problems.

The term "information" is used with very differing meanings and is commonly used attributively to refer to books, journals, databases, and other physical objects regarded as potentially informative. Access to a potentially informative document depends on identifying, locating, and having affordable physical access to it. However, for someone to become informed, to become more knowledgeable, requires more: The reader needs to be able to understand and evaluate what is in it. If what is found is rejected or not understood, then little informing will have been achieved. Much has been written in recent years on the possible impact of new technology on "the library of the future." This is nothing new. It could be that long term visions have a beneficial effect in stimulating debate and thought. However one may suspect that little of the rhetoric and few of the specific technological proposals have been of much direct help to those with the heavy responsibility of planning for the future of any particular library: the administrators, funders, librarians, and library users developing five or ten year plans, contemplating the high cost of a major new library building, or worrying about the relationship between the familiar technology of paper and the less familiar, unstable technology of computers. The problems of existing libraries are severe.

Visions of electronic libraries seem uncertain and suspect. Even if such a vision seems good, it is not at all clear that plausible paths of development from here to there have been adequately mapped. Redesigning library services has been written on three assumptions:

— There has been insufficient attention to strategic planning, that is, the making of decisions relative to a three to ten year time frame. Researchers seek to examine the middle ground between the large literature on possible options among the tactical and operational decisions made day-to-day and month-by-month and the sweeping visions of endless, interlinked electronic villages. The latter offer little continuity with present experience and can make those who are dependent on existing services understandably nervous. Some people are enthusiasts for electronic solutions; other want to avoid the high cost of continuing present operations.

— A disproportionate amount of attention has been paid to new information technology. It is not really that too much attention has been given to it, but rather that not enough critical attention has been given to the characteristics of the familiar technology of paper. What is familiar tends to be transparent. It may take some conscious effort to appraise critically and evaluatively. They are so accustomed to.

— There is, in fact, considerable experience on which our strategic planning can be based, more than is generally realised.

The purpose being pursued in library service is the provision of access to books, journals, and other informative materials.

Libraries have never had a monopoly since much of what is in demand is also available in personal collections, bookshops, from personal contacts, and, indeed, from other sorts of libraries. However, even if it is not a monopoly, it is clearly the major role and niche of library service. Now, in addition to the customary difficulties in providing library service, the radical changes in the technology available as means for providing service leaves the future unclear.

In such a situation need to be prepared to retreat to first principles. Library service is a busy, service-oriented activity, with a deeply-rooted emphasis, reflected in the professional literature, on practical and technical matters, on means, rather than on ends, and tactics rather than strategy. There is so much more written, for example, on how to build collections than on the roles that collections play. There is so much more on how to create catalogs than on how catalogs are used. Nevertheless, there is currently a healthy awareness that major changes are likely and a recognition, for example, of some convergence between library services, computing services, and telecommunications services, of probable changes in the publishing world, and that library management is, at least in part, concerned as much with the management of service as with the management of books.

References

Duranceau, E., "Beyond print: revisioning serials acquisitions for the digital age", in W. Jones (ed.) *E-Serials: Publishers, Libraries, Users and Standards*, The Haworth Press, 1998.

Hildreth, Charles, *On-line public access catalogue: the user interface*, Dublin, Ohio, On-line Computer Library Centre, 1982.

Howard, S., 1997, Trade-off decision making in user interface design." *Behaviour and Information Technology* 16, 1997: 98-109.

Hulser, Richard P., Digital Library: Condent Preservation in a Digital World, *DESIDOC Bulletin of Information Technology*, 17 (6), 1997.

International Federation of Library Associations and Institutions (IFLA), *Position paper on copyright in the electronic environment*, October 1996.

7

Digital Library, Origin, Resources and Preservation

Origin of Digital Library

The term "digital library" is simply the most recent in a long series of names for a concept that was written about long before the development of the first computer. The idea of a "computerized library" that would supplement, add functionality, and even replace traditional libraries was invented first by H.G. Wells and other authors, who caught the imagination of millions with speculative writings about "world brains" and similar fanciful devices.

There is general agreement that much of the early actual application of computers to information retrieval was stimulated by the prominent scientist Vannevar Bush, who wrote about the "memex," a mechanical device based on microfilm technology that anticipated the ideas of both hypertext and personal information retrieval systems. The first real-world applications of computers to libraries began in the early 1950s with IBM and punched card applications to library technical services operations, and with the development of the MARC (machine-readable cataloging) standard for digitizing and communicating library catalog information.

In 1965, J. C. R. Licklider coined the phrase "library of the future" to refer to his vision of a fully computer-based library, and ten years later, F.W. Lancaster wrote of the soon-to-come "paperless library." About the same time Ted Nelson invented and named hypertext and hyperspace. He also analyzed some of the problems to be identified later in this paper in some detail, but never built an operational system. Many other terms have been coined to refer to the concept of a digitized library, including "electronic library," "virtual library," "library without walls," "bionic library," and others.

The relatively recent use of the term "digital library" can be traced to the Digital Libraries Initiative funded by the National Science Foundation, the Advanced Research Projects Agency, and the National Aeronautics and Space Administration in the United States. In 1994 these agencies granted 24.4 million dollars to six U.S. universities for digital library research, impelled by the sudden explosive growth of the Internet and the development of graphical Web browsers. The term was quickly adopted by computer scientists, librarians, and others. Thus, while the term "digital library" is relatively new, work in bringing digitized information resources to libraries has a history spanning several decades.

The most inclusive view takes a digital library to be, as its starting point, essentially what the Internet is today. But from this extreme perspective it can be seen that the metaphor of the traditional library fails in several respects. A digital library contains digital representations of the objects found in it. Most understandings of "digital library" probably also assume that it will be accessible via the Internet, though not necessarily to everyone. But the idea of digitization is perhaps the only characteristic of a digital library on which there is universal agreement.

A digital library may be organized and represented in the form of object surrogates created by human specialists or it may be entirely unorganized, with no "added value" whatever, using free text searching of the objects themselves — rather than object surrogates — to gain access to the objects in the library. The digital coherence of the objects, the near elimination of distance or physical location as an important consideration, and the existing computer and communications infrastructure will give rise to a myriad new possibilities for enriching and redefining what we think of as a library. But there may be a tradeoff. We may be asked to give up some important properties to gain new ones.

The traditional research library has a physical location, embodied in its physical building. Most of the objects in the library are information resources of some kind. The works are also selected. Criteria for the selection process are defined, and these criteria typically include measures of quality.

The objects (information sources) in it are organized — classified, catalogued, and indexed by human beings, in what are called value-added processes. Authority control is a key feature, in which names of authors, variants of works (editions), and subject headings or descriptors are all controlled.

The concept of authorship and ownership are extremely important in a traditional research library, in which various forms of an author's name are brought together in a name authority file. Surrogates of the objects in the library — called index records, or in digital library terminology, metadata — are created for purposes of representing the value added by catalogers and indexers. Data are recorded in dozens of specific fields and subfields of these records, and are "finely searchable." That is, highly specific searches can be conducted on particular combinations of fields or subfields of the index records. Retrieved records are linked to the objects themselves, which can then be obtained and used. The treatment of authorship and ownership in the traditional research library reflects the importance of these ideas in traditional scholarly communication, in which scholars and scientists cite in reference lists the authors and works from whom they have borrowed ideas, words, or facts, thus paying intellectual debts and acknowledging original authorship.

Ownership of intellectual property is central to publishing and scholarship. Plagiarism — stealing the words of others without attribution — is considered unethical in scholarly writing and science. Formal legal rights of ownership are also defined by national and international copyright law. The objects in a traditional research library have certain properties as well. First, they are fixed — they do not normally change, or if they do, various editions are identified and considered to be different from one another. Objects are also permanent — they do not normally disappear from a collection. A variety of services to users are offered by librarians who work in the traditional library.

These include assistance with searching for information resources, reference and research services, readers advisory services, and others. A traditional research library typically offers only limited access to materials and services; access to certain services may be restricted to certain classes of potential users. Use of basic services in many traditional research libraries is free for defined user populations. Some of these libraries are large, tax-supported research institutions.

There are many definitions, ranging from the electronic catalog that describes physical items in a "brick and mortar" library to advanced multimedia environments housing all-digital collections. H. Thomas Hickerson, Cornell University's Associate University Librarian for Information Technologies & Special Collections, believes it is time to erase the line between physical and digital libraries. "A major portion of library activities are technology-supported and have been for years. The Internet has had an incredible impact, but libraries have a history of managing large systems and using technology to deliver bibliographic information," Hickerson says.

Sun Microsystems defines a digital library as the electronic extension of functions users typically perform and the resources they access in a traditional library. These information resources can be translated into digital form, stored in multimedia repositories, and made available through Web-based services. The emergence of the digital library mirrors the growth of e-learning (or distance learning) as the virtual alternative to traditional school attendance.

As the student population increasingly turns to off-campus alternatives for lifelong learning, the library must evolve to fit this new educational paradigm or become obsolete as students search for other ways to conveniently locate information resources anywhere, any time.

Digital libraries began to appear on the campus in the early 1990s as research and development projects centered within computer science departments, sometimes funded by government grants. Campus librarians were often uninvolved in these early projects, which focused on digitization technology, metadata schemes, data management techniques, and digital preservation. Dan Greenstein, former director of the Digital Library Federation and now head of the California Digital Library, characterizes this experimental period as the "second-generation digital library," exploring new opportunities and developing new competencies.

With this new knowledge in hand, Greenstein suggests that the third-generation digital library abandoned this experimentation and the "build it and they will come" philosophy that characterized early digital collections, focusing instead on fully integrating digital material into the library's collections through a modular systems architecture. "This modular approach is fundamentally liberating since it permits libraries to think creatively about how to build upon services supplied by others." As these projects matured and led the way toward more practical digital library implementations, the library began to take a more central role.

Digital library use shifted to a large and diverse campus audience, and information technology (IT) groups began to partner with the library to develop campus-wide standards for the deployment and operation of digital libraries as an integral part of the education enterprise. This development paralleled the development of heightened student requirements for access to library resources. With the advent of the Internet, individuals' expectations for access to information have increased dramatically.

It is no longer considered practical or acceptable to travel to a specific location during certain hours to locate needed information. Library patrons are not satisfied to locate an item of interest that is housed at yet another physical location, request the item, and then wait days or weeks for the item to arrive at the building where it was requested. Patrons increasingly expect instant access to all the information resources they require, from any location, at any time, and from any device. This is the objective that the digital library is fulfilling. With digital libraries, an individual can:

— Gain access to the holdings of libraries worldwide through automated catalogs.

— Locate both physical and digitized versions of scholarly articles and books.

— Optimize searches, simultaneously search the Internet, commercial databases, and library collections.

— Save search results and conduct additional processing to narrow or qualify results.

— From search results, click through to access the digitized content or locate additional items of interest.

All of these capabilities are available from the desktop or other Web-enabled device such as a personal digital assistant or cellular telephone. Additionally, the user can customize his or her information request so that search results reflect individual needs and preferences. Sun considers personalization the next killer application, creating a more valuable and richer user experience in the digital library environment.

These components might not all be part of a discrete digital library system, but could be provided by other related or multi-purpose systems or environments. Accordingly, integration is a consistent issue cited by digital library developers. To interoperate with the existing library infrastructure, the digital library must be designed to work with existing library catalogs and incorporate industry standards, formats, and protocols.

The term "digital library" is often used to describe any multimedia management system holding digitized information, but this does not mean it will deliver true library application functionality. Thus, these digital library components must also be tailored to capture, encode, and deliver information according to the standard practices adopted by the library industry. Because of the rapid pace of technological change, some standards are concrete and others are emerging.

Throughout the world, libraries, museums and archives are digitizing the important documents and images of our culture, both to preserve them for future generations and to make them more accessible to our own. As digital imaging technology has advanced, so have opportunities for preservation of irreplaceable artifacts. Today, students, researchers, information professionals, and the general public can directly access many of the world's rarest artifacts-from high-quality images of each page of the Gutenberg Bible to a digital likeness of the Mona Lisa-right at the desktop or other Web-enabled device, at any time and from any location. Audio recordings of historic speeches or exotic birdcalls, video clippings from televised news programs, geospacial data, and more are being delivered directly to the desks of students and researchers.

Through the 1990s, digital library projects were largely experimental activities. Digital library techniques came about through research sponsored by the U.S. National Science Foundation (NSF) and the U.K. Joint Information Systems Committee (JISC). In 1999 these projects began expanding internationally when NSF linked its digital library research program with similar activities being undertaken by JISC, resulting in the JISC-NSF International Digital Library Initiative. The objectives of this three-year program were to:

— Assemble collections of information that were not otherwise accessible or usable because of technical barriers, distance, size, system fragmentation, or other limits.

— Create new technology and the understanding to make it possible for a distributed set of users to find, deliver, and exploit such information.

Evaluate the impact of this new technology and its international benefits. through research sponsored by the U.S. National Science Foundation (NSF) and the U.K. Joint Information Systems Committee (JISC). In 1999 these projects began expanding internationally when NSF linked its digital library research program with similar activities being undertaken by JISC, resulting in the JISC-NSF International Digital Library Initiative. The objectives of this three-year program were to:

- Assemble collections of information that were not otherwise accessible or usable because of technical barriers, distance, size, system fragmentation, or other limits.
- Create new technology and the understanding to make it possible for a distributed set of users to find, deliver, and exploit such information.
- Evaluate the impact of this new technology and its international benefits.

Development of Digital Libraries

The development of digital libraries must be considered in the overall context of initiatives to unify the IT structures of the campus and to transform the learning process through innovative technology. Economic, social, and cultural pressures are forcing schools and universities to reinvent themselves. As in the business process re-engineering activities of the last decade that transformed corporate enterprises, education organizations are now viewing themselves in a new light.

New types of students and changing student expectations are driving the integration of core campus functions and deployment of student services on the Web. Fragmented, monolithic approaches are falling away as educators realize the need to link learning and administrative resources in a more effective way to become a "knowledge enterprise," the 21st century version of the traditional campus. During the past decade steep declines in the cost of commodity components, combined with the availability of high bandwidth networks, have made sophisticated IT applications for education affordable.

A mix of sophisticated digital and Internet-based services and rapidly expanding global digital content have made possible a "virtual learning environment" (VLE) that delivers the capability to enhance the classroom experience or conduct learning apart from a physical campus. The digital library is a core component of this VLE. "These developments are extending the role of the library, and changing the relationships between the library and other parts of the academic enterprise," according to Clifford Lynch, Director of the Coalition for Networked Resources and a noted authority on digital libraries.

The NSF in the United States has joined with the JISC in the United Kingdom to sponsor a major research program called "Digital Libraries and the Classroom: Testbeds for Transforming Teaching and Learning." This program will promote the use of large-scale, distributed digital content and advanced networking technologies for learning. Running from 2002 to 2007, the sponsored projects are expected to demonstrate how integrating recent technical developments with digital content improves the learning experience of students and provides new models for classroom instruction.

Descriptive metadata

This metadata provides information that a) allows discovery of collections or objects through the use of search tools, and b) provides sufficient context for understanding what has been found. When collections become large or when searching multiple collections (such as over the Internet) the discovery of objects of interest becomes a "needle in a haystack" exercise.Without agreed-upon metadata standards and the discipline of capturing and storing appropriate descriptive metadata, all but the smallest digital collections would be useless.

Metadata for individual objects varies by the type of object, but would include such things as its title, what it is, who created it, contributors, language, when it was created, where it is located, the subject, etc. At the collection level, users should be able to determine the scope, ownership, any access restrictions, and other important characteristics that would assist in understanding the collection. Probably the best-known descriptive metadata standard for libraries is MARC (MAchine-Readable Catalog) used for cataloging books and other publications.

MARC has served the traditional library well, but was not designed for describing images, sound files, and other new media types. An important emerging descriptive metadata standard for images and other multimedia objects is Dublin Core, a group of 15 items of information designed to be simple to understand and use. Dublin Core was designed to provide a very widely accepted mechanism to allow discovery, but with the option for different communities of users to adapt and customize it by adding more fields of particular importance to the community. In this way, the same base standard can be used for a wide variety of purposes and business models.

Structural metadata

The second type of metadata is structural metadata. This describes the associations within or among related individual information objects. A book, which consists of pages and chapters, is one of the most straightforward examples of structural metadata. The structural metadata would explain how individual page images make up individual chapters, and how chapters make up the book. There could also be individually imaged figures, and structural metadata could also relate these to chapters or to a list of all figures in the book. Structural metadata aids the user in navigating among individual objects that comprise a compound object.

Administrative metadata

Administrative metadata facilitates access,management, and preservation of the digital resource. It can describe the viewer or player necessary to access the object, automatically opening that viewer or player when a user selects that resource. It can describe attributes such as image resolution, file size, or audio sampling rate. It can provide a record of how and when an object was created as well as archival and rights management information.

An important emerging standard for interoperability of digital collections is the Metadata Encoding and Transmission Standard (METS), which provides a uniform framework for managing and transmitting digital objects. The Making of America II project (MOA2) developed an encoding format for descriptive, administrative, and structural metadata for textual and image-based works. Supported by the Digital Library Federation and the Library of Congress, METS builds upon the work of MOA2.

It provides a format for encoding metadata necessary for both management of digital library objects within a repository and exchange of such objects between repositories (or between repositories and their users). Leading academic and research libraries are citing METS as an important standard for digital library interoperability, and seem to be rallying behind this standard.

As libraries increasingly focus on building gateways that direct patrons both to the library's own content and to networked digital resources owned or controlled by other entities, rights management becomes a major concern. “In constructing a digital library service environment, the library becomes responsible for configuring access to a world of information of which it owns or manages only a part,” says the California Digital Library’s Dan Greenstein. “Accordingly, the digital library is known less for the extent and nature of the collections it owns than for the networked information space it defines through a range of online services.”

In this type of cooperative resourcesharing environment, mechanisms for identifying information users and their access privileges are essential. With increased use of the Internet to buy, sell, or license the use of documents, images, video, and other copyrighted content in digital form, comes the need to protect that content from unauthorized use once it is outside the control of the publisher or distributor.

Digital content is very easy to copy and disseminate with little or no loss of quality. Accordingly, the ability to positively identify library patrons and their associated access privileges is required to assure that materials are being accessed and used by the appropriate parties. From a more practical perspective, it is also useful to integrate these identification and authorization mechanisms with other campus requirements, providing an environment where individuals can use a common facility for a “single signon” identification process shared with other campus computing applications.

Ideally, a common authentication/authorization process would be capable of positively identifying any computer user, linking that user to groups of other users with similar access requirements, and passing the user’s identity and access profile to all campus computing applications that require such intelligence. A student enrolled in a particular class should be able to seamlessly access reserve materials in digital form (held in the digital library system) as well as online course materials available through the curriculum management system, the student’s enrollment in the course being verifiable through the course registration system.

Libraries place high value on preserving the irreplaceable contents of their collections, making the historical and cultural artifacts of our civilization available for future generations. Stanford University’s Michael Keller comments, “Libraries are communications devices from preceding generations to succeeding generations. Preservation of scholarly publications are tremendously important.” Fire prevention systems, environmental controls, and microfilming initiatives guard against catastrophic loss of irreplaceable items. Even the move from acid to alkaline paper in publishing has worked for long-term retention of printed items.

In 1991, the American Library Association published a preservation policy outlining the responsibilities of the library profession for preserving access to information of all forms. In 2001, that policy was updated to reflect changes brought about by the Internet. The preamble of the revised policy states: "Librarians must be committed to preserving their collections through appropriate and non-damaging storage, remedial treatment of damaged and fragile items, preservation of materials in their original format when possible, replacement or reformatting of deteriorated materials, appropriate security measures, and life-cycle management of digital publications to assure their usefulness for future generations."

With digitized resources, it would seem that preservation would be much easier to achieve, especially since an unlimited number of copies can be created of the individual object. There are, however, a number of issues that complicate the maintenance of digital objects over long periods of time:

— *Deterioration of media*: Stone tablets have a considerable advantage over today's digital media for long-term storage. The problem of deterioration limits the useful life of today's digital media to between 5 and 50 years, while librarians debate how to retain the artifacts of our civilization for thousands of years to come.

— *Evolution in type and format of media*: In addition to the concerns of physical deterioration of media, we must be aware of the challenges posed by changes in media type and format. In the relatively recent history of personal computer use, we have seen an evolution from 5-1/4" floppy disks to higher density 3-1/2" diskettes to high-density zip disks, all requiring different physical disk drives and reader software. Optical storage technology is next, and there will undoubtedly be continual change in storage technologies.

— *Changes in applications and operating systems*: New software constantly appears on the horizon, rendering older versions obsolete. The hardware required by applications and operating systems software also changes over time. Any information stored in a given software/ hardware environment will eventually be rendered obsolete through technological obsolescence, most likely before deterioration of the actual storage media occurs. Today, locating a system capable of reading 20-year-old Visicalc spreadsheet files or Multimate word processing files is a difficult proposition; in 50 years' time it will likely be impossible.

— *Preservation of processing results*: Some digital resources exist only fleetingly as a program runs and cannot be preserved as static objects. Preservation of such resources requires maintenance of the program and the surrounding operating environment in operable form. Of course, not all digital resources have the same preservation requirements. "We are more concerned about persistence and authenticity of the collection of images than the long-term preservation of the surrogate," explains David Bearman, director of the Art Museum Image Consortium (AMICO). "Museums are in the business of pre-serving the real thing." The skill set of the archivist, establishing criteria for selection of content to be preserved, will become even more essential as the amount of digital content expands.

Today, most digital libraries follow a schedule of copying archived digital resources to address the issue of media deterioration. As organizational standards for formats and applications evolve,many libraries also convert the objects over time to maintain readability. Specific preservation policies and best practices, however, are not well developed. The Research Libraries Group (RLG) is an international member alliance, including universities and colleges, national libraries, archives, historical societies, museums and independent research collections, and public libraries dedicated to "improving access to information that supports research and learning."

The National Library of Australia sponsors an initiative called "Preserving Access to Digital Information" (PADI) with the goal of providing mechanisms that help ensure that digital information is managed with appropriate consideration for preservation and future access. PADI recommends these strategies for long-term preservation of digital collections:

1. The migration of digital information from one hardware/software configuration to another or from one generation of computer technology to a later one offers one method of dealing with technological obsolescence.

2. Adherence to standards will assist in preserving access to digital information.

3. Technology emulation potentially offers substantial benefits in preserving the functionality and integrity of digital objects.

4. Encapsulation, a technique of grouping together a digital object and anything else necessary to provide access to that object, has been proposed by a number of researchers as a useful strategy in conjunction with other digital preservation methods.
5. It is universally agreed that documentation is an important tool to assist in preserving digital material. In addition to the metadata necessary for resource discovery, other sorts of metadata, including preservation metadata, describing the software, hardware and management requirements of the digital material, will provide essential information for preservation.

Deployment of portal technology has occurred side-by-side with digital collection development and access. As libraries create, license, or negotiate access to more and more digital content, the need for an easy-to-use interface becomes increasingly important. Library portals typically include an online catalog of materials as well as gateways to collections of digital resources accessible to the user.

Broadcast search tools allow library users to search all of these sources simultaneously with a single query. Portals may include electronic reference services ("ask a librarian"), personalization features ("my bookshelf," custom intelligent searches), and other research tools. Enriched content, such as author biographies and book reviews, tables of contents, and jacket images can be provided to supplement the online catalog. Some libraries have built interactive features into their portals, allowing development of virtual communities.

The resulting nonprofit organization, the Art Museum Image Consortium (AMICO) now includes more than 35 major museums in the United States, Canada, and the UK. As the museums grew their digital collections and usage increased, they found that the task of dealing with requests by students and faculty took increasing amounts of time. AMICO provides a more efficient means of dealing with the work of rights management and access by clearing a licensed set of rights and delivering access to the consolidated collections through a variety of distribution mechanisms.

More than three million AMICO Library subscribers access not only the images, but also find detailed provenance information, curatorial text, multiple views, and other related multimedia for many of the works. AMICO maintains the half-terabyte master repository in a custom-developed relational database that is growing by 20,000 works per year. Current challenges include expanding the multilingual capabilities of the user interface to encourage more internationalization of membership and use, as well as encouraging the inclusion of more multimedia items in the collection. Clearing digital rights for works sought for inclusion in the AMICO Library also remains a continuing challenge.

The University of California at Berkeley has been in the forefront of digital library innovation for many years. Projects begun at Berkeley included the creation of specifications for encoding electronic finding aids that are used to access special collections and archives. These specifications later evolved into the XML-based Encoded Archival Description (EAD). Current work involves development of a modular object management environment, called GenDL (for "Generic Digital Library"). GenDL includes three components that can be thought of as three separate systems:

— The Web-based content management system, where creation and maintenance of the digital content is controlled. Descriptive, administrative, and structural metadata is created and linked to digitized or born-digital content. The resulting digital library objects are then encoded to the METS standard.

— The preservation repository (a joint project with the California Digital Library), where the digital content is managed to ensure its integrity and longevity.

— The access system, which is used to discover, display, and navigate objects that may have complex internal organizations (i.e., structural metadata).

Having undertaken one of the world's most aggressive digitization programs, Cornell library has been a developer of best practices and a leader in the field of digital libraries. As a Sun Center of Excellence for Digital Libraries, Cornell has served as a co-developer with Endeavor Information Systems for the product "ENCompass," a specially tailored multimedia management system intended for library implementations. Although Cornell has gained international recognition for its computer science advances in digital library technology, this university also recognizes the value of off-the-shelf products.

Cornell has attained recognition for the substantial digital collections it has developed. One of the best known is the "Making of America" collection, a multi-institutional digitization initiative making available primary sources of 19th century American culture and history, including popular magazines like Harper's, Atlantic Monthly, and Scientific American. To date, more than 900,000 pages, which are full-text searchable and freely accessible over the Internet, are in the collection.More than 40 other digital collections have been established, ranging from audio recordings of rare birdcalls to digital facsimiles of essential works in the literature of witchcraft and demonology, drawn from Cornell University's Rare Book Collection.

There are several strategic digital library priorities. One is to establish a central repository for all information resources deemed worthy of long-term maintenance. The repository's aim is to support the total lifecycle of those materials. Harvard University has a very large and decentralized library system including more than 100 libraries and 35 major research collections. There is no hierarchy tying these libraries into a single organizational group.

Harvard's digital library activities are designed to provide a common technology infrastructure, consulting assistance, and guidance on policy issues to all of the Harvard libraries. Unlike many universities, Harvard has established major funding to support the development of a comprehensive infrastructure for digital libraries. The $12 million, 5-year program is called the "Library Digital Initiative," deliberately emphasizing the library orientation of the program. The goal of centrally funding this initiative to serve the decentralized network of libraries is to create incentive for participation in a common, standardized solution featuring a robust production IT environment and common practices for digitizing, reformatting, metadata creation, digital licensing, preservation, and migration of objects, etc.

The central Oracle repository supports all types of multimedia objects and a set of catalogs. A portal sits over the catalogs, allowing cross-catalog searching. Although born digital information is at the heart of the program, a program of internal grants has also been established to foster additions to the collection. It is expected that there will be a lot of activity devoted to the interface with learning systems in the future. There will also be increased emphasis on scholarly communication and the libraries' role in capturing the university's intellectual output.

The problems associated with storing back issues of printed journals and locating articles of interest in those back issues led to the creation of JSTOR, an electronic archive of scholarly journals. JSTOR began as a pilot project sponsored by the Andrew W. Mellon Foundation in 1990. Ten journals in economics and history were selected initially, and all back issues were digitized. High-resolution images of each page were captured and linked to a text file generated with optical character recognition software. Table of contents indices were developed as well, to provide search and retrieval of journal content of interest. When five test libraries showed enthusiasm about the space savings and ease of access, JSTOR was born.

In 1995 JSTOR was established as an independent non-profit organization with the goals of providing a trustworthy archive of important scholarly journals, reducing the cost of accessing these materials, and assuring their long-term preservation. JSTOR now provides 1,100 user institutions worldwide access to 169 journals. Originally written in Perl, the Web interface has been ported to Java. Java's object-oriented approach makes it easier for JSTOR's geographically distributed developers to quickly write small pieces of reusable code. More than five million requests per month are satisfied through three sites at Princeton, the University of Michigan, and the University of Manchester.

The entire JSTOR archive requires 2.2 terabytes of storage for more than eight million pages of journal content. Usage has been growing at a rate of 50% per year, with rapid growth among international users. There is also increasing emphasis on allowing access to the JSTOR archive by secondary schools and public libraries. The University of Maryland has opportunistically grown its unique digital collections, beginning with the Performing Arts Library and the Broadcasting Archives. Both were highly motivated to make their holdings more accessible and usable.

A 1996 implementation of a commercial multimedia management platform had mixed results, due to the difficulty of integrating the product into the existing environment and the lack of specific library functionality. The University of Maryland has since taken a different approach, becoming an Ex Libris "Premier Partner" for the Ex Libris "DigiTool" product. This involves full implementation of the Ex Libris digital asset management product, as well as ongoing participation in product design, development, and testing. The implementation will emphasize streaming audio and video, as well as images. The university's goal is an environment that handles all types of digital objects.

Advanced object management technologies are envisioned to assist users in accessing the Performing Arts Library audio collections. An example of an enhanced digital service is the capability of displaying sheet music images simultaneous with the music being played. "It's good to have a vendor who works with library problems as a mainline business. Other commercial products don't necessarily map to the library business," says University Dean of Libraries Dr. Charles Lowry. Lowry also cites the ability to integrate the digital library software into the Web-based user interface as a benefit, so users can access the physical collection catalog in the same way as the digital collections. It is also important to the University of Maryland that the digital library software supports. National Information Standards Organization (NISO) and National Institute of Standards and Technology (NIST) standards and protocols

Stanford University is well known for its pioneering work in digital library development and electronic publishing. Stanford has participated in both phases of the NSF Digital Library Initiative, provided online publishing services to nearly 100 scholarly societies, developed extensive digital collections, and is currently implementing an advanced digital repository. Stanford has entrusted the responsibilities of University Librarian, Publisher of the University Press, Publisher of the HighWire Press, and Director of Academic Computing to a single individual at Stanford.

This assignment has fostered functional synergy that has integrated many information management activities across these disciplines and facilitated coordination between related activities such as digital repository and learning management system development. After putting up many digital collections on custom-developed systems, the Stanford Libraries have selected the "TEAMS" multimedia management software from Artesia Technologies as the base for its new digital repository. It is also utilizing Luna Imaging's "Insight" software for managing high-resolution images, and it will utilize the METS standard for managing multimedia objects.

"METS is tremendous, an XMLimplemented generalized metadata environment that lets you describe and interrelate any digital entity.We'll be able to store objects one time in one repository, encode them using different descriptive metadata, and make them available to all different types of applications on campus," explains Stanford Libraries' Chief Information Architect Jerry Persons. The repository will handle authentication using Kerberos certificates and will include rights management and charging mechanisms.

In future, the pace of change in digital library technology and its applications has accelerated in recent years as the focus has begun to shift from R&D to full-scale deployment. Several key trends are emerging and will continue to gain momentum:

— The shift from text and image-based systems to audio and video will continue.

— As network bandwidth becomes more economical and streaming technologies improve, increasing numbers of institutions will have access to the practicality of full multimedia solutions.

— Broadly accepted best practices will emerge for digitization, rights management, preservation, metadata encoding, and other key digital library processes. The library discipline is highly collaborative and has a history of sharing successful approaches. Debate about these issues will recede as proven techniques mature and spread.

— Standards will move from the discussion and trial stage to widespread adoption.

It is clear that digital library technology is becoming an essential enabler of library services. In fact, one recent posting to a digital library e-mail list commented that the term "digital library" is starting to sound as anachronistic as "horseless carriage."

Online Library Resources

There is no truly reliable or single source of information on the growth of electronic journals. A study of the World Wide Web archives of the e-journal and magazine electronic announcement list NewJour reveals that in 1989, fewer than 10 e-journals were available. They were created in basic ASCII (.txt) form and had to be distributed in small chunks, lest they crash the mailboxes of subscribers. Today, many large publishers around the world, both for-profit and not-for-profit, maintain Web sites that make available their full collections of print journals (with only limited back-file runs, so far) to subscribers.

Given this penetration of new technologies into scholarly, scientific, and popular journal and magazine publication, a list such as NewJour will one day soon no longer be needed. In this decade (or even half-decade), most print magazines and journals will have a Web version, if they do not already have one. Furthermore, although for the moment it is convenient to think of print and Web versions as providing the same or identical information, the two styles are already beginning to pull apart and will only diverge further.

Not only will the same name ultimately denote collections of content that are in fact very different, but some of the e-journals also will evolve into new genres. The prevailing vision is that this wealth of journal literature will be linked through indexing services and search engines and cross-linked internally online; indeed, this vision is rapidly being realized. For as long as print versions continue to be published, tracking and collecting will be much more difficult. The most significant problem for ubiquitous electronic access is that of long-term archivability and preservation, an issue that begs to be solved if publishers and libraries are not to maintain costly parallel print and electronic systems.

So far, very few electronic journals (or any other resource) have had to survive on the Internet for even one decade. While some experts say that long-term sustainability is a trivial matter, studies suggest high costs and tremendous uncertainties. Fundamental to these uncertainties is the matter of ownership, which libraries rarely have, given that electronic information produces no fixed artifact for libraries to possess and cherish. While rapid growth characterizes scholarly and research journals, the committee found similar or even faster growth in the even broader universe of all continuing publications that includes popular magazines and newspapers as well as annual reports, directories, series, and so on.

Standard periodical indexing and abstracting services began to become available electronically in the 1970s through specialized vendors such as Dialog and BRS, whose proprietary systems required the mediation of expert searchers; by the mid-1990s, they were available through easy-to-use Web interfaces for any licensed subscriber. Thus it is no surprise that the journal articles cited by these sources would become quickly available online. However, books—such as novels and scholarly monographs, for example—have seemed far less susceptible to electronic transformation.

While some books are consulted in bits and bytes (for particular facts or small sections), many (the argument goes) need to be deliciously savored and contemplated from beginning to end, and an online screen is hostile to such prolonged congenial or intense reading. "You can't take it to bed or to the beach or onto the plane with you," is the oft-heard lament. The vision now being articulated by many players in the book publishing industry and its partners (in printing, distribution, and software) is that the full text of all published books, at least from mainstream publishers, will exist on vast electronic information servers, there to be channeled to the output of the reader's choice: traditional print formats or digital formats (by accessing a local copy on a PC or portable device or by viewing a remote copy through the Web). That is, the authoritative source file of many books may soon be an electronic version that can generate various derivative versions.

The e-book may be on the verge of acceptance and success because of the convergence of large computer servers, big network pipelines, rapid progress in developing e-book standards, and the increasing sophistication and utility of handheld book-reading devices, as well as business partnerships to take advantage of all this. Like e-journals, e-books also have a history that goes back to the 1980s.

In the mid-1990s, an entrepreneur making a car trip with his wife had a vision of "the world's largest bookstore," a virtual shop in which the discerning reader could obtain every book—or nearly every book—currently in print. Jeff Bezos, founder and CEO of Amazon.com, Time Magazine's Person of the Year for 1999, achieved his dream: situating bookselling at the core of e-commerce and radicalizing the bookstore concept, to say nothing of notions of business success. Through the Web, the Amazon.com shopper fills a virtual shopping cart with the desired books, which are delivered a day or two or three later to the reader's address of choice.

Through Amazon.com, large collections of books have come one step nearer to their readers—and no library has played a part in this dramatic convergence of reader and book. In the case of the virtual superstore, the reader controls the atmosphere, which need not be as public as a library or bookshop and may be as comfortable as reading in a lounge chair wearing fuzzy slippers and a dressing gown. Most significantly, the rise of the book superstore has implicitly changed the overall economics of access to books and information.

Where once a good public library was the best and most accessible source of materials for many, if not most, communities, bookstores of similar size may be a few doors down the block, open longer hours, and with enough copies of popular titles to satisfy almost all comers. And, most libraries and physical bookstores are dwarfed by online bookstores. These book superstores offer a remarkably wide range of library-like services—lectures, discussion groups, ready access to books, a sense of community. What they do not yet offer is information service--labor-intensive, provided by experts—but it is probably not wise to predict that they will not continue to expand their range.

For now, it is most noticeably the information navigation functions of the library--the instruction in finding, filtering, and evaluating information from a welter of available sources—and its provision of historical depth that the bookstores make the least attempt to supplant. Borders began its career with claims about the literacy and helpfulness of its staff, all of whom had to pass a test to demonstrate their book lore as a condition of employment. Despite this, the library is less than ever a primary supplier of access to new and current books. Libraries continue, however, to be strong in providing access to both older and more specialized material.

Another implication of the shift in the economy of information is that collecting and storing materials are arguably somewhat less the jobs of the library than before. The current emphasis is on services. Indeed, many public libraries have always had this bias, retaining from among older books only those of continuing interest to their readers, while clearing out shelf space for what a current generation demands.

In any case, the superstores and Amazon.com have by no means reached the end state of the publishing industry's book-to-reader vision, nor do libraries seem to have much of a role in that next vision either. The concept of books on demand has been in gestation for some time. For example, in the early 1990s, Xerox partnered with a few large publishing houses in an OD experiment. The products were acceptable, but computer servers and network pipelines were less capacious than today and so the results were slow. The need to resolve rights and permissions issues also posed a significant challenge. The concept needed time to ripen, and ripen it has.

Most individuals, organizations, and publishers agree that at the very least, the traditional book format is facing competition from formats that do some things better. In 1999, the American Historical Association announced an electronic book prize to be awarded annually for several years to half a dozen brilliant dissertations in various fields of history, dissertations that take full advantage of the converging multimedia capabilities that computers and networks can offer and books cannot. The results will enliven the books, attract readers, promote the new medium as a viable one for serious scholarship, and give young scholars a leg up.

Challenge in Utilising Digital Technology

The challenge in utilising digital technology for enhanced access, is the need to secure that investment, and guarantee long-term access to that information. The role of digital technologies as a preservation strategy is a contentious issue, with the traditional school of library preservation clinging to microfilm as the preferred reformatting medium for long term archival storage. The challenge is to react pro-actively, to look forward to consider ways of minimising identified future risks associated with new media, and to look back into the past to understand the nature and development leading to their creation.

Digital information and electronic resources have transformed academic research fundamentally. As the price of print materials, such as scholarly journals continues to rise, the accessibility and functionality of electronic versions become more attractive, and libraries invest more heavily in new technologies. A related issue in the need to preserve digital resources is a growing reliance of libraries as service providers on digital technology, which must impact on our institutional goals. Digital technologies find their place in the preservation strategies of research libraries in the opportunities presented to one such goal - in improved public access to on-line digital surrogates. Digitisation is now a mainstream activity of the Campbell Collections of the University of Natal, aimed at collecting, preserving and organising historical material of national and international importance in a manner that is widely accessible.

The retrieval of digital images offers a significant technological advance as a vehicle for integrated access to visual representations of historic photographs, art and ethnographic artefacts - together with traditional library resources. Preservation digitisation has focussed on reformatting rapidly deteriorating materials, with the aim of preserving the intellectual content, as separate from the medium or carrier. Because one is able to make repeated copies of digital files without the informational loss associated with analogue copies, the impact of the technology is beguiling.

Complete digital conversion comprises two process, the capture by scanning of digital data, and that of the associated metadata, wrapped as a digital object and stored using containers to hold the objects and related software modules. The integrity of the digital file is threatened by alterations to the contextual data file, and the loss of the linking mechanism between the two is the same as deleting the contextual information.

The improvements in storage media are so great as to drive market forces. Longevity of a floppy disk common until a year or two ago, can be estimated at between one and ten months. CD longevity is estimated between 10 and 100 years. Other advantages can be found in the aggregation of larger quantities of information to facilitate data management. 650Mb of data can be stored on a CD, current disk storage capacity is moving in excess of 72Gb, the equivalent of 113 CD's. Migration of information is commonly associated with archival storage. We have all known software upgrades to "orphan" or render unreadable, files created under an earlier version.

The most serious problem facing managers of digital collections, is not unstable media, but data format and software obsolescence. Transforming information from one digital format to another, migration is an essential strategy for persistent adherence to international standard formats. Infrastructure risks include the presence or lack of persistent institutional support, in terms of funding, hardware, software and staff to manage the repeated migration of digital collections. Emulation of software and hardware platforms aims to use the power of present computer technology to function as if it were the technology of a previous generation.

Rather than repeated create new versions of a digital document, recent experimentation has shown that it is possible to develop a set of specifications for the building of emulators that can render the content of digital documents on future unknown platforms. The representational information contains all the technical characteristics, including format, navigational structure such as a table of contents, application software, and the computer specifications and system requirements necessary to read that document. Secure systems technologies provide stable environment for digital archives. When preservation strategies have not been applied to systematic digital archiving and all else fails, it may become necessary to work out how to read the stored bits. Because of the manner in which magnetic media are written, it is possible, given sufficient resources, to recover much material believed lost.

Long term preservation of digital resources is feasible through the implementation of sound policies at the inception and in the development of digital libraries. The challenge lies in the need for libraries to move pro-actively in establishing digital collection development programme in an electronic environment that is conducive to preservation. The collaboration of a wide community of information professionals was responsible for developing new strategies for data management and storage for the preservation of digital information resources.

The interaction between library, archive and museum professionals, together with information technology specialists, helped to clarify the myriad technical issues. There are digital imaging projects underway at some libraries in South Africa, and a number of problems have been encountered that are difficult to overcome in isolation. The equipment is expensive, especially if it is state-of the-art, software varies in quality and local support is often lacking. Standards have not been agreed upon, and vary from one project to another.

Standard Generalized Markup Language (SGML) an international standard designed to promote text interchange, provides a definition of a document structure that can be used to encode the logical structure and content of any defined document and known by any remote system. Extensible Markup Language (XML), a simpler dialect of SGML has since been adopted, using the information community-based document type descriptions of the Text Encoding Initiative (TEI) and Encoded Archival Description (EAD), to build an infrastructure that enables interoperability between heterogeneous systems. The most comprehensive preservation strategy currently evolving is that of a collection-based persistent archive system.

A persistent archive operates in two phases, the first comprising capture of digital data wrapped as XML digital objects and ingestion to archival disk storage, using containers to hold objects along with relevant metadata and software modules for future emulation. The second is in the opposite direction, with containers brought out of storage and loaded onto new possibly new information management systems, and returned to a new, and possibly new archival storage system. The result is a product with the ability to scale its capabilities by adding resources when required.

By differentiating between the storage of the bits that comprise the digital object and the related information carried by the metadata it is possible to create an infrastructure for life cycle management for digital preservation. In fact, information products, like electronic documents and digital objects are particularly important because they represent the purest form of Electronic Commerce. Indeed Electronic Commerce, with its greatly reduced cost of production and distribution makes many new knowledge businesses practical that were previously impractical.

For example, a fully realized infrastructure for Electronic Commerce would make it practical for authors to charge pennies for paragraphs and still make a profit - because the author can reach millions world-wide over the Internet, who can pay and download the paragraph at little or no cost to the author. Electronic commerce does not completely address collaborative design and manufacturing activities, although they do share many of the same sorts of activities. The publication of compelling electronic catalogs, advertisements, and product information requires the same set of electronic publishing tools, as the author of an electronic document or digital object for a digital library.

In the ultimate "wired" society; collaborative design and manufacturing could decompose to hundreds of specialty firms that meet, negotiate and contract with each other over the network, which they would then use to purchase, sell, distribute, and assemble the various components that make up a product or service. Policies regarding customer satisfaction and return should be negotiated prior to this activity, and made part of the contract between buyer and seller. For larger, more complex, orders, distribution may involve more than two parties and entail complicated distribution coordination strategies. An ancillary distribution service involves acting as a fiduciary, and holding goods, certificates, bonds, stocks, etc., in trust. Account activity is particularly important to corporate customers and suppliers. Both buyer and seller must reconcile all electronic transactions in the accounts receivable and accounts payable, inventory information, and accounting systems.

In the information age, a large percent of the commerce will never be embodied physically. Information products are enabled by information technology and not just distributed more efficiently by it. These products can consist not just of electronic publications, catalogs, videos and the like, but can include interactive video games, software programs, electronic keys and tokens, customized design specifications, even electronic keys that can open to hotel rooms, cars, storage compartments, and airport boarding gates.

Furthermore, these information products are not just created entirely by the service provider, but can be designed or customized by the customer, adding a customer-driven activity call "design" to the purchase cycle. Indeed, information products can be continuously added to, modified, and morphed, as they pass along a chain of users. It is also likely that for these products ordering, billing, payment, and distribution would likely all happen simultaneously. Some micro-payment schemes for use over the Internet have been proposed that are significantly weaker than those being proposed for the more traditional payment schemes. The argument is that one can safely sacrifice security for processing efficiency when the transactions are low value enough.

The argument is that it is much more important to minimize the amount of computational and communications resources needed to effect payment than to ensure the integrity of the transaction—that the loss of a penny here or there will not be consequential enough to matter. But, this may not be the case when the revenue is being allocated across many parties, each getting only a small portion of the payment, and where the profit margins may be extremely thin. The user acceptability of these new forms of payment is also questionable. Advocates point to gas meters, and telephone bills, as proof of the acceptance of bills with small payments based on usage.

But, the complexity of these bills certainly pale by comparison to the sorts of bills that users might expect to see in some future "wired" world of micro-payments. Imagine sitting down to reconcile a bill comprised of thousand of penny items. Each item is small enough, but the total will probably be large enough to command attention. Also, these all these examples of usage billing are coming from businesses that have been run as a monopoly - the user has had no other alternative offered them. When given the choice, users have often opted for a more certain, fixed flat fee, even if that fee is slightly greater than their historical usage pattern. The cost of usage billing and accounting may be unacceptably high in the future economics of the "wired" society.

Hybrid Library Resources

The hybrid library tries to use the technologies available to bring things together into a library reflecting the best of both worlds. The hybrid library is on the continuum between the conventional and digital library, where electronic and paper-based information sources are used alongside each other. The challenge associated with the management of the hybrid library is to encourage end-user resource discovery and information use, in a variety of formats and from a number of local and remote sources, in a seamlessly integrated way. The hybrid library should be designed to bring a range of technologies from different sources together in the context of a working library, and also to begin to explore integrated systems and services in both the electronic and print environments.

The hybrid library should not, then, be seen as nothing more than an uneasy transitional phase between the conventional library and digital library but, rather, as a worthwhile model in its own right, which can be usefully developed and improved. This kind of library has been given other labels. The concept of the gateway library, for instance, seems to be one which describes a similar idea.

Hybrid Electronic Access and Delivery in the Library Networked Environment (HeadLine) is a 3-year programme, undertaken by the London School of Economics, the London Business School, and the University of Hertfordshire. It aims to design and implement a working model of the hybrid library in actual academic environments, providing access to a wide range of library materials, regardless of physical form, from a single web interface. The user-centered model employed by HeadLine defines authentication as a predominant issue, since the system must store information about users and their personal preferences, as well as details of resources they have rights to access by virtue of their membership of a given academic community.

In this respect, HeadLine seeks to link otherwise disparate sources of data—which may range from institutional MIS databases to browser bookmarks files—that serve to define users attributes and preferences. Authentication therefore plays a key, dual role: firstly, in securing personal data privacy, and secondly, in controlling which resources may be used. A major goal of HeadLine is the promotion of the single sign-on approach for access to networked information resources: once authenticated into a HeadLine system, the user should not be required to supply further passwords for subsequent resource access or requests.

Moreover, this facility should function consistently, independent of the user's current location. HeadLine therefore engages directly with the complexities of differing schemes of access control for resources available over an open network infrastructure. The creation of a practical, robust, yet flexible authentication model will depend on its simultaneous ability to address users as individuals and to conform to current and future developments in computer access control technology. Authentication establishes the identity of a user within a given context; its companion process—authorization—controls the levels of permitted access to resources for that user identity.

Network operating systems inherently provide this degree of administrative control; however, their locus of influence is confined to the organizations that deploy them. The open network environment of the Internet operates without any such centralised, enclosing authentication scheme; the new era of ubiquitous networked information services has rapidly exposed the limitations of authentication techniques in common use for the past three decades. Problems inevitably arise as users attempt to move between resources where different access restrictions apply.

Traditional techniques of access control employing user identifier and password combinations are becoming unsustainable due to their high administrative overhead and practical shortcomings: loss, unauthorized transfer, or theft. The password proliferation scenario familiar to librarians, information managers, IT personnel and computer users themselves is symptomatic of this problem. A number of current, widely deployed access control techniques, such as IP address filtering, rely upon a continuity of identification rather than upon an absolute identification of an individual.

HeadLine aims to formulate an authentication model that can encompass the need to store users' attributes and data privacy whilst remaining sufficiently extensible to incorporate subsequent developments in third-party authentication methodologies. Many enabling technologies already exist which can be used to achieve this deep integration. However, in some key areas there is currently an absence of tools. There is, perhaps most significantly, an absence of standards-based ways of communicating with many external services.

In an ideal world, these would be supplied by the data providers themselves in the form of an Application Programming Interface (API). Agora is developing a hybrid library management system (HLMS) to provide integrated access to heterogeneous discovery, location, request and delivery services. Agora is led by the University of East Anglia, with UKOLN, Fretwell-Downing Informatics, and CERLIM (the Centre for Research in Library and Information Management) as partners. A prototype system has been made available to provide a focus for development.

It encompasses a range of social science resources, including abstract and indexing services, library catalogues, archive databases and subject gateways. It will demonstrate two scenarios: cross-domain searching for mixed media with authentication; and search through to delivery for monographs and serials. The feedback on the Agora prototype will be sought from professional staff at the library associate sites. The Agora broker is based on the MODELS Information Architecture (MIA). This is a conceptual framework for managing distributed services. MIA suggests some principal components of such systems and provides a common vocabulary for both systems developers and information managers.

In implementing MIA, Agora will be exploring some key areas of concern for distributed service development. It is hoped to find some workable and scalable solutions which will be shared with the relevant communities via targeted dissemination activities. Most libraries today are, in fact, already hybrid libraries—they own and subscribe to a range of resources and services which are supplied in a variety of formats and media: print monographs and serials, electronic journals, abstract and indexing services on CD-ROM, music CD-ROMs, etc.

Many electronic resources are accessed on remote servers. An increasing number of end-users are also accessing these services from outside the home institution: users and services are both distributed. However, there is currently no uniform way of managing and providing integrated access to these hybrid resources. Users are forced to interact with each service individually and waste time in repeating the same steps to search different systems. At the same time, using different interfaces also increases the risk of inefficiencies—such as failure to discover relevant resources because of unfamiliarity with one service's idiosyncrasies.

In a discover/locate/request cycle, the user will also be forced to re-enter the same data when he or she moves from one stage to the next. Agora is using the Z39.50 protocol as the 'glue' to link services together and provide true integrated access via a single interface. Although Agora is principally concerned with developing an infrastructure for managing hybrid libraries, the development of understanding and the acquisition of new hybrid library management skills are equally important to producing a working demonstrator.

Consequently, the Agora hybrid library management system will be a key tool for demonstrating potential service scenarios to a range of library and information communities. The issues facing these hybrid library are those facing all library and information services. The aspects of their programmes the writers have chosen to highlight here are now—and will continue to be—at the centre of contemporary information provision.

Many archives' most significant holdings are not commercially produced recordings but are unpublished recordings of various types. Such works include radio broadcast recordings, television sound tracks, "live" musical or dramatic performances, ethnographic field recordings, and interviews. It is in these recordings in which rights issues are most complex and in need of study, and perhaps adaptation, as they relate to preservation. When a for-profit or nonprofit corporate body, such as a broadcast network/station/producer or a music producer, creates these unpublished recordings, that body often owns the rights to the recording.

As with commercially distributed published recordings, unpublished recordings are usually interpretations of music or literary underlying works that are commonly protected by copyright. In the United States, federal copyright protection was not available for sound recordings until 1972. However, state and common laws protect these recordings until the year 2067, no matter when they were created. This means that, in effect, the law grants greater protection to sound recordings than to print materials.

The radical transformations that have made digital formats the predominant form of sound recording have made available to the public more types of sound recordings, and greater numbers of hours of audio, than ever before. As a result, research library administrators responsible for collection development policies must regularly reevaluate their long-range goals as well as their day-to-day acquisitions. No longer are acquisitions limited to physical items offered by retailers and in catalogs, or bought on their behalf by contracted purchasing representatives.

Rather, librarians and archivists face a plethora of technologies, platforms, and genres. In the consumer arena, the digital audio revolution began in the early 1980s, when the compact audio disc format was introduced. Public adoption of the CD format burgeoned beyond anyone's expectations. The public, and libraries, were attracted by the lack of surface noise and hiss that was commonly heard on LP and 78-rpm records and cassette tapes and by the CDs' touted invulnerability to normal wear.

The sound on compact discs was criticized by audiophiles, collectors with high-end playback equipment, and other consumers, but most consumers never heard their arguments or the aural evidence. In fact, the 44-MHz, 16-bit sampling rate, or amount of compression, selected by the creators of the compact discs was a compromise that sacrificed sound quality at the expense of time capacity of the discs.

Initially, the content of compact discs replicated that of the LP discs they would supersede. However, record companies gained significant profits from the re-release of older catalog issues, in addition to new releases. Serious sound archives dedicated to documenting the history of music and sound recording continue to acquire LP and 78-rpm discs for their unique repertoire and their audio quality. Stored properly, these discs will last many years, but they deteriorate from repeated playback. Moreover, high-quality disc playback equipment is expensive. With compact discs came myriad recording reissues.

The complete recording careers of hundreds of notable classical, jazz, blues, and rock artists have been thoroughly documented on thousands of CD reissues. These discs and sets have enabled libraries to build research-level, encyclopedic collections of important musicians and recording artists. These are recordings that libraries might not have obtained otherwise, either because of inaccessibility or the expense of obtaining and maintaining the original records. Two important points related to reissues must be emphasized. The first is that most comprehensive jazz, blues, and classical reissues are produced outside of the United States in countries where older recordings are no longer protected by copyright.

In most European countries, the copyright on a sound recording is 50 years from the original date of recording. Although liberal foreign copyright laws enable publication of thousands of previously out-of-print recordings, the quality of these reissues varies greatly. While the producers of comprehensive reissues make thorough searches to locate one copy of every recording an artist has made, the copy used is often generations away from the master recording and is in only mediocre condition. To compensate for the condition of the source recordings, many producers of reissues misrepresent the original recordings with signal processing: overuse of noise reduction, sound equalization, and limiting tools in order to reduce the surface noise found on the source.

Today, many archives are rethinking their acquisitions policies, preservation techniques, and delivery systems. The sheer number of new audio materials made available through the World Wide Web is astounding.

Interoperability

Interoperability among heterogeneous collections is a central theme of the Core Integration. The potential collections have a wide variety of data types, metadata standards, protocols, authentication schemes, and business models. They are managed by large numbers of organizations, some of which have grants from the NSF, but most of which are independent. Some are well funded, but many have limited resources. Some were established specifically for education, but most are not designed primarily for education. All have their own priorities. The Site for Science strategy for interoperability was first articulated in a memorandum that was distributed among the Core Integration demonstration projects in fall 2000. The goal of interoperability is to build coherent services for users, from components that are technically different and managed by different organizations. This requires agreements to cooperate at three levels: technical, content and organizational.

- Technical agreements cover formats, protocols, security systems, etc., so that messages can be exchanged.
- Content agreements cover the data and metadata, and include semantic agreements on the interpretation of the information.
- Organizational agreements cover the ground rules for access, preservation of collections and services, payment, authentication, etc.

Defining these agreements is hard, but the central challenge is to create incentives for independent digital libraries to adopt them. The traditional approach to interoperability is for all participants to agree to use the same standards. If each service implements a comprehensive set of standards then interoperability follows. However, experience has shown that interoperability through comprehensive standardization is hard to achieve.

Adoption of common standards provides digital libraries with valuable functionality, but at a cost. Some costs are directly financial: the purchase of equipment and software, or hiring and training staff. More often the largest costs are organizational. Rarely can a single aspect of a digital library be changed in isolation. Introducing a new standard requires inter-related changes to existing systems, altered work flow, changed relationships with suppliers, and so on. It is important to recognize that there is no best point on these curves. Every point is optimal for some purpose.

For example, libraries have developed a framework for interoperability based on the Z39.50 protocol, the Anglo American Cataloguing Rules and

MARC. This combination of standards provides an excellent choice for libraries, because they value the functionality and have catalog records in this form, but the cost of adopting these standards is high unless an organization already has metadata that meets them. Hence, few other collections of information on the Internet have adopted these standards because, for most other organizations, the cost of adoption is high relative to the functionality gained.

A heterogeneous digital library, such as the NSDL, will include some collections that support powerful standards, such as Z39.50 or SGML, but must expect that most collections will use standards with lower functionality, such as HTTP or HTML, because of the lower cost of adoption. Current research and development on web information systems and digital libraries are often aimed at such changes. For instance, text-based applications clearly gain functionality if they support a range of scripts beyond English. There are three levels of digital library interoperability:

— Federation

— Harvesting

— Gathering

Federation

Federation can be considered the conventional approach to interoperability. In a federation, a group of organizations agree that their services will conform to certain specifications. The libraries that share online catalog records using Z39.50 are an example of a federation. Another federation is the ADEPT project for geospatial materials, led by the University of California at Santa Barbara, one of the partners in the Core Integration production team [Alexandria]. The principal challenge in forming a federation is the effort required by each organization to implement and keep current with all the agreements. Since the cost of participation is high, typical federations have small but dedicated memberships.

Harvesting

The difficulty of creating large federations is the motivation behind recent efforts to create looser groupings of digital libraries. The underlying concept is that the participants agree to take small efforts that enable some basic shared services, without being required to adopt a complete set of agreements. The Open Archives Initiative (OAI) is based around the concept of metadata harvesting. Each digital library makes metadata about its collections available in a simple exchange format.

This metadata can be harvested by service providers and built into services such as information discovery or reference linking. Two members of the Site for Science team act as the executive for the OAI, and Site for Science was one of the alpha test sites for the metadata harvesting protocol. Metadata harvesting was first developed by the Harvest project in the early 1990s, but the approach was not widely adopted.

The concept was revived in 1998/99 in a prototype known as the Universal Preprint Server. This prototype concluded in favor of metadata harvesting as a strategy to facilitate the creation of federated services across heterogeneous preprint systems. The OAI work, which is derived from this experiment, emphasizes the core functionality that can be achieved by digital libraries sharing metadata. It minimizes the cost by using a simple protocol based on HTTP, by providing software that is easily added to web servers, and by documentation, training and support.

While services built by metadata harvesting are usually less powerful than those provided by federations, the burden of participating is much less. As a result, many more organizations are likely to join and keep their systems current. This is confirmed by the rapid acceptance of the metadata harvesting protocol of the OAI.

Gathering

Even if the various organizations do not cooperate in any formal manner, a base level of interoperability is still possible by gathering openly accessible information using a web crawler. The premier examples of this approach are the web search engines. Because there is no cost to the collections, gathering can provide services that embrace large numbers of digital libraries, but the services are of poorer quality than can be achieved by partners who cooperate directly.

Some of the most interesting web research at present can be thought of as adding extra function to the base level, which will lead to better interoperability, even among totally non-cooperating organizations. Even though the concept of a fully semantic web is a pipe dream, it is reasonable to expect that the level of services that can be provided by gathering will improve steadily.

Metadata

In an ideal world all the collections and services that the NSDL wishes to encompass would support an agreed set of standard metadata. The real world is less simple. However, the NSDL does have influence. The prospect of obtaining NSF's funding provides useful incentive for collections. The Site for Science metadata strategy is based on two principles. The first is that metadata is too expensive for the Core Integration team to create much of it. Hence, the NSDL has to rely on existing metadata or metadata that can be generated automatically. The second is to make use of as much of the metadata available from collections as possible, knowing that it varies greatly from none to extensive. Based on these principles, Site for Science, and subsequently the entire NSDL, developed the following metadata strategy:

— Support eight standard formats
— Collect all existing metadata in these formats
— Provide crosswalks to Dublin Core
— Assemble all metadata in a central metadata repository
— Expose all metadata records in the repository for service providers to harvest
— Concentrate limited human effort on collection-level metadata
— Use automatic generation to augment item-level metadata
— Metadata formats

Early in 2001, the NSDL Standards and Metadata Workgroup, which represents all NSDL projects, identified the following list of preferred metadata element sets.

Digital Preservation

Today, information technologies that are increasingly powerful and easy to use, especially like those that support the World Wide Web, have unleashed the production and distribution of digital information. Such information is penetrating and transforming nearly every aspect of our culture. If we are effectively to preserve for future generations the portion of this rapidly expanding corpus of information in digital form that represents our cultural record, we need to understand the costs of doing so and we need to commit ourselves technically, legally, economically and organizationally to the full dimensions of the task.

In the face of rapid technological obsolescence and to overcome the problem of media fragility, archivists have adopted the technique of "refreshing" digital information by copying it onto new media. Copying from medium to medium, however, also suffers limitations as a means of digital preservation. Refreshing digital information by copying will work as an effective preservation technique only as long as the information is encoded in a format that is independent of the particular hardware and software needed to use it and as long as there exists software to manipulate the format in current use.

Otherwise, copying depends either on the compatibility of present and past versions of software and generations of hardware or the ability of competing hardware and software product lines to interoperate. In respect of these factors- backward compatibility and interoperability-the rate of technological change exacts a serious toll on efforts to ensure the longevity of digital information.

Digital information today is produced in highly varying degrees of dependence on particular hardware and software. Moreover, it is costly and difficult for vendors to assure that their products are either "backwardly compatible" with previous versions or that they can interoperate with competing products. Jeff Rothenberg, has suggested that there may be sufficient demand for entrepreneurs to create and archive emulators of software and operating systems that would allow the contents of digital information to be carried forward and used in its original format. Refreshing digital information by copying it from medium to medium and the possibility of maintaining a complex set of emulators describe two distinct points on a continuum of approaches to preserving digital information.

However, neither refreshing nor emulation sufficiently describes the full range of options needed and available for digital preservation. Instead, a better and more general concept to describe these options is migration. Migration is the periodic transfer of digital materials from one hardware/ software configuration to another, or from one generation of computer technology to a subsequent generation. The purpose of migration is to preserve the integrity of digital objects and to retain the ability for clients to retrieve, display, and otherwise use them in the face of constantly changing technology. Migration includes refreshing as a means of digital preservation but differs from it in the sense that it is not always possible to make an exact digital copy or replica of a database or other information object as hardware and software change and still maintain the compatibility of the object with the new generation of technology.

Users of intellectual property are unsure about what rights are conveyed with the use of a particular digital information object and about how much such use is worth. Government representatives seek in the public interest to manage the powerful changes that accompany digital technologies, but are unsure about what levels of influece are available to them and how to generate appropriate public policy. The state of the copyright law, which was generated and developed in an analog world but is applied in an increasingly digital universe, is itself confusing and uncertain.

And all of these concerns are exacerbated by the fact that bits know no borders. The costs and the technical, legal and organizational complexities of moving digital information forward into the future raise our greatest fear about the life of information in the digital future: namely, that owners or custodians who can no longer bear the expense and difficulty will deliberately or inadvertently, through a simple failure to act, destroy the objects without regard for future use.

Viewed developmentally, the problem of preserving digital information for the future is not only, or even primarily, a problem of fine tuning a narrow set of technical variables. It is not a clearly defined problem like preserving the embrittled books that are self-destructing from the acid in the paper on which they were printed. Rather, it is a grander problem of organizing ourselves over time and as a society to maneuver effectively in a digital landscape. It is a problem of building-almost from scratch-the various systematic supports, or deep infrastructure, that will enable us to tame anxieties and move our cultural records naturally and confidently into the future.

For digital preservation, the organizational effort-the process of building deep infrastructure-necessarily involves multiple, interrelated factors, many of which are either unknown or poorly defined. One of the biggest unknowns is the full impact on traditional information handling functions of distributed computing over electronic networks. Digital archives are distinct from digital libraries in the sense that digital libraries are repositories that collect and provide access to digital information, but may or may not provide for the long-term storage and access of that information.

Digital libraries thus may or may not be, in functional terms, digital archives and, in fact, much of the recent work on digital libraries is notably silent on the archival issues of ensuring long-term storage and access. Conversely, digital archives necessarily embrace digital library functions to the extent that they must select, obtain, store, and provide access to digital information. Many of the functional requirements for digital archives defined thus overlap those for digital libraries.

Many traditional libraries, archives and museums, as institutions, have taken and may well continue to assume digital library and archival functions. Certified digital archives will have available to them a critical fail-safe mechanism. Such a mechanism, supported by organizational will, economic means and legal right, would enable a certified archival repository to exercise an aggressive rescue function to save digital information that it judges to be culturally significant and which is endangered in its current repository.

The current repository may be a digital library, another digital archives, or some other individual, organizational, public or private source of digital information. Without the operation of a formal certification program and a fail-safe mechanism, preservation of the nation's cultural heritage in digital form will likely be overly dependent on marketplace forces, which may value information for too short a period and without applying broader, public interest criteria.

Such development is necessary for and will contribute powerfully to the overall growth of an information-based society and economy. We can afford to continue and increase economic and social investments in digital information objects and in the repositories for them on the information superhighway if, and only if, we also create the archival means for the knowledge the objects and repositories contain to endure and redound to the benefit of future generations. The digital world is still too new for us to describe fully the life cycle of the information objects that do now or will in the future reside there, but what surely unites the community of actors in their various information-based activities is their common purpose in support of the pursuit of knowledge.

The pursuit of knowledge is a process in which the emergence of new knowledge builds on and reconstructs the old. Knowledge cannot advance without consistent and reliable access to information sources, past and present. It is the archival function in the system of knowledge creation and use that serves to identify and retain important sources of information and to ensure continuing access to them. How reliable the archival process proves to be in the emerging digital environment hinges on the trustworthy operation of digital archives and on their ability to maintain the integrity of the objects they are charged to preserve. For digital objects, no less than for objects of other kinds, knowing how operationally to preserve them depends, at least in part, on being able to discriminate the essential features of what needs to be preserved.

Digital technologies increasingly serve to integrate information resources. Text, numeric data, images, voice, and video have heretofore resided in print or other analog media for storage and transmission. When they are encoded digitally, either by conversion or at the point of creation, these various kinds of resources share layers of technology-a common means of storage and transmission- that allows them to be brought together and used in both old and new ways.

Multimedia and hyperlinked objects on the World Wide Web represent some of the new kinds of information and new ways of knowing in the digital realm that bring together the traditional forms of information and transform their use. The application of computer hardware and software has also generated other new kinds of information objects, including the products of simulation, remote sensing, computer-aided design (CAD) and geographic information (GIS) systems. These objects come into being and exist as creatures of the digital environment; if nurtured well, digital technologies will certainly beget still other kinds of information objects, which we can now only anticipate. The processes of preserving digital information will vary significantly with the different kinds of objects-textual, numeric, image, video, sound, multimedia, simulation and so on-being preserved.

Whatever preservation method is applied, however, the central goal must be to preserve information integrity; that is, to define and preserve those features of an information object that distinguish it as a whole and singular work. In the digital environment, the features that determine information integrity and deserve special attention for archival purposes include the following: content, fixity, reference, provenance, and context. What digital archives are trying to preserve after all is the intellectual substance contained in information objects. The notion of content, however, is itself a complex idea that operates at several different levels of abstraction.

To preserve the integrity of objects in their charge, digital archives must decide at which level, or levels, of abstraction they are defining information content. At the lowest level of abstraction, all digital information objects consist of simple bitstreams of 0s and 1s. One can distinguish objects from one another merely by distinguishing the configuration of bits. Preserving the integrity of an information object in this sense means preserving the bit configuration that uniquely defines the object. There are various well-established techniques, such as checksums and digests, for tracking the bit-level equivalence of digital objects and ensuring that a preserved object is identical to the original. Defining content as a collection of bits, however, is often too limited and simplistic to be useful.

In the digital environment, as we have seen, ideas are typically embedded in particular formats and structures that are dependent on hardware and software technologies subject to rapid change. In addition to character set issues, digital archives must also grapple with the means of representing and preserving textual content embedded in layout and structure. Markup systems, such as implementations of TeX and the Standard Generalized Markup Language (SGML), do exist as platform-independent mechanisms for identifying and tagging for subsequent layout and retrieval detailed structural elements of documents. The use of TeX and its variants, for example, is relatively common among scholars in some scientific disciplines such as mathematics and computer science, and the federal government and scholarly publishers are increasingly employing the SGML standard in documents that they produce and distribute electronically. Beyond these relatively specialized segments, however, word processing and desktop publishing systems still dominate the market for the creation of documents with complex structure and layout, and the software for such use typically models and stores document structure and layout in proprietary terms.

Although software may provide mechanisms for converting documents to common interchange formats, use of such mechanisms often results in the loss or inadequate rendering of content such as page structures and the layout of headers, footers and section headings. The preservation of images comprises another example of the ways in which content, defined in terms of structure and format, poses integrity problems for digital archives.

Image resolution, accuracy of color representation and compression for storage all require attention, but the interaction of these structural factors tends to pit judgments about the quality of content against the need for its efficient archival storage and use. In general, one can express the tradeoffs as follows: the higher the resolution and the richer the color register, the larger the file size and more costly the storage. At the highest level of abstraction, digital archives define content in a way that transcends the limits of the hardware and software systems needed for reading and interpreting the bits of an information object and for rendering it for use in a specific format and structural representation; that is, they define content in terms of the knowledge or ideas the object contains.

The measure of integrity in the preservation process thus turns, at least in part, on informed and skillful judgments about the appropriate definition of the content of an digital information object-about the extent to which content depends on its configuration of bits, on the structure and format of its representation, and on the ideas it contains-and for what purposes. The process of identifying and preserving a digital information object as a whole and singular work goes well beyond considerations of content. It also depends, for instance, on the way that the content is fixed as a discrete object. If an object is not fixed, and the content is subject to change or withdrawal without notice, then its integrity may be compromised and its value as a cultural record would be severely diminished.

The acts of production and broadcast establish radio and television programs as discrete objects. And the act of publication marks a specific version or edition of a literary work. In each of these cases, it is virtually impossible to change or withdraw the cultural record that the release of an information object establishes. On the digital landscape, by contrast, it is still relatively easy for a creator to alter or retract previously released information. Such actions can eliminate or overlay significant content and thereby corrupt the record. To address these problems, a wide range of cryptographic techniques, such as watermarking, already exist for various kinds of digital information objects.

These could serve well to mark and identify specific, canonical versions and editions of textual, audio and visual works, and to establish trusted, protected channels of distribution for those objects. However, the standards and infrastructure and the policies and practices for applying such techniques to the creation of fixed versions of digital information objects still need considerable development. Absent such development and the fixity of information that would result, digital archives face considerable challenges in trying to preserve the integrity of digital objects.

Some kinds of digital objects present the problem of fixity of information in yet another way. An increasing number of networked information resources are better modeled, not in terms of versions or editions of works, but as continuously updated databases. The financial communities also depend on large, continuously updated databases. There is no natural way to fix these resources at the database level, no natural set of publication points for the objects as a whole. Their integrity, or singularity, as databases resides in the coherence of the database as a whole and in the continuousness of the updates.

To preserve the integrity of such information resources, the complete record of changes has to be built into the design of the database and fixed at the record level. In the absence of such a preservation-oriented design, digital archives may have no choice but to fix the database artificially in time and capture a series of snapshots of its state at periodic intervals as a way of preserving its integrity. Information objects come into being and acquire their distinctiveness in relation to various other objects in an information space.

There are several factors contribute to the unique identification of digital information objects. Two of the most important factors are the Uniform Resource Name (URN) and the Uniform Resource Locator (URL). The URL refers to the specific place where a digital object resides and is currently the dominant method of object location on the World Wide Web. The weakness of the URL, however, is that it may frequently change, especially as an object migrates from one machine to the next.

By contrast, a name, the URN, is supposed to apply uniquely and permanently to a distinct object and to designate it independently of its particular location at any point in time. URNs today exist more in concept than in practice. Thus, resolving the name and location for variant digital works and thereby providing consistent reference to them means moving from a conceptual design of the relation between names and locations to an operational reality through the implementation of naming authorities, which assign URNs, and and the development of digital services that translate names into currently valid URLs.

For archival purposes, however, there are two other qualities of digital information objects that a reference system must take into account. Provenance has become one of the central organizing concepts of modern archival science. The assumption underlying the principle of provenance is that the integrity of an information object is partly embodied in tracing from where it came. To preserve the integrity of an information object, digital archives must preserve a record of its origin and chain of custody.

For some information objects, the formal process of publication creates a trusted channel of distribution and serves to establish a sophisticated record of provenance, at least from the creator through the point of release. In the digital environment, as in other domains, individuals produce and accrete much information that relates to their private lives and to their public roles and responsibilities, including their means of livelihood.

The archival challenge for establishing the provenance of such objects is to find ways to preserve an understanding of the corporate policies and processes and roles and responsibilities thus represented in the information system and its products. In some cases, the instrumentation produces data in the service of individual experiments or of clinical practice; in other cases, remote sensors gather streams of observational data about physical systems in space or on earth.

In the end, the investment that digital archives make in establishing the provenance of objects in their care serves to preserve the integrity of digital information in two distinct ways. First, a tracing of chain of custody from the point of creation helps to create the presumption that an object is authentic, that it is what it purports to be and that its content, however defined, has not been manipulated, altered or falsified. The second effect of establishing provenance through a chain of custody is to document, at least in part, the particular uses of the object by the custodians. In thus creating a record of use, the archival concern with provenance is intimately related to the notion of context as a matter of information integrity.

As network-based objects, such as video and records of confidential transactions, make their way into digital repositories, an archival account of their integrity must include an account of the features of the network context that supports their existence. Finally, the wider social environment plays a significant contextual role that contributes to the integrity of digital information objects. Networked information, for example, depends on specific policy and implementation decisions that address the bandwidth, security and other qualities of the network and related technical infrastructure.

Preservation Description Information (PDI)

An important function of the OAIS is deciding what parts of the Content

Information are the Content Data Object and what parts are the Representation Information. In addition to Content Information, the Archival Information must include information that will allow the understanding of the Content Information over an indefinite period of time. The specific set of Information Objects, which are required for this function, is collectively called Preservation Description Information (PDI).

The PDI must include information that is necessary to adequately preserve the particular Content Information with which it is associated. It is specifically focused on describing the past and present states of the Content Information, ensuring it is uniquely identifiable, and ensuring it has not been unknowingly altered. This information is typical for all types of archives and has been classified in the context of traditional archives. However, the class definitions must be extended for digital archives. The following definitions are preserving Digital Information:

Reference Information: This information identifies, and if necessary describes, one or more mechanisms used to provide assigned identifiers for the Content Information. It also provides those identifiers that allow outside systems to refer, unambiguously, to this particular Content Information. Examples of these systems include taxonomic systems, reference systems and registration systems. In the OAIS Reference Model most if not all of this information is replicated in Package Descriptions, which enable Consumers to access Content Information of interest.

Context Information: This information documents the relationships of the Content Information to its environment. This includes why the Content Information was created and how it relates to other Content Information objects existing elsewhere.

Provenance Information: This information documents the history of the Content Information. This tells the origin or source of the Content Information, any changes that may have taken place since it was originated, and who has had custody of it since it was originated. This gives future users some assurance as to the likely reliability of the Content Information. Provenance can be viewed as a special type of context information.

Fixity Information: This information provides the Data Integrity checks or Validation/Verification keys used to ensure that the particular Content Information object has not been altered in an undocumented manner. Fixity Information includes special encoding and error detection schemes that are specific to instances of Content Objects. Fixity Information does not include the integrity preserving mechanisms provided by the OAIS underlying services, error protection supplied by the media and device drivers used by Archival Storage. The OAIS needs to explicitly decide what the exact definition of Content Information is in order to be able to ensure that it also has the PDI needed to preserve the Content Information. Once the Content Information has been determined, it is possible to assess the Preservation Description Information.

Packaging Information: The Packaging Information is that information which, either actually or logically, binds or relates the components of the package into an identifiable entity on specific media. For example, if the Content Information and PDI are identified as being the content of specific files on a CD-ROM, then the Packaging Information may include the ISO 9660 volume/file structure on the CD-ROM.

The Packaging Information does not necessarily need to be preserved by an OAIS since it does not contribute to the Content Information or the PDI. However, there are cases where the OAIS may be required to reproduce the original submission exactly. The OAIS should also avoid holding PDI or Content Information only in the naming conventions of directory or file name structures. These structures are most likely to be used as Packaging Information.

Descriptive Information: To preserving information, the OAIS must provide adequate features to allow Consumers to locate information of potential interest, analyze that information, and order desired information. This is accomplished through a specialization of the Information Object called Descriptive Information, which contain the data that serves as the input to documents or applications called Access Aids.

A library is not a last resting place for the books contained there but a place where information and ideas live and breathe in new minds. The digital age brings, here as elsewhere, opportunities and challenges. The Library can now provide access to some objects without assuming any responsibility for preserving them. The acquisition of materials and their integration into a library's collections traditionally have implied a responsibility to preserve those items for use by future generations. Its preservation responsibilities using a variety of professionally accepted practices:

— Providing adequate storage conditions (e.g., proper environmental controls and appropriate binding and shelving);

— Reformatting materials from their original fragile formats and media to more stable media (e.g., microfilming newspapers and brittle books, transferring audio recordings to more stable media, and copying content on nitrate and acetate film to more stable polyester film bases); and

— For a small percentage of rare and unique materials with intrinsic value in their original formats, restoring originals through conservation treatments.

The library also has a long history of providing leadership in the broader field of preservation. Over the last two centuries, it has conducted research and led efforts in areas such as binding and shelving books, proper environmental conditions for storage, use of microfilm for preservation, and mass deacidification of paper. The Library faces challenges in digital preservation that are widely recognized and shared by many other libraries and archives. They include the following:

— *Fragile storage media*—Digital materials are especially vulnerable to loss and destruction because they are stored on fragile magnetic and optical media that deteriorate rapidly and that can fail suddenly from exposure to heat, humidity, airborne contaminants, faulty reading and writing devices, human error, and even sabotage.

— *Technology obsolescence*—Digital materials become unreadable and inaccessible if the playback devices necessary to retrieve information from the media become obsolete or if the software that translates digital information from machine- to human-readable form is no longer available.

— *Legal questions surrounding copying and access*—Libraries, archives, and other cultural institutions have limited and uncertain rights to copy digital information for preservation or backup purposes, to reformat information so that it remains accessible by current technology, and to provide public access.

All organizations with responsibilities for preserving digital information are seeking better technical solutions, model policies, best practices, and clearer guidelines regarding legal and intellectual property issues. In US, Library Congress (LC) providing leadership or contributing actively to solving critical problems of digital archiving and long-term preservation. Until now, LC seems to have assumed a wait-and-see attitude toward its role in preserving digital information created outside the walls of the Library itself;

this was probably exacerbated by the absence of a director for the Preservation Directorate.

The Library's collecting policies and mechanisms with regard to born-digital materials are closely tied to its preservation capabilities. As long as traditional collecting mechanisms guarantee a steady stream of print, other analog materials, and tangible digital objects such as CD-ROMs into the Library's collections, there is an illusion that little significant content is being lost. The absence of significant digital content in the Library's collections removes a sense of urgency about digital preservation, and the lack of organizational capacity to preserve many types of born-digital information discourages the Library from taking on responsibilities that it is not prepared to fulfill.

The methods for doing this include traditional collecting and custodianship and developing relationships with publishers, other research libraries, other national libraries, bibliographic networks and utilities, government agencies, and archives. Traditionally, the acquisition of materials through purchase, exchange, or deposit and their cataloging into the Library's permanent collection entailed a commitment to preserve those materials. In the digital environment, libraries will assume a wider variety of roles and responsibilities with regard to preservation.

One of the first steps that librareis needs to take in adapting its collecting practices to accommodate born-digital information is to delineate clearly its responsibilities for preserving digital information. As libraries identifies the areas in which it will assume the lead responsibility for digital preservation, other organizations can adjust the scope of their digital collections accordingly. Just as the Library cannot ignore the problem of digital preservation, so also it cannot be expected to do it all. If libraries does not set clear boundaries around its digital preservation responsibilities, then many people may assume unrealistically that the Library will be the repository of last resort for everything worth keeping.

The Library of Congress must act as the owner and primary custodian for the digital collections it creates. This is a logical extension of the Library's current efforts to preserve the digital resources that it creates through the retrospective conversion of materials for the National Digital Library Program (NDLP), compilation of public-domain materials, and cataloging. The Law Library's Global Legal Information Network (GLIN) maintains an online database composed primarily of searchable legal abstracts in English of foreign laws and regulations enacted in selected countries since 1976 and over 20,000 full texts of legal instruments since 1995.

In addition, libraries has preserved its bibliographic database of some 12 million machine-readable catalog records representing the books, serials, maps, sound recordings, manuscripts, and visual materials in its collections by migrating these data successfully from older legacy systems to the new Integrated Library System. The Library can also logically be expected to serve as owner and primary custodian of materials for which it has a unique mandate and of digital resources that it has unique responsibilities for acquiring.

The Library's role in registering copyright and enforcing mandatory deposit law creates a unique opportunity for the Library to collect digital information that might otherwise vanish from the historical record. One particular concern with regard to preservation is how deposited items will be identified for integration into LC's permanent collection and which parts of LC will look after long-term preservation requirements. It is not clear when (or if) CORDS will begin retaining and preserving complete digital objects in a systematic way rather than maintaining only registration information and a digital signature of the object being registered.

In some cases, only the digital signature will be kept in CORDS, to verify potential alterations to a digital document or copyright infringements. It is also unclear whether the Copyright Office will assume responsibility for the long-term preservation of the digital content deposited in CORDS or whether some or all of this task will pass to Library Services. The Library needs to determine whether CORDS is intended to serve solely as a registration and deposit mechanism or whether it should also include a repository for digital materials with long-term value.

In the paper world, each library that decided to provide its users with a given resource both obtained and conserved its own copy of the object. This replication in the paper world served as a powerful fail-safe mechanism, helping to ensure long-term accessibility through the uncoordinated but distributed maintenance of independent copies. (The only coordination between libraries took place when materials deteriorated to the point where reformatting was required. At that point, a library would check in national databases to see whether another library had already reformatted the item.)

In the digital environment, in which much content is distributed through the centralized services of a publisher, it is not clear where the preservation responsibility lies. The Library has begun experimenting with arrangements that may help clarify its role in these instances. It is now necessary to move from these early experiments to the development of a coherent, overarching strategy for digital preservation. There are no formal arrangements that define LC's role in long-term maintenance and preservation of the portions of the NDLP that are currently in the custody of other participating institutions. Although the committee does not question the participating institutions' commitment, in principle, to preserving the digital content they have contributed, a variety of unforeseen circumstances could prevent them from doing so. This is a particular concern because of the funding model for the NDLP and the emphasis to date on digitization and the development of access mechanisms.

An important next step for the NDLP is to develop standards and agreements for long-term stewardship that define when and under what circumstances LC will serve as the fail-safe mechanism or repository of last resort. Repositories are systems for storing digital objects in a robust and managed fashion. They protect data from inappropriate access, facilitate the recording of appropriate metadata to allow the management of objects, and provide delivery facilities for both curatorial and user access.

The Library has recently acquired, through a gift, the TEAMS system developed by Thompson Publishing. TEAMS supports both object and metadata storage and maintenance and has been implemented in a variety of corporate settings. Its use by LC represents the first implementation of TEAMS in a traditional library application. The committee supports the development of a repository system as an important next step for the NDLP and agrees that this work needs to be stepped up, but it has reservations about the directions that LC is taking.

Although accepting donated hardware and software helps to mobilize private support for LC and may reduce expenditures in the short run, contributions like these can also commit LC to proprietary systems and methods that in the long run will limit the Library's ability to federate its collections with those of other repositories and interoperate easily with potential partners. One approach is for LC to coordinate its efforts to develop a repository system with those of other organizations that are using the reference model for the Open Archival Information System (OAIS). This high-level model does not specify any particular implementation of an archival information system, nor does it define standards accession, description, data management, or distribution.

The OAIS model is important for digital preservation standards and strategies because it defines the functions and requirements for a digital archive through an international standard that vendors and producers of digital information can reference. If the OAIS reference model is widely adopted (and there are indications that it will be), then it may provide the framework for a network of cooperating and federated repositories. US National Archives and Records Administration is adopting this model for some of its digital archiving requirements and is working with the San Diego Supercomputer Center on one specific implementation.

In general, for LC to develop the capacity to serve as a fail-safe mechanism, it will need to acquire a much more extensive technical infrastructure and greater expertise in a wide variety of file types and formats. While they are important experiments, neither the NDLP repository nor CORDS yet offers solutions to LC's responsibility to preserve born-digital content created outside the Library. In the case of NDLP, LC has been working with materials converted to digital form, and for these materials it has taken the lead in setting standards for formats, metadata, naming conventions, and other technical attributes.

But for born-digital materials, especially those created outside the Library, LC is unlikely to have the leverage to define or limit the formats and structures that are used. In the experimental period of the dissertation project, ProQuest is presenting dissertations in the portable document format (PDF) directly to the Copyright Office. These are being accepted as the best edition, cataloged using the cataloging specifications offered by ProQuest, verified by examiners in the Copyright Office, and stored at ProQuest. That is, registration is handled by the Copyright Office but the deposit is virtual. This arrangement presents LC with no immediate need to preserve the materials.

Because of intellectual property law and the uncertainty of some publishers regarding the deposit of copies of digital works, institutions with long-term preservation responsibilities must seek and develop new means of ensuring continuing access to the valuable documentation of history, culture, and creativity. One possible approach is contractual agreements with rights holders who maintain digital information in off-site repositories, with provisions for deposit in a library or other institution should the publisher cease to maintain the information.

Some publishers have agreed to provide perpetual access to their materials as one of the conditions of a license. The Library has initiated an experiment in reaching such an agreement with ProQuest. The committee believes that such arrangements need to be tested carefully and that other models need to be explored as well. The way in which librarians work must be totally reconceptualized for these fail-safe mechanisms to work.

Library needs to articulate carefully a policy identifying the subset of digital materials for which it will assume long-term curatorial responsibility, taking into account the following:

— The burden of preserving digital collections is daunting and must be shared with other archiving institutions.

— The archiving and preservation of digital resources normally accessed over the Internet will not take place as a by-product of normal access but must be explicitly pursued. Simply assuming that preservation will be carried out somewhere across numerous replicated research collections will not be a solution for networked resources.

Both considerations argue for libraries to define the scope of their archiving roles, in order that responsibilities be distributed across the archiving libraries of the world. The archiving and preservation responsibility is a long-term one that will serve researchers in generations to come. One advantage of digital materials is the potential to distribute preservation responsibilities among a wide variety of partners so that each institution preserves only a designated portion of the global digital record.

With careful planning, coordination, cooperative agreements, and clearly articulated boundaries around its curatorial collection, the Library could assume long-term preservation responsibility for a much smaller portion of the digital corpus than it did for the paper one. Some redundancy is necessary for backup and security purposes, but less redundancy is needed for digital collections than was required in the past because access no longer requires physical proximity to materials. Distributed curatorial responsibility will be achieved only with leadership from LC and cooperation with many partners.

A variety of roles can be envisioned for the Library in a collaborative effort among libraries, publishers, government agencies, and other stakeholders to define the parameters of distributed digital collections and delineate the roles and responsibilities of various parties for access and long-term maintenance of important digital works. One of LC's roles could involve coordination with other national libraries. Several European national libraries and the national libraries of Canada and Australia have launched programs to collect and preserve the digital portions of their national bibliographies.

If the mechanisms to acquire and preserve the digital national bibliographies of some countries succeed, LC could be relieved of responsibility for preserving most digital materials from those countries. At that point, it could concentrate its curatorial efforts on works created or published by Americans or that reflect important aspects of U.S. history, policy development, and culture. Some other countries would need help.

For the foreseeable future, many developing countries will not have the resources to preserve their digital heritage. Curatorial responsibility for these collections could be shared by LC and other libraries that have well-developed repository systems rather than assuming that LC will serve as the repository for all significant materials globally. There are many other opportunities to divide up long-term preservation responsibilities by subject area or domain. LC already cedes responsibility for materials in medicine, agriculture, and education to the national libraries set up for those subject domains. In addition, the National Archives and Records Administration preserves records of the federal government that have long-term value for documenting U.S. government, policy development, and history. A clear delineation of LC's long-term curatorial responsibilities would be critical as a means to avoid unachievable commitments to long-term preservation and enable the Library to preserve materials that it is best suited or uniquely able to collect and maintain.

Many national libraries, university research libraries, national archives, bibliographic utilities, and organizations with large holdings of digital information are actively pursuing solutions to the problems of digital preservation. Although the Library of Congress might have been expected to provide leadership in this area as it once did in others, LC has at best played only a minimal role in these initiatives. As a consequence, it has little awareness of potential solutions that are emerging from joint research and development projects and has not contributed much to this important national and international problem for the library community.

Ensuring its leadership in digital preservation will require the Library to hire or develop relevant expertise. The Library should join and, where possible, lead or facilitate national and international research and development efforts in digital preservation. There are opportunities for the Library to learn from and contribute to such efforts in preserving born-digital information and converting certain types of information to digital form as a preservation strategy.

To make it a safe haven for preservation purposes, the Library should take an active role--including working with the Congress if necessary--in efforts to rework intellectual property restraints on copying and migration.

Even if LC carefully defines its roles and responsibilities along the continuum from serving as a portal to acting as the primary custodian for digital materials, there is an urgent need for it to enhance its technical capacity and expertise in digital preservation. Such preservation will involve a wide range of activities, including the following:

— "Protecting the bits"—The making of backup copies, periodic recopying to new media, and regular checking of object coherence and validity are required to make certain that rarely accessed materials remain technically sound. Access will be enhanced to the extent that archived materials remain online rather than, say, being stored on media such as tapes, which must be mounted manually.

— Archiving appropriate copies—For many digital materials, the format most useful for current services (say, a PDF file or a GIF image) is not the most robust for long-term archiving (SGML, XML, or TIFF may serve better). A preservation program must encompass the selection and archiving of the appropriate formats for long-term use and then the derivation of current-use copies appropriate to the technological base of today's users. It must also work with users to help them undertake these tasks.

— Maintaining appropriate metadata—All preservation activities will depend on the completeness and quality of the metadata for the objects to be preserved. It will be critical for the Library to monitor developments in metadata standards and follow best practices for metadata as they develop.

— Migrating formats—Even the most careful selection of archiving formats cannot ensure that objects will be useful in the decades to come. It will be necessary to migrate objects periodically from one archival format to another. Such processes must be carefully designed and executed to ensure minimal loss of content (it is impossible to ensure that all such migrations will be loss-free). Some works, such as those that include active software (e.g., Java applets), may raise particularly difficult issues.

— Conducting research and development—Only a handful of institutions are likely to face digital preservation challenges on the scale or scope of those that LC faces in the coming years. This makes it unlikely that LC will be able to import models and solutions for all of its preservation needs. An active program of research and development in digital preservation is needed to solve immediate preservation problems--technical, legal, and economic—at LC and to provide guidance to other libraries and archives.

— Educating the relevant communities—Especially in this transitional period, when digital materials are new and preservation practices are still in flux, institutions and particular communities will need to be educated about digital preservation: What is the state of the art? What factors must be taken into account in planning for preservation? LC is well situated to participate in such efforts and possibly to take the lead.

A robust preservation program will employ curators and preservation staff with knowledge of the formats of materials in their collections and of appropriate metadata standards and practices and an understanding of the issues involved in migrating objects from one format to another. It will require well-developed production services for creating the specified metadata, sound and robust repository services, and periodic quality checking and copying of objects in the collection.

In the future, libraries will also need to make much more extensive use of digitization for preservation. Some professionals consider digital objects—whether born digital or turned digital—unacceptable as preservation masters because their longevity is uncertain. In some cases, however, digital conversion may offer the only viable means of salvaging and preserving certain materials, such as audio recordings in obsolete analog formats. The Library has used digitization to preserve severely damaged black-and-white negatives and some audio and video records on magnetic media.

The challenges of digital preservation make it easy to overlook the benefits that libraries could enjoy by rapidly enhancing its capacity to collect and preserve digital information. Digital storage media are very compact, making it possible to store enormous quantities of information in a very small amount of space. Digital information can be managed and handled more automatically. More significantly, whatever libraries collects and preserves in digital form has the potential to be made accessible to anyone, anywhere, on any day of the week or at any time of the day.

References

Ackerman, Mark, S., Roy T., Fielding, "Collection Maintenance in Digital Library", *Digital Libraries 95: The Second Annual Conference on theory and Practice of Digital Libraries,* June 11-13, 1995, Austin, Texas USA.

Curtis, P. and D. A. Nichols, *MUDs Grow Up: Social Virtual Reality in the Real World*, 1993.

Halbert, Debora, "Weaving Webs of Ownership: Intellectual Property in an Information Age", Dissertation Draft, Stanford Law and Policy Review, Vol. 5, Copyright 1994.

Hartley, S., et al. "Enhancing teaching using the Internet", *Report of the Working Group on the World Wide Web as an interactive teaching resource. SIGCSE/SIGCUE ITiCSE '96*, 218-228.

Nikolaou, C, and M. Marazakis, "System Infrastucture for Digital Libraries: A Survey and Outlook", *SOFSEM'98, Lecture Notes in Computer Science 1521*, Springer, 186-203, 1998.

8

Online Library Services

Libraries have an inherent obligation to provide information service to support the educational, recreational, personal and economic endeavors of the members of their respective communities, as appropriate to the libraries' individual missions. Information services in libraries take a variety of forms including direct personal assistance, directories, signs, exchange of information culled from a reference source, reader's advisory service, dissemination of information in anticipation of user needs or interests, and access to electronic information. A library, because it possesses and organizes for use its community's concentration of information resources, must develop information services appropriate to its community and in keeping with the American Library Association's Library Bill of Rights. These services should take into account the information-seeking behaviors, the information needs, and the service expectations of the members of that community. Provision of information in the manner most useful to its clients is the ultimate test of all a library does.

Online Library Services in Asia and Pacific

Among the East Asian countries, Japan is by far the most advanced in terms of using information technology to provide the best possible information services to its users, although the Republic of Korea would almost be on a par with Japan. China, for its part, is still very much in the process of laying down the infrastructure in its bid to become a networked society in the near future. There are several major libraries and information centres in Japan involved in the provision of science and technology information as well as related information services.

In China, the Institute of Scientific and Technical Information of China (ISTIC) is one of the largest information services in that country. Established in October 1956, ISTIC is under the auspices of the State Science and Technology Commission or SSTC. ISTIC at present has a staff in excess of 1,100, and an annual allocation of funds averaging about 15 million yuan. The allocation covers about 70% of the budgetary requirements of the institute; the other 30% is generated from income from its information services.

In the Republic of Korea, the government rationalized the various information services along specialized lines in 1990, with the rapid growth of its information industry. One of the foremost is KINITI (Korea Institute of Industry and Technology Information), created in 1991 and responsible for industrial and technological information. ETRI (Electronic Technology Research Institute) responds to the industrial information needs, and KORDIC (Korea Research and Development Information Centre) is the national science and technology information service system. KINITI is a non-profit organization under the umbrella of the Ministry of Trade, Industry and Energy, and has 208 staff members at present.

The mission statement of the National Library of New Zealand is to contribute to the building of a learning society and enterprise economy within New Zealand by supporting the creation of an environment where information is readily available and widely used. It collects, preserves and makes accessible an important part of the documentary heritage of New Zealand.

The National Library of Australia (NLA) maintains the Australian Bibliographic Network (ABN) national bibliographic database, which now contains over 11 million records. The utility has over 1,400 institutional clients. The NLA is responsible also for Ozline, an online retrieval service providing access to thirty-five Australian databases. The NLA is now engaged in the complete redevelopment of ANB and Ozline.

In common with New Zealand, the Commonwealth Scientific and Industrial Research Organization (CSIRO) Information Services is the mainstay of the information infrastructure for science in Australia. It publishes fourteen independently reviewed journals of Australian science, the Australian Bibliography of Agriculture, an index to all CSIRO publications, the Australian Rural Research in Progress database, Science and Geography Abstracts (SAGE), some thirty book titles a year and about twenty video titles a year, and provides access to nearly thirty databases on the Ozline network.

The education and training of librarians and information professionals in East Asia and Oceania seems to be a major preoccupation in all the countries under review. Both formal degree programmes and short-term non-degree programmes are well established. As far as Japan is concerned, Matsumura thinks that the state of library and information science (LIS) education is rather contradictory.

Prior to 1978, library and information science education in China was available only at Wuhan University and Beijing University. In 1978, Wuhan University established a department of library and information studies offering programmes at both undergraduate and postgraduate levels. In the same year, ISTIC also began to train postgraduate students. Many universities or institutions of higher education started to offer library and information specialization during the next ten years and some major information institutions set up education and training programmes to train information personnel. At present, a total of about seventy universities and colleges offer information studies programmes in China. These institutions are distributed over twenty-three provinces, autonomous regions and municipalities.

Richardson reports that there are two main providers of formal librarianship training in New Zealand, although the New Zealand Library and Information Association (NZLIA) has a continuing education officer who coordinates, organizes and publicizes other training courses, meetings and initiatives. Other universities and polytechnics are also increasingly providing courses in areas such as records management and information systems that are of interest to librarians.

Education for the library and information sector in Australia is continually being improved and some innovative courses are being offered, with emphasis on the provision of continuing professional development courses and of education for people in isolated areas of Australia. In the Pacific, two institutions offer education and training for library and information work: the University of the South Pacific (USP) in Fiji, and the University of Papua New Guinea (UPNG) in Papua New Guinea.

USP offers a degree-level diploma programme in Information and Library Studies. The UPNG, for its part, provides library and information studies through its South Pacific Centre for Communication and Information in Development (SPCenCIID). Its librarianship programmes are offered at three levels: Certificate, Diploma and Bachelor's degree. A Certificate in Information Studies is offered by the centre, as well as a specialist Diploma in Teacher-Librarianship and a B.Sc. in Information Management. These correspond to position levels within libraries across Papua New Guinea.

The range of problems in the region related to education and training is rather wide: non-standardized curricular offerings in training institutions, leading to thc uneven quality of graduates (Japan); the uneven quality of instruction provided by training institutions, and their pressing need for more financial support (China); the acute lack of training institutions and teachers; and the need for more and better distance education programmes to train librarians in far-flung areas.

Most of the major countries in East Asia and Oceania are either starting or are already at an advanced stage in networking their libraries and databases. This is due partly to the importance attached by these countries to information as a tool for national development. Nowhere is this more apparent than in Australia and New Zealand, where information industries are at advanced stages of development.

In 1995, operational control of AARNET, a high-speed computer telecommunication network that connects Australian users to the Internet, was taken over by Telstra, Australia's major telecommunication carrier. The NLA's online catalogue and all the major Australian databases are accessible via AARNET. In New Zealand, NZBN is an online computer system that links most public, university, government and special libraries in New Zealand to a central bibliographic database maintained by the National Library.

NZBN's prime function is to support libraries throughout New Zealand in their reference, interloan, cataloguing and acquisitions activities. There are over 260 member libraries. Kiwinet, the National Library's online database service with a focus on New Zealand information, supports thirty-two databases of published information covering current affairs, New Zealand law, proposed legislation, politics, science, trademarks, education and health.

In the Pacific, Fiji, Noumea, Tonga, Vanuatu, Papua New Guinea and other countries have access to Internet services and are connected by e-mail. Fax, e-mail and the Internet provide the main routes through which information is communicated, disseminated and delivered. Currently existing regional information systems are the Pacific Information Centre (PIC), the Pacific Islands Marine Resources Information System (PIMRIS) and the Population Information Centre for the South Pacific, all based at the University of the South Pacific in Suva, Fiji.

In China, the fastest developing data communications centres are Beijing and Nanjing, although in South China cities like Shanghai and other free trade zones are not lagging behind. The most prominent service providers at present are the China National Public Data Network (CNPAC), CHINAPAC, Springnet International, Beijing Posts and Telecommunications Public Mailboxes, the Internet, and Finance and Trade Networks.

Local initiatives in networking, most of which use CHINAPAC, are the National Computing and Networking Facility of China (NCFC), the Tsinghua University Network (TUNET), the Chinese Academy of Sciences Network (CASNET), Peking University Network (PUNET) and the Chinese Education Research Network (CERNET). At present, PUNET users can access one of the largest scientific literature collections in China.

In addition, a major library information retrieval system is being developed under the auspices of Beijing University. Japan embarked in 1994 on the establishment of the Inter-Ministry Research Information Net-work (IMnet), envisioned to be a seamless research information network that links national research institutes and other public research organizations, both in the country and abroad.

The Republic of Korea, like Japan, has a well-developed information industry, with the natural consequence that it has well-established national information networks. For instance, the Korea Research Environment Open Network (KREONet) and the Korea Education Network (KREN) are public-based communication networks for science information. Both of these networks were established to serve the information needs of the academic and research communities.

The goal of KREONet, started in 1988, is to connect all the computing facilities of R&D institutes in the Republic of Korea (120 organizations currently are connected and the network is operated by the Systems

Engineering Research Institute (SERI)). KREN was established in May 1990 and is supported by the Ministry of Education. It has three components: the inter-university network, the library network and the educational administration network.

The library network component of KREN includes all national libraries, major public libraries, university/college libraries and special subject libraries. The goal of the library network is to con-nect by 1997 the 350 libraries scattered throughout the Republic of Korea using nineteen regional switching centres. The effort, which is being co-ordinated by the National Central Library, has to date already standardized the KOMARC (Korean MARC) format to KS (Korean Standard), developed six domestic bibliographic databases, developed and distributed the library application software KOLAS for personal computers, and distributed UNIX-based software.

Finally, the DNS (Dacom-Net Service) is the most popular data communication network in the Republic of Korea today. It is operated on a commercial basis by the Data Communication Corporation of Korea (DACOM). DACOM had a monopoly of the country's data communication market since its establishment in 1982, but with government deregulation of such services in 1991, more than ten companies have started to provide similar services.

India has one of the world's largest populations of qualified scientific and technical personnel, yet about half its people cannot even sign their names. This wide-spread illiteracy, while dampening demand for printed materials, calls for extensive information transfer through audio, video and multimedia products. Most of the countries have introduced vernacular languages in official work and higher education, and others are making efforts to do so.

However, a knowledge of English is fairly widespread, except in countries like Viet Nam and Indonesia, where the early colonial rulers were French and Dutch respec-tively; these countries also have introduced English as the second language in their education systems. Such foreign-language proficiency has prompted several transnational information companies to set up a base in the region for their international operations. Politically, the region has experienced turbulence from the time the countries were freed from the shackles of colonial rule soon after the Second World War.

While Viet Nam, the Lao People's Democratic Republic and Cambodia are still striving hard to recover from the damage inflicted on their socio-economies by prolonged war and civil conflicts, a civil war still rages in Afghanistan. The other countries currently have more or less stable political systems, except for sporadic militancy and separatist movements.

Some of the countries, like Bhutan, are heavily dependent upon the agricultural sector, whereas Singapore draws 62% from the service sector, followed by Bangladesh, Sri Lanka and Thailand, Pakistan and the Philippines. Since the propensity to use information in agriculture is lower than in manufacturing and services, the higher sectoral contribution to agriculture would signify a low demand for information. One could infer from the above that the demand for information, especially library-based information, may not be high.

Technologically advanced countries like India, Indonesia, Pakistan and the Philippines are also no better off; they have 8 to 10 telephone lines per 1,000 population. The state of school libraries in the region is more or less uniformly poor. When some of the schools do not even have trained teachers, it is too much to expect that they will have professional librarians. If by chance they do have a librarian', it is one of the teachers in the school who is given the additional charge, with or without proper training, of managing the library. When many schools cannot afford to provide appropriate furniture for their students, setting up libraries is well beyond their dreams. With the limited resources at their disposal, they can acquire only a few textbooks and cheap story books.

In India the implementation of the National Literacy Mission has brought out the need to provide reading materials at the school and village levels; how this will be organized remains to be seen. The National Library of Indonesia's scheme of providing short introductory training for teachers with the possibility to accumulate credits, and the endeavour of the Centre for Library Development to set up model school libraries in twenty-six provinces, are experiences to learn from.

In India, since independence in 1947 there has been a proliferation of universities and R&D organizations. However, in terms of collections, very few universities are information-rich. The disparity is more pronounced when they are compared with professional institutions like the five Indian Institutes of Technology—each with annual acquisitions of over US$500,000—and the Indian Institute of Science with US$1 million.

Even in terms of services, the academic libraries are way behind the community of national laboratories—the forward-looking step of the small Gulbarga University in subscribing to CD-ROMs in place of print products may be cited by way of exception only. Strengthening higher education libraries in Indonesia started as late as 1988 with World Bank support. Now all forty-five universities and institutions have well-developed libraries. Progress has been equally marked in the nine university libraries of Malaysia. The libraries in Thailand are well-developed in terms of services. A process of organization is under way for the 105 university and college libraries of Viet Nam.

In Myanmar, lack of funds has constrained library development in the three univer-sities and specialized institutions. However, irrespective of the attention that library development received, the tale of woes, such as lack of financial resources, dearth of space and shortage of trained staff, remains more or less the same across the countries of the region. Differing perceptions of the role that the national library and the public library system should play in intellectual, societal and literacy development, and varying levels of investment and workforce inputs, have given rise to widely dissimilar patterns of development.

Equipped with a local area network (LAN), it prepares a wide range of computerized products and assumes the co-ordination responsibilities for the national library networking project. The high point in national and public library movements is found in Singapore. The report of the Library 2000 Review Committee in 1994, the IT 2000 plan, and an information technology usage survey in 1992 had set the pace for the development of the National Information Infrastructure. The Library 2000 plan will see the establishment of a constellation of libraries of all kinds.

In contrast, the National Library of India provides only traditional services. The Indian National Bibliography of the Central Reference Library is way behind its schedule. The national libraries in specific subject areas—that is, science at the Indian National Scientific Documentation Centre (INS-DOC), medicine at the National Medical Library and agriculture at the Indian Agriculture Research Institute—are in a better state.

INSDOC publishes Indian Science Abstracts, which is now on schedule and compiles the National Union Catalogue of Scientific Serials in India, available online. The National Library of Pakistan, on the other hand, was inaugurated as recently as 1993. The computerized preparation of the

Pakistan National Bibliography and special directories has been initiated. Since 1992, in Viet Nam, all provincial public libraries have been provided with PCs for the creation of local databases. After establishing linkages with the National Library in 1994, the provincial public libraries derive assistance for database development from the National Library and in return contribute new records to the national union catalogue.

The existing Nepal National Library is being reorganized to contribute to the improvement of literacy through pilot public and school library services, in close association with the Basic and Primary Education Programme. As in the case of India, the public library service in Indonesia, the Philippines and Thailand is thinly spread. The units are understaffed and underfinanced. It is proposed to improve outreach to rural areas, which is low, by using bookmobiles. Specialized services are offered by organizations of diverse legal and economic status. The most prominent of these are the national information and documentation centres such as BANSDOC in Bangladesh, INSDOC and the Defence Scientific Information and Documentation Centre in India, the Centre for Scientific Documentation and Information (PDII-LIPI) in Indonesia, the Pakistan Scientific and Technological Information Centre (PASTIC), and the National Centre for Science and Technology Information and Documentation (NACESTID) in Viet Nam.

These national centres are better endowed in terms of financial and human resources, and better equipped. Their activities usually include partly or fully computerized library services, database development and database services, document supply services, specialized training, compilation of the national union catalogues, and the like. Library and information units attached to national laboratories, industries, government departments and executive agencies provide information services in specific subjects; for example, the petroleum company and law library in Brunei Darussalam, the Bangladesh Agricultural Research Council, the National Chemical Laboratory, Central Leather Research Institute, Central Food Technological Research Institute, Central Manufacturing Technology Institute and National Institute of Immunology in India, the rubber and palm oil institutes in Malaysia, the Royal Nepal Academy of Science and Technology and the Agricultural Projects Services Centre in Nepal, the Pakistan Forest Institute, the Natural Resources Energy and Science Authority of Sri Lanka (NARESA), and the National Research Council of Thailand.

These organizations generally have enough resources to invest in information materials, equipment, space and human resources. In the larger national interest, the resources of such closed groups should be made accessible to a wider user base. A forward-looking step in this direction has been taken by the following Government of India programmes: the National Information System for Science and Technology (NISSAT), the Bio-technology Information System (BTIS) and the Environmental Information System (ENVIS), which support specialized information facilities around existing nuclei and enable their ser-vices to extend to the national community of users.

The Philippines also has programmes of a similar nature. The Science and Technology Information Network (SciNet-Phil) is a consortium of libraries and information centres in twenty-one agencies under the Department of Science and Technology. It has been designed to promote and improve the flow and use of scientific and technical information through resource-sharing.

In Pakistan, development has followed two paths: one for science and technology, covering major sectors like agriculture, industry, energy, medicine, water resources and general science and technology; and the other including the National Library, the National Documentation Centre and the National Archive Centre.

International assistance has helped to develop similar facilities in the Sri Lanka Scientific and Technical Information Network (SLSTINET), Viet Nam's (NACESTIO) and Indonesia's IPTKnet. Computer applications in the region were at a low level until the advent of micro CDS/ISIS, software developed by UNESCO.

Because it is distributed frcc of charge, its use has grown at an exponential rate in the region. In India, the CDS/ISIS installation base has grown to about 1,300, with about 3,000 application specialists trained through about 200 low-cost work-shops. The software is used for database development, maintenance of personnel records, patient records in hospitals, and so on.

A comprehensive library automation package called SANJAY, based on CDS/ISIS, has been developed for small and medium-size libraries. Interfaces for local language handling have been developed in India, Thailand and Viet Nam. MINISIS, a package developed by the International

Development Research Centre (IDRC) in Canada, is also popular in the region, but the growth in its applications base is constrained owing to the relatively uncommon hardware platform that it requires.

Some more affluent institutions use software like VTLS, ATLAS, URICA, TINLIB and TECH-LIB in minicomputer, mainframe computer, network and client-server environments. Few countries in the region have made efforts to develop library software indigenously.

Growing awareness of the need for resource-sharing, the all-round resource shortage, an increase in computer installations or access facilities in libraries, an enhanced skill base, and improved telecommunication facilities within and across geographical regions have been responsible for the recent spurt in library networking activities.

In Bangladesh a comprehensive project on automation and networking of science and technology libraries is currently under implementation. In contrast, India has adopted a three-pronged approach:

— metropolitan library networks in major cities;

— countrywide networks of academic and research institutions, such as INFLIBNET; and

— sectoral networks on bio-informatics and the environment.

Since the beginning of the 1990s, the use of CD-ROM databases has grown at a rapid pace. This was catalysed by UNESCO, which provided workstations complete with CD-ROM drive and selected CD-ROM databases to a few expert institutions in the region; these small facilities had a great demonstration value.

Now, of course, utilization of CD-ROM products such as MEDLINE, AGRICOLA, AGRIS and CABI is relatively common in almost all countries. Perhaps MEDLINE has the largest installation base, owing to the generous support provided by the World Health Organization (WHO).

Conversion of databases to CD-ROM has yet to take off, as large databases that can reasonably occupy an entire CD-ROM are few, unless collaborative inputting arrangements like those of AHEAD are arranged. Accessing database hosts in Europe, North America and Japan may not be a technical problem for the South Asian countries, but payment for searches could be. As yet no large commercial host has appeared in the region.

Information Market

Singapore, Malaysia, Thailand, India, Sri Lanka and Viet Nam have taken measures to develop the national information market. The most notable endeavour is the Industrial Technological and Market Information (ITMIN) network of Sri Lanka. This network of databases is a public limited-liability company whose shareholders are a mix of public and private agencies.

The company, also assisted by the United Nations Development Programme (UNDP), the United Nations Industrial Development Organization (UNIDO) and the Government of Sri Lanka in the initial stages, is mandated to set up the backbone for a national information infrastructure, to strengthen and upgrade industrial, technological and commercial information activities in the country, to enhance professional capabilities in related spheres, to facilitate the sharing of knowledge and skills among information technology professionals and end-users, and to provide information services to foreign investors.

In India commercialization is being independently pursued by almost all programmes, including the National Information System for Science and Technology (NISSAT) and the National Informatics Centre (NIC), and some of the larger libraries have opened their facilities to outside clientele on a daily/monthly/annual fee basis or on a block-grant basis. The concept of marketing is widely discussed in various forums. This is just the beginning.

The all-round budget crunch and consequent need to supplement resources through revenue generated by selling information products and services, the general demand to improve access to information for a wider user base, and increased appreciation of the fruitful role that information could play in decision-making systems will invariably force greater use of marketing concepts in the future. The region also displays a wide diversity in education and training. In the Philippines formal library education started as early as 1914 at the University of the Philippines, and in India in 1937 at the University of Madras (non-formal training was initiated in 1901 at the National Library, Calcutta). In contrast, a Bachelor's level course was introduced in Nepal only in 1995/96 at Tribhuvan University.

The Library Association of Bangladesh (LAB) plays an important role in library education by running a one-year postgraduate diploma course and conducting a six-month certificate course twice a year in four different cities. The National Administration of Educational Management has an elaborate programme for school librarians. Library Science is also a part of Bachelor of Education courses. In India, an entire range of facilities for formal education is available today, but only those offered by INSDOC and the Indian Statistical Institute's Documentation Research and Training Centre keep in step with technological developments.

Efforts made by regular university departments to modernize are handicapped by poor budgetary support. Among several distance educational facilities, the one run by the Indira Gandhi National Open University (IGNOU) is worth mentioning for its excellent course materials which include television broadcasts, video clips and contact programmes run by its regional centres.

Trans-country programmes like APINMAP helped in identifying common problem areas and in exploring solutions on a co-operative basis, thereby providing an ideal ground for testing the concept of Technical Co-operation among Developing Countries (TCDC). Community Learning and Resource Centres (CLARC), an initiative taken by the General Information Programme of UNESCO, aims at improving the downstream information services, in parallel with the development of library and information institutions at the national level.

The pilot projects of CLARC were conceptualized to develop an approach that would make literacy classes better understood and appreciated by the target group -that is, people in rural, isolated and depressed areas of developing countries. The objective was also to strengthen institutional linkages between the target community and existing resources and facilities at the national and local levels. After case-studies in Bangladesh, Indonesia, the Philippines and Thailand, the concept was implemented in the Lao People's Democratic Republic, the Philippines and Viet Nam. CLARC has been used most notably to develop a project for nineteen depressed provinces of the Philippines under the Social Reform Agenda of the President.

Mosques also served as repositories of human knowledge and played important cultural and educational roles similar to those of present-day schools and public libraries. Two current Arab universities—Zeituna in Tunisia and Al-Azhar in Egypt—date back to that era. Many Arab libraries, particularly national and academic libraries, are attempting to reassemble their former manuscript collections that are now scattered all over the world. The Arab League Educational, Cultural and Scientific Organization (ALECSO) established the Arab Manuscript Institute for this purpose.

The Al-Albait Foundation in Amman, Jordan, has collected 1,600 catalogues of Arabic manuscripts. Arabic books were first printed in Europe in 1514 (Rome) and 1620 (Paris). Arab libraries and information centres in their present sense date back to the nineteenth century, or even more commonly to the present century. Presently all types of libraries are represented in most Arab states, with variations in levels of progress. Five Arab states, namely, Djibouti, Kuwait, Oman, the Sudan and Yemen, do not have a national library, although Oman has the nucleus for one, and Kuwait, the Sudan and Yemen have libraries or information centres that perform part of a national library's functions.

Moreover, the national libraries in Lebanon and Somalia have suffered great damage from civil war. The first national library in the region was that of Algeria, established in 1835, while the most recent is the Jordanian National Library, established in 1990. Some are also national archives as in Egypt, Iraq, Jordan and Morocco. With the exception of the UAE, all Arab states with or without national libraries have legal deposit laws or regulations. Jordan's law is the only legislation that covers computer software. In the Sudan, with no national library, legal deposit is entrusted to the National Archives.

But enforcement of legal deposit legislation is far from satisfactory in the region as a whole, particularly concerning official publications, and comprehensive coverage of all types of materials produced in the country has not yet been achieved. Dissertations, for instance are entrusted to the Ein-Shams University Library in Egypt, and printed music to the National Music Conservatoire in Tunisia. Moreover, all national libraries, except in Morocco, claim that they collect materials relating to their respective countries or written by their citizens and published elsewhere, but it is evident that they all lack the mechanisms for doing so. Few Arab countries have copyright laws.

An Arab copyright agreement, however, was signed in 1981 by fourteen states. All national libraries except in Lebanon, Mauritania and Somalia publish national bibliographies. They differ in frequency; all are annual except Algeria, Egypt and Tunisia. The contents also vary as most cover commercially published materials while some cover government publications, school textbooks, periodi-cals and dissertations.

International Standard Book Numbers (ISBNs) have been applied in Egypt, Morocco and Saudi Arabia, while Jordan and Tunisia are in the process of introducing them. An Arab stan-dard (ASMO 521) is available for ISBN, but few Arab states have introduced it as a national standard. Lists of periodicals are separate from the national bibliographies and tend to be published at irregular intervals. No such lists have been published in Bahrain, the Libyan Arab Jamahiriya or Mauritania. Algeria and Morocco have ISSN data-bases.

International Standard Serial Numbers (ISSNs) are comprehensively applied only in Morocco and Saudi Arabia. Some journals have been assigned ISSNs directly from the International Serial Data System in Paris. An Arab standard (ASMO 581) is available for ISSN, but again few Arab states have introduced it as a national standard. Although some states have made attempts to publish indexes of periodical articles, mostly through centres other than national libraries, the national libraries in Saudi Arabia and the Syrian Arab Republic are the only ones doing this on a regular basis. The former comprehensively covers Saudi Arabian serials, while the latter covers eighteen newspapers and fifty-two journals and is published quarterly.

Education has progressed relatively fast during the second half of this century. Nevertheless, illiteracy is still high at more than 43% of the population at the age of 15 years and over. This rate varies a lot among individual states, as it is Education is developing quantitatively rather than qualitatively. Schools ignore, for instance, individual learning and a shift from a teacher-oriented to a student-oriented educational system. School libraries are not contributing to the educational process in its modern sense.

Most existing libraries in the preschool and first levels are no more than a cupboard in an inaccessible office of the school. The other weak point is the staffing, sometimes nonexistent, but mostly only part-time or insufficiently qualified. Moreover, concern about school libraries only starts at the second level, when it is too late for the student. The shift from a traditional school library to a resource centre is very rare; instead, some resource centres are established outside the school environment, presumably to serve a number of schools (Jordan has established three such centres).

The Union of Arab Universities (UAU) signed an agreement in 1986 with the University of Jordan Library naming it as depository library for Arab theses. Since then, the library has issued an index of deposited titles, and some 6,000 titles have been received. Various other higher education institutions offer post-secondary education for a period of two to three years, or technical degrees. They are mostly state-financed, except in Egypt and Jordan where some are private, and concentrate mainly on vocational and technical education.

Responsibility is distributed among different government agencies in most states: municipal, local government, ministry of education or ministry of culture. In a few cases, however, libraries are private. No kind of co-ordination or co-operation exists. Human resources are very inadequate. Services are very traditional except in a few instances, such as the King Abdul Aziz Public Library in Saudi Arabia and the Abdul Hameed Shoman Foundation Library in Jordan, both of which are fully automated using MINISIS.

The latter offers a unique service by having a computer library with fifteen computer workstations for both adults and children. Most users are students from all levels of education, emphasizing the educational rather than the recreational function of the public library. Children's libraries may be part of the public library, whether separate or sharing the same premises, or independent. Interest in children's literature and libraries is rather unsatisfactory. Special libraries are those found in government and public agencies as well as private ventures such as banks, chambers of commerce and industry, companies, societies and research centres.

They all tend to be rather small, varying in quality and size from a few hundred to tens of thousands of volumes, but no data are available from any Arab state. As compared to others, some of these libraries are advanced as regards automation and link with online services, and are interested in the Internet. Most of the more advanced ones are from the public sector: central bank libraries in Egypt, Jordan, Kuwait, Morocco and Tunisia; the Ministry of Finance in Saudi Arabia and the Ministry of Planning in Kuwait. In the private sector, libraries in commercial banks, business and industry are now feeling the pressure to provide effective information services.

With the exception of Morocco (where the school reports to the Ministry of Planning which has been recently disbanded), the schools of library and information science are all university departments, mostly in faculties of arts, but also in faculties of social sciences or education. There is no such school in Djibouti, Mauritania, Somalia, the UAE or Palestine.

Kuwait has one post-secondary department and Jordan has two, while Algeria, the Sudan and Tunisia have a diploma programme in addition to formal university study. Unfortunately, Jordan has suspended its postgraduate diploma as of 1995. Teacher/student ratios are below international standards in most schools. The curriculum is mostly unbalanced as courses unrelated to librarianship and information science account for about 43% of the entire BA programmes.

Modern information technology is creeping slowly into the curriculum, with the Moroccan school the best equipped. A recent development, hopefully signalling better co-operation, co-ordination and harmonization, is the formation of the Society of Arab Library Schools (1993), located in Rabat, Morocco.

As the role of library schools in training is too often unsatisfactory, continuing education activities are run by library associations, library sections of the ministries of education, some national information centres, some national libraries and some regional and international organizations. But this training is not carried out systematically, and no follow-up programmes are ever done anywhere.

Conferences and seminars are held in the region both nationally and regionally, although the latter are diminishing owing to the severe financial crises Arab organizations are facing. On paper, there are twelve library associations at the national level in ten states. But it is difficult to assess their activities in concrete terms. For instance, only the Jordanian Library Association has continued issuing its quarterly journal, Risalat al-maktaba since 1965.

There are four other regional associations: the Arab Federation of Libraries and Institutions (AFLI), established in Tunis in 1985, the Arab Association for University Libraries, established in Kuwait in 1976 (no longer existing), the Arab Branch of the International Council on Archives (ICA) and the recently formed Society of Arab Library Schools. The American Society for Information Science (ASIS) has a Gulf branch.

Arabic professional library literature is rather weak; current journals (other than those intended for bibliographical control) number only nine titles for all the Arab states put together. The other important part of library literature is the provision of working tools in Arabic. For cataloguing purposes, the Anglo-American cataloguing rules (AACR2) were arabized and published by the Jordanian Library Association, while all International Standard Bibliographic Descriptions (ISBDs) were arabized and published by ALECSO.

The eleventh and twelfth abridged editions of the Dewey Decimal Classification (DDC) were translated and modified by ALECSO. Filing rules were prepared and published by the Arab League Documentation Centre (ALDOC). Format, based on the Common Communication Format (CCF) of UNESCO, was prepared by the Jordanian National Information Centre. Sixty-two Arab Standards on documentation and information based on International Standards Organization (ISO) standards were issued by the Arab Organization for Standardization and Metrology (ASMO) before it ceased to exist as an independent Arab Organization.

Since 1990 it has become a department of the Arab Industrial Development and Mining Organization (AIDMO), and no further standards have been issued in the field of information. Subject headings and thesauri have also been published, although the former cater for small and medium-size libraries. There are now four general lists and three specialized, while there are sixteen specialized thesauri, two monolingual, and the remainder bilingual or trilingual. The list of Medical Subject Headings (MeSH) also is being translated.

The Secretariat-General of the League of Arab States, through ALDOC, took the initiative to create an Arab network (ARIS-NET). ALDOC accomplished this through many practical measures: organizing meetings, publishing manuals and bibliographies, holding regional and national training courses, arabizing MINISIS and CDS/ISIS, and preparing Guidelines for Preparing a National Policy for Information Systems and Services in the Arab World. The latter was distributed among Arab states, but no state has applied it since 1989 and the project has faded out, with no more action being taken since 1992.

Telecommunications in most of the Arab states are developing much faster than libraries and information services. Those still suffering are mainly Mauritania, Somalia and the Sudan. Some, such as the Gulf states and Tunisia, have already developed their national data transmission networks. Many recently automated libraries and information centres are now using local area networks (LANs). The problem that has not been solved is the creation of national and Arab information networks.

Consequently, large library collections of between 100,000 and 500,000 books, periodicals, unpublished manuscripts and non-book materials are not uncommon in many African university libraries. Significantly more modest resources are typical of academic libraries at lower levels. However, the downturn in the economic fortunes of African countries during the last decade or so has had a devastating effect on the quality of library services in academic institutions, virtually all of which are publicly funded.

Most of them can no longer afford to buy new books, and large proportions of periodical subscriptions have been cancelled. With a corresponding inability to switch to the new information technologies, African university libraries in particular, and African academics in general, face a dim future indeed. International assistance agencies, such as the World Bank, are beginning to respond positively to the grave situation by implementing massive rehabilitation projects, designed to restore services essentially to what they were in the 1970s and early 1980s.

For instance, the World Bank has recently granted a US$15.8 million development loan to the Senegal Government for the improvement of library services in the Cheikh Anta Diop University of Dakar. This programme includes the renovation and the extension of the central library, the renewal of the collections, the purchase of equipment, computerization of the libraries and further training for the staff.

Special libraries have fared marginally better than their academic counterparts only because they are generally smaller, concentrating on well-targeted sectors of African economies—industry, agriculture, health, etc.—and without the responsibility of providing services to students. But the need to adopt modern information processing and delivery services is probably greater and more urgent in this sector—a need that remains unmet mainly as a result of severe funding constraints.

Public and school library services are in a state of decline throughout most of Africa because the largely external initiatives which established them have not been sustained by adequate indigenous funding, effective literacy campaigns and indigenous publishing in the local languages. Consequently, old, foreign books continue to feature prominently on the shelves of many an African public or school library, on the questionable premise that it is better to have something to read than nothing at all! It is difficult to escape the conclusion, therefore, that the development of public and school library services is still very low down the priority lists of most African governments.

Modern computer-based library and information services are beginning to make an appreciable impact in Africa, especially in the relatively well-endowed international research organizations. There is growing evidence that the International Institute of Tropical Agriculture's (IITA's) success story (published in the African Journal of Library, Archives and Information Science, which described how the services of a large library were successfully computerized), is beginning to have the desired multiplier effects in the region.

However, inadequate funding and insufficient numbers of appropriately trained and motivated human resources constitute the main obstacles to more success stories of this kind. The proceedings of a recent Seminar on Information Provision to Rural Communities in Africa strongly suggest that African governments may, at last, be addressing the fundamental issue of bringing library and information services to the vast populations of non-literate and rural communities in francophone, lusophone and anglophone African countries.

As African governments, in collaboration with multilateral and bilateral development assistance agencies and international and non-governmental organizations, invest more resources in the development of this vital sector of African library and information services, the long-awaited measurable impact may not be long in coming. The African private sector is dominated by the activities of big multinational corporations which specialize in such capital-intensive enterprises as mineral exploration and marketing, banking and finance, manufacturing, and trading in primary commodities. In virtually all cases, the headquarters of the enterprises are outside Africa, from where specifically African policies are determined and controlled.

Consequently, direct private sector investment in African library and information services, in support of the corporations' Africa-based enterprises, is not common. Indigenous initiatives in this highly competitive area are relatively new and small, with little or no attention to the development of indigenous library and information services, so far. With the exception of the biggest enterprises, such as the well-known mining conglomerates of South Africa and the giant manufacturing and marketing United Africa Company of Nigeria, it is, indeed, difficult to locate effective library services in the African private sector.

However, the increasing digitization of information services has been a boon to private enterprises, including those operating in Africa, which have appropriate resources and international connections to capitalize on the fast-growing business of transborder data flow. There is little evidence that

African governments are even aware of the serious implications of telematics and transborder data flow in their development efforts. And yet, the evidence is strong that transborder data flow affects the international economic exchanges of all countries, and that African countries in particular are not getting much from the value-added direct benefits resulting from the processing and distribution stages of the raw data which they produce.

Trade in information goods and services, for instance, has increased exponentially over the past three decades, partly in the context of growing trade in services generally. Increasingly, it is being recognized that data flows are commodity flows (either in their own right or because they are closely related to trade flows in other areas, such as shipping) and that, therefore, the subject should be regarded as an economic issue. It has also been established that transnational corporations are the major exporters of data and that their information flow activities must be closely monitored in the overall interests of both generator and recipient countries.

The information advantage of transnational corporations may place domestic enterprise at a competitive disadvantage, thus hindering the emergence of indigenous capacities in host countries. This factor also bears directly on the bargaining positions of these corporations vis-à-vis states and groups within states (for example, trade unions). Evidently, Africa has much to ponder on this sensitive and potentially lucrative aspect of information services. Electronic commerce is beginning to make a noticeable appearance on the African business scene, especially in the region's international capitals of Addis Ababa, Dakar, Johannesburg and Nairobi.

In other locations, experimental or embryonic initiatives have not blossomed, largely because of severe limitations in telecommunication infrastructure and anachronistic or nonexistent information and informatics policies. The land areas and populations of most African countries are small; only Nigeria and South Africa have sufficiently large populations to justify the establishment of large national library and information systems.

South Africa's relatively sophisticated national library system is a model for other African countries in organization, funding support and comprehensive coverage of services normally associated with national libraries worldwide. The system comprises three national libraries: the South African Library, the State Library (in Pretoria) and the National Library for the Blind. The South African Library and the State Library have deposit privileges, as do the Library of Parliament in Cape Town, the Natal Society Library in Pietermaritzburg and the Bloemfontein Public Library.

The South African Library, founded in 1818, is the national centre for collecting and preserving legal deposit, and rare and unique material, with the additional responsibility of compiling retrospective bibliographies and indexes of Southern African materials. In 1990 it established a Centre for the Book to stimulate interest in the book and reading and to provide a meeting forum for publishers, booksellers and librarians. The State Library, founded in 1887, is responsible for co-ordinating the national book-stock, exchange programmes with other countries, interlibrary loans, redistributing surplus material and compiling the South African National Bibliography, which continues Publications Received in Terms of Copyright Act No. 9 of 1916, issued by the State Library from 1933 to 1958.

It also co-ordinates the exchange of bibliographic records and national and international bibliographic standards. The South African Library for the Blind was founded in 1919 and became a national library for the print-handicapped in 1969. It produces and provides books in Braille and on tape, and offers a service for blind students throughout the country. Unfortunately, the National Library of Nigeria has not, so far, fulfilled many of the expectations described either in the 1964 Act which established it or in the revised National Library of Nigeria Act of 1970.

It provides rudiments of national library and information services, using several rented and dysfunctional buildings in Lagos, separated by many kilometres of often chaotic roads. In 1975 and, again, roughly a decade later, all seemed set to commence the construction of a building complex befitting the National Library of Nigeria. On both occasions, political rather than economic reasons seemed to have frustrated the implementation of an important national project.

Web-based Resources

Websites are sometimes used as front ends, or user interfaces, for accessing an organisation's database(s). Site users search prepared lists or put together their own searches which, in turn, query the content of a database. The information returned from these queries is displayed as an HTML (hypertext mark-up language) document to the user. In many cases, documents exist as objects in a database. Each document will have its own unique identifier, usually reflected in the URL. This means that a user can bookmark the particular document and return to it later without reconstructing the original search query (provided the document has not been deleted from the database).

Even if the site's main or top-level pages are static, dynamic data access websites raise some additional issues for agency recordkeepers. Not all users 'see' the same website. At designated levels, the pages displayed on users' browsers are based on what they ask for, therefore user queries are an integral part of generating the website and may need to be captured. Information contained in databases behind the site may be continually changing. An increasing number of websites are being built which generate all of the pages 'on the fly'. This means that the component parts of each individual page—its content, structure and presentation—are generated dynamically using a combination of databases and style sheets based on:

— a stored set of user preferences;
— a stored set of access profiles;
— a user query; and/or
— the capabilities of the user's browser.

In these situations, the website does not exist in any single or easily capturable form. Each user sees a different 'site' based on their stored preferences and access rights, current needs, and the capabilities or limitations of the technology they are using. Although the end result for the user might be a set of static pages, the processes which build the pages involve the use of a number of software tools. This is the point at which websites become more like software applications than electronic publications.

Agencies need to consider how to archive dynamically generated web resources in a fully functional state. The major issues these sites raise for agency recordkeepers is the need to choose whether to use an object-based or an event-based approach to keeping records of web resources and activities. That is, an agency needs to determine whether it wishes to focus on keeping records of:

— the individual transactions between clients (users) and servers (agencies); or
— the objects that comprise the content of the site at any given time.

Following are the fundamentals of good web-based recordkeeping:

— Take a systematic approach
— Assign and document responsibilities
— Determine requirements for records
— Apply metadata
— Capture records into a recordkeeping system

In keeping records of web-based activity, there are certain fundamental procedures that all agencies should observe. These rules are not unique to web-based recordkeeping. They are commonsense approaches which organisations, as a matter of course, should implement as part of their regimes for managing information resources—whether these are web resources, electronic or paper-based records, or data in legacy systems.

Effective web-based recordkeeping relies on pursuing a systematic approach that is generally applicable to all records, regardless of format. The following strategies are applicable to all electronic records, regardless of format.

— Promulgate agency policy on making and keeping records of web-based activity
— Formulate a plan for capturing and maintaining these electronic records
— Formulate an electronic records preservation plan
— Implement specific website maintenance procedures

Three or four different groups of agency staff may have responsibility for making and keeping records of web-based activity and resources. They are:

— content authors;
— website administrators;
— recordkeeping practitioners; and
— information technology staff, such as network managers or data administrators.

Although the spread of responsibilities may vary from agency to agency, the important point is that responsibilities need to be assigned to individuals or positions, and documented. If an agency has a high public profile and is particularly open to public scrutiny, it is liable—and may be called to account for—the material on its public website. A major component of an agency's internal accountability process should be assigning and documenting responsibilities for web-based recordkeeping.

One example of the type of responsibility that must be assigned and properly documented is the capturing of individual records of web-based activity into a formal agency recordkeeping system. It would make sense to assign this responsibility to either the content author, or to agency publications staff or to recordkeeping staff, rather than to the websit administrator. However, an agency might choose to extend some recordkeeping responsibility to the website administrator.

In this scenario, a procedure might be written which requires the website administrator to inform responsible staff when material has been posted to or removed from the website. This would help to ensure that the relevant administrative metadata is appended or linked to the original record in the recordkeeping system. Before determining specific strategies and actions for keeping records of web-based activity, agencies need to know which records they need to create, and how long those records should be retained. The National Archives of Australia has developed a number of tools, including the DIRKS Manual, to assist agencies to ascertain recordkeeping requirements and to determine the need to create, capture, retain or dispose of records.

Agencies must decide what records of their web-based activities are needed to support operational needs and to satisfy broader organisational accountability requirements and community expectations. An agency's decision to keep or not keep records of its web-based activity must, as with all records, be made on the basis of an assessment of business risks, costs and benefits. In particular, agencies must assess the business risks of not enabling full accountability for their actions.

Agencies also need to be aware of their responsibilities under the Privacy Act 1988 with regard to capturing and maintaining records containing personal information. These responsibilities extend to keeping records of web-based activity. Where a website publication exactly replicates a printed publication, it is sufficient to maintain the printed version of the publication as the record that is captured into the agency's recordkeeping system. If, however, the website version contains significant web-based functionality that is not adequately replicated in the printed version, then web-based records of the publication must be captured into the agency's recordkeeping system.

Decisions regarding how often an agency needs to take snapshots of public web resources will vary from agency to agency. These decisions should be based on an analysis of the risks faced by the agency in relation to its web-based activities. Web resources which go beyond being a publication, include those that are highly interactive, or serve as the front end of organisational databases and provide a unique response to queries and requests. In these circumstances, the records that should be captured are the requests made and the unique resources that are delivered in response to the queries.

Access to Online Collections

In this rapidly changing environment, libraries must continue monitoring trends, assessing their performance by seeking feedback from current users, and anticipating the needs of future users. To meet and anticipate these needs of the academic and research communities, libraries are collaborating as never before, forming partnerships both within and outside their own institutions, often sharing control in order to effect critical change. While circumstances will vary from library to library, the results of the task force survey demonstrate many ways that libraries are responding to user expectations.

Libraries are expanding the amount and variety of high-quality information resources that are directly available to academic and research users via the Web. They are also expanding the definition of collections to include "born-digital" content that is neither owned nor licensed by the library. The varied efforts toward this goal may be characterized as follows: changing collection development policies to emphasize the acquisition of electronic resources, engaging in digitizing and electronic publishing projects, and assuming responsibility for managing and servicing born-digital content that resides outside the domain of the library.

Even in the electronic and networked environment, the economic model continues to feature the library as the central agency on campus that buys and/or manages information resources on behalf of the institution. Libraries have shifted the focus of their collection development policies to the acquisition of more electronic content, much of it via consortia. While aggregate data documenting the quantity of e-resources currently being made available by libraries has proven elusive, there is data on the spending trends.

Over the last decade the average percentage of a research library's materials budget that is spent on electronic resources has grown from 4% to 16%. One hundred six ARL university libraries report spending more than

$132 million on electronic resources in 2000-01. The vast majority of that was spent on electronic serials and subscription services, expenditures which have increased sharply, from just $11 million in 1994-95 to more than $117 million today. To support this increased spending on electronic content, libraries have reallocated resources from the purchase of print. The extent of such reallocations will vary depending on institutional user expectations and financial circumstances.

Many libraries have adopted a policy of adding the e-version of journals when available and are showcasing titles of e-journals available to users via the Web by making this a staff priority and by applying software management tools for titles included in aggregated electronic databases. The processes for selecting, budgeting, and acquiring electronic materials are continually changing and greatly differ from those for the selection and management of print. The print process is orderly: discrete amounts of money are allocated by discipline, the marketplace is fairly predictable, and materials are selected and ordered using established procedures.

By contrast, the processes for selection and management of electronic resources are chaotic. The migration from print to electronic varies in speed and extent by discipline; electronic products are interdisciplinary and expensive, giving rise to selection by committee; projections for future funding are guesswork; and archiving and content control are problematic. Legal and negotiation skills are now mandatory. To complicate matters, decisions are often made through a consortium. The process for acquiring electronic resources turns the traditional acquisitions and user service model topsy-turvy.

In building electronic collections, libraries must also constantly respond to changing publisher behavior. The most profound influence on a library's collection management and access strategies has been the extraordinary price increases for scholarly journals, combined with publishers' use of licensing to define the terms under which a library may make the content available and to whom. It is reasonable to speculate that these phenomena, driven by some of the larger publishers but now employed widely, make up one of the forces that prompted libraries to blend the previously distinct operations of collection management and access.

Some libraries have fully embraced initiatives stimulated or endorsed by SPARC (the Scholarly Publishing and Academic Resources Coalition) and other affordable publishing venues and are using acquisitions funds as investments in the future of scholarly communication. These libraries focus acquisitions on publications from scholarly societies and less expensive publishers, nonprofit and for-profit, that provide high-quality titles at affordable prices. These less expensive titles tend to be the most highly ranked by faculty but labor intensive to obtain, since each publisher has only a few titles and often lacks sales and technical staff. These libraries try to consistently view collection expenditures as investments, and to seek out publishers likely to contribute to a sustainable future for scholarly information.

Libraries are also supporting open access projects that experiment with alternatives to the current subscription-based funding model or the current journals-based publishing model for scholarly communication. These approaches are seen as those of a good citizen, especially in an institution whose needs for funding include many urgent priorities in addition to library needs. These libraries are investing in initiatives that may help solve the long-term problem of high prices for journals.

Online Catalogues

It is clear that the role of the online catalog has changed. That catalog has become one of many databases available to users; libraries are linking to and from the catalog to integrate all of these resources. In recognition of this broader role for the library catalog, some libraries are considering modifying cataloging to favor timely access to a wider variety of formats. One proposal called for reallocating funds that are devoted to describing books and journals to materials that are proportionately underrepresented in today's catalogs, such as films, music, photographs, and digital objects.

Libraries are also reconsidering their current efforts to collect and catalog free Web resources, concluding that these labor-intensive activities can be avoided by perfecting nascent machine harvesting and cataloging techniques. A small number of libraries and library organizations are participating in experiments funded by The Mellon Foundation to test the application of harvesting and search engine technologies. Using the recently developed OAI metadata harvesting protocol, these libraries are delivering information from the "hidden Web" not normally found by Internet search engines and from databases with retrieval formats that present special processing or presentation problems.

For example, several libraries are working with vendors to adapt existing portal software into multifunctional products with features and services desired by users in research communities. Other examples of library involvement in development of software applications are ILL management systems, instructional tutorials, management of content and services for digital libraries, and institutional repositories. Although where information resides matters less to the user, the library as place—the physical entity—remains more important than ever and performs a host of functions vital to learning and research. Much research library space is busier than ever before.

Library facilities are being reconfigured to provide space for collaborative learning and research. There are classrooms and media labs where faculty and librarians may interact in providing student learning experiences, group study spaces, and community spaces where students can meet to discuss ideas. The transformation of library space has also become an opportunity to attract new academic collaborations such as writing studios and academic skills tutoring. Library space is now seen as learning space on an equal footing with classrooms and laboratories.

Libraries are being renovated to expand e-access and foster community by providing electronic classrooms, wireless data networks, offering laptops, and expanding library hours. Libraries are establishing spaces called "information commons" where library reference services are offered jointly with information technology support. At the same time, libraries are responding to decreasing use of in-person reference service by combining service points and shifting resources to online reference service and online tutorials. To make the best use of prime real estate, libraries are adopting new approaches to managing large print collections by using storage centers with delivery services for less frequently used materials and engaging in cooperative approaches to long-term preservation copy retention.

The branch or departmental library remains valuable but its role too is changing. While access to information and library services is far less geographically based, branch and departmental libraries still play a role in development of community and serve as sites for collaboration. Yet, in the Internet world there are opportunities to rethink the role of multiple libraries and their configuration within an institution. One library reported establishing a program to replicate the opportunities for personalized services and contacts that characterize branch library service without the cost of creating additional branches.

Some of the same opportunities for reorganization may present themselves when libraries work in collaboration with other libraries outside their institutional boundaries. Libraries are active participants in building awareness among researchers, faculty, and students of uses of high-quality content and information technology in teaching and research. Curriculum review and changing expectations for teaching faculty present opportunities for libraries to contribute expertise and resources.

Libraries provide classrooms; training and consulting in finding and evaluating information; and assistance with creating electronic theses and dissertations, displaying and visualizing data, publishing journals on the Web, and using geographic information systems (GIS) and remote sensing. Libraries are embracing change—being willing to change what libraries do and how it is done—and, as a result, are reorganizing their operations and re-deploying staff to respond to the new environment.

Open Access

The advent of the Internet, the World Wide Web, and digital technologies has revolutionized scholarly communication. Creative applications of these technologies are leading to innovations in the conduct of research as well as in the conveyance of ideas to readers. And the growing availability and application of these technologies has dramatically altered how readers may discover, gain access to, and use information. As positive and liberating as these developments are for many researchers, authors, and readers, they have also accelerated the commodification of information and drives by some content industries to make their channels of information distribution more secure.

As a result, changes are taking place in copyright, license/contract, and related laws that govern the management and use of intellectual property. For the most part, the changes result in more limited access and more restrictive uses for copyrighted material. It is no surprise then that, as the laws change to secure content for publishers, there is a negative impact on those in the educational and research communities where the creation, dissemination, and use of intellectual property is expected and, in fact, forms the very core of learning and research.

Historically, the library and academic communities looked to copyright law as the policy framework for balancing competing interests of creators, publishers, and users of copyrighted works. To achieve its constitutional purpose to promote the progress of science and the useful arts, copyright law provides a copyright owner with a private monopoly to reproduce, distribute, perform, display, and revise a work, while simultaneously providing exceptions for the special circumstances of education and libraries. This balance has been significantly eroded as copyright and other laws have been revised to apply in the digital and networked environment.

Changes in the laws have come from many directions but are largely driven by players who are part of a large and diverse commercial marketplace seeking changes in the legal framework in order to maximize their profits from e-commerce in publishing and entertainment. The rules promoted by these players to govern a sizeable, general marketplace of users do not lend themselves well to the educational and research communities because, with a few notable exceptions, they do not provide for the special qualities and needs of education and scholarship.

Even in licensing, where libraries have made some progress in negotiating broad uses for their communities, efforts to legitimize mass-market licenses could eliminate fair use and erode the willingness of providers to negotiate at all. In the U.S. and Canada as well as other parts of the world, the library community has been actively engaged in policy debates as laws have been revised, consistently advocating the need to retain a balance among the interests of creators, owners, and users. Our involvement has been significant but these efforts have not been able to stop the economic and political forces of the marketplace that now so clearly dominate society.

It is critical that library community advocacy activities be sustained so there is no further erosion of the balance of interests among creators, copyright owners, and users. At the same time, it is essential for the community to step back, assess the current reality, and consider additional strategies for achieving our commitment to "promote equitable access to and effective use of recorded knowledge in support of teaching, research, scholarship, and community service." The current environment clearly favors commercial interests and thus mitigates against effective use of intellectual property for purposes of education and research.

After many years of the library community's struggle to retain the balance in copyright law, scientists and scholars have cast a new light on the debate. Researchers have come to depend on new technologies for rapid peer-to-peer communications and sophisticated searching and manipulation of data. They have begun to insist that publishers support articles with large datasets, image files, and simulations. And, as the original authors, they are demanding open, easy access to the literature as soon after publication as possible.

Some publishers have been resistant to open access, fearing loss of revenues and loss of control over their content. To date, librarians have exhibited mixed responses to open-access initiatives. Some librarians, like their scientific and scholarly colleagues, see open access as an opportunity to exploit technology more fully in support of research and teaching; others express concern, particularly with the Public Library of Science, that some libraries will cancel journal subscriptions thereby motivating publishers to raise subscription prices and increasing the overall cost of access. Now is the time for librarians to fully embrace the goal of open access, and join with scholars, scientists, and their institutions in working toward this goal.

References

Achatz B and H. Chen, "Digital Libraries: Technical Advances and Social Impact", *Computer*, vol. 32, February, 1999.

Bailey, C.W., 'Public-Access Computer Systems', *Information Technology and Libraries*, 12, March 1993.

Barker, P., *Electronic Books and Libraries of the Future*, Electronic Library, 10, 3, 1992.

Gopal Krishan, *Digital Libraries in Electronic Information Era,* Authorspress, New Delhi, 2000

Harvery, Ross, *Preservation in Libraries: Principles, Strategies and Practices for Librarians*, London: Bowker-Saur, 1993.

Hulser, Richard P., Digital Library: Condent Preservation in a Digital World, *DESIDOC Bulletin of Information Technology*, 17 (6), 1997.

Rajashekar, T.B., Digital Libraries, *Information Studies*, Oct. 1995.

Bibliography

Ackerman, Mark, S., Roy T., Fielding, "Collection Maintenance in Digital Library", *Digital Libraries 95: The Second Annual Conference on theory and Practice of Digital Libraries,* June 11-13, 1995, Austin, Texas USA.

Association of Research Libraries, *Intellectual Property: An ARL Statement of Principles*, Adopted by the ARL Membership, May 1994.

Bailey, C.W., 'Public-Access Computer Systems', *Information Technology and Libraries*, 12, March 1993.

Barker, P., *Electronic Books and Libraries of the Future*, Electronic Library, 10, 3, 1992.

Bawden, D., *User-oriented Evaluation of Information Systems and Services,* Aldershot: Gower, 1990.

Bearman, D., "Archival methods", *Archives and Museum Informatics*, 3(1): 17-27, 1989.

Berninghausen, David K., "Report of Intellectual Freedom Committee to Council, Dallas, June 25, 1971", *American Libraries* 2: 891, September 1971.

Boisvert, R., P. Tang, "The Architecture of Scientific Software," pp. 273-284, *Data Management Systems for Scientific Applications,* Kluwer Academic Publishers, 2001.

Brandt, D. Scott, "Evaluating Information on the Internet", *Computers in Libraries* 16(5), May 1996: 44-46, 1996.

Brunner, R., S. Djorgovski, A. Szalay, "Virtual Observatories of the Future," pp. 257-264, *Astronomical Society of the Pacific Conference Series,* Vol. 225, June, 2000.

Burk, Dan L., *Transborder Intellectual Property Issues on the Electronic Frontier.*

Chen, C., "Global Digital Library Development," *Knowledge-based Data Management for Digital Libraries,* Tsinghua University Press, pp. 197-204, 2001.

Computer and Internet Security, US, Library of Congress, Retrieved September 10, 1999 from the World Wide Web, 1999.

Conway, Paul , *Preservation in the Digital World,* Washington, D.C.: Commission on Preservation and Access, 1996.

Discussion Paper for Intellectual Property or Public Knowledge: A Roundtable Discussion of Copyright in the Nineties, Concordia University, April 7, 1995.

Duranceau, E., "Beyond print: revisioning serials acquisitions for the digital age", in W. Jones (ed.) *E-Serials: Publishers, Libraries, Users and Standards*, The Haworth Press, 1998.

Fox, E. A., *Source Book on Digital Libraries*, Virginia Tech, Department of Computer Science, TR 93-35, 1993.

Frey, D. and R. Adams, *A Directory of Electronic Mail Addressing and Networks*, O'Reilly and Associates, Inc., Sebastopol, CA, January 1990.

Gopal Krishan, *Digital Libraries in Electronic Information Era*, Authorspress, New Delhi, 2000.

Graham, Peter S., *Intellectual Preservation and Electronic Intellectual Property.*

Halbert, Debora, "Weaving Webs of Ownership: Intellectual Property in an Information Age", Dissertation Draft, Stanford Law and Policy Review, Vol. 5, Copyright 1994.

Hartley, S., et al. "Enhancing teaching using the Internet", *Report of the Working Group on the World Wide Web as an interactive teaching resource. SIGCSE/SIGCUE ITiCSE '96*, 218-228.

Harvery, Ross, *Preservation in Libraries: Principles, Strategies and Practices for Librarians*, London: Bowker-Saur, 1993.

Hentoff, Nat, *The First Freedom: The Tumultuous History of Free Speech in America*, New York, Delacorte Press, 1980.Englewood Cliffs, N. J: Prentice Hall, 1964.

Hildreth, Charles, *On-line public access catalogue: the user interface*, Dublin, Ohio, On-line Computer Library Centre, 1982.

Howard, S., 1997, Trade-off decision making in user interface design." *Behaviour and Information Technology* 16, 1997: 98-109.

Hulser, Richard P., Digital Library: Condent Preservation in a Digital World, *DESIDOC Bulletin of Information Technology*, 17 (6), 1997.

International Federation of Library Associations and Institutions (IFLA), *Position paper on copyright in the electronic environment*, October 1996.

International Publishers Association, *Position Paper on Libraries, Copyright and the Electronic Environment of the International Publishers Copyright Council (IPCC)*, 22 April 1996.

Jenkinson, Edward B., *Censors in the Classroom: The Mind Benders,* Carbondale, Ill: Southern Illinios University Press, 1979.

Jensen, Michael, *Need-Based Intellectual Property Protection and Networked,* University Press Publishing.

Johnson, C.A., "Retrospective Conversion of Three Library Collections", *Information Technology and Libraries*, 1982.

Kahle, B., *Archiving the Internet*, Paper submitted to Scientific American for March 1997 issue, 1997.

Kantor, P.B., *Objective Performance Measures for Academic and Research Libraries*, Washington, DC: Association of Research Libraries, 1984.

Kelleher, J., E. Sommerlad, and E. Stern, *Evalution of the Electronic Libraries Programmes: Guidelines for e-Lib Project Evaluation*, London: Tavistock Institute, 1996.

Lee H W., Networked, electronic and virtual library: Libraries of the 1990s, *Jl. of Educational Media and Library Sciences,* 32 (2), 1995.

Lynn, M.S., "Digital Preservation and Access", *Collection Management* 22, nos. 1998.

Ma, Y. *A., Semiotic Analysis of Icons on the World Wide Web*, Paper presented at the Annual Conference of the International Visual Literacy Association, Chicago, 1995, (ERIC Document Reproduction Service, ED 391481).

Malwad N. M., *et al* (ed.), *Digital Libraries: Dynamics storehouse of digitised information,* New Delhi, New Age International, 1996.

Marchionini, G., and H. Maurer, "The Roles of Digital Libraries in Teaching and Learning", *Communication of the ACM,* Vol. 38, No 1, 67-75, 1995.

Marshall, A.D, and S. Hurley, "The Design, Development and Evaluation of Hypermedia Courseware for the World Wide Web", *Multimedia Tools and Applications*, 3, 5-31, 1996.

Moy, Naomi, *CyberSpace Reference Library: the Virtual Reference Collection*. Carson, CA: CA State University at Dominguez Hills, 1997.

Nikolaou, C, and M. Marazakis, "System Infrastucture for Digital Libraries: A Survey and Outlook", *SOFSEM'98, Lecture Notes in Computer Science 1521*, Springer, 186-203, 1998.

Oboler, Eli, M., "Defending Intellectual Freedom: The Library and the Censor", *Westport*, Conn: Greenwood Press, 1980.

Philip, H. Young, "Visions of Academic Workplace in a Brave New Future", *Library and Future: Essays on Library in the Twenty-First Century*, New York, Haworth Press, 1993.

Plaisant, C., Marchionini, G. Bruns, Komlodi, T. A. &, L. Campbell, *Bringing Treasures to the Surface: Iterative Design for the Library of Congress National Digital Library Program,* 1997.

Platoff, A., Shackle, L. and Mazurkiewicz, O., 1998, *Arizona State University Libraries: Help Using the Library,* 1998.

Raitt, David, (ed.), *Libraries for the New Millennium: Implication for Managers*, London, Library Association Publishing, 1987.

Rajashekar, T.B., *Digital Libraries, Information Studies,* October, 1995.

Schatz, B., and H. Chen, "Digital Libraries: Technical Advances and Social Impact", *Computer,* vol. 32, February, 1999.

Sproull, L., and S. Kiesler, *Connections: New Ways of Working in the Networked Organisation*, MIT Press, Cambridge, MA, 1991.

Wusteman, J., "Electronic Journal Formats", *Programme* 30, October 1996.

Index

H

I

K

L

M

N

O

P

R

S

T

V

W